Easter Island

—CHILE—

0   1   2   3   4 km

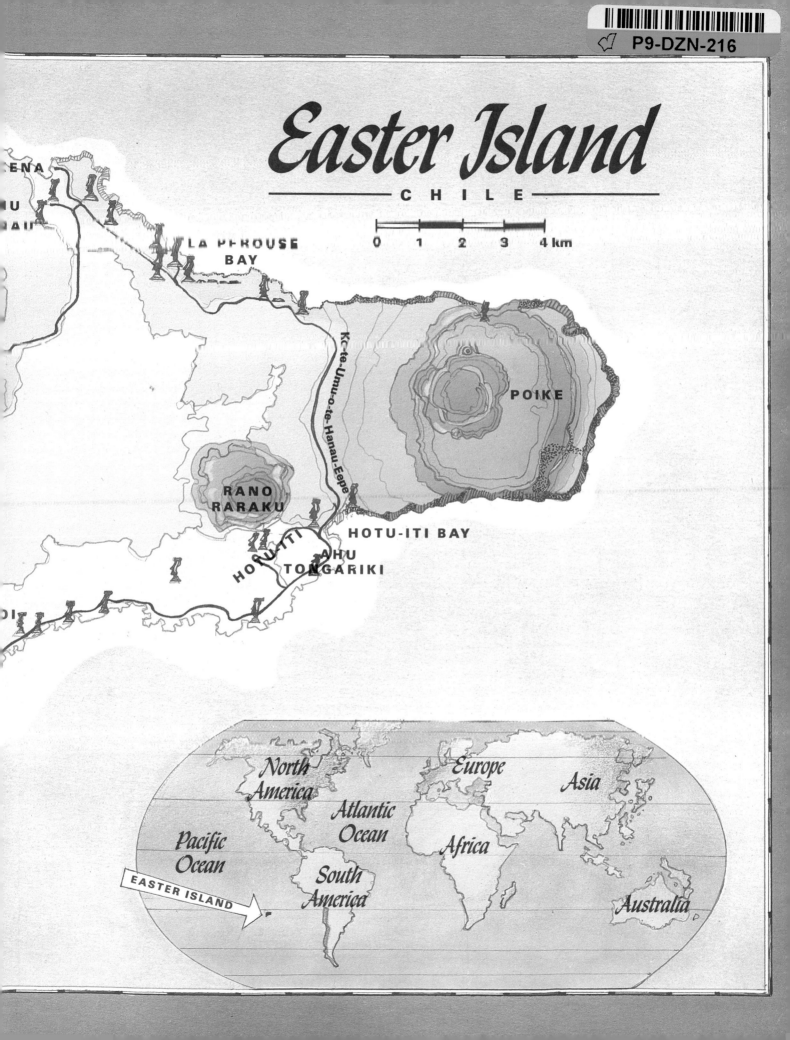

LA PEROUSE
BAY

Ko-te-Umu-o-te-Hanau-Eepe

POIKE

RANO
RARAKU

HOTU-ITI BAY

HOTU-ITI

AHU
TONGARIKI

North
America

Europe

Asia

Atlantic
Ocean

Pacific
Ocean

Africa

South
America

Australia

EASTER ISLAND

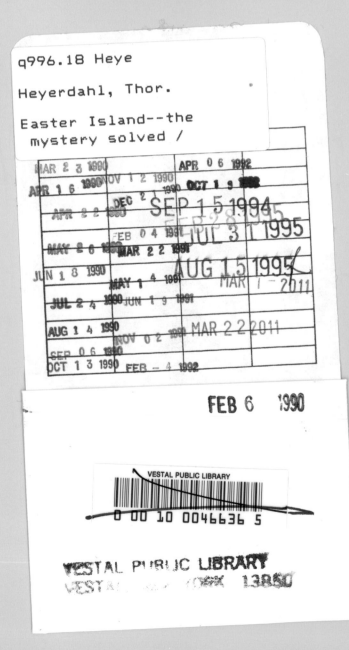

"Everywhere is the wind of heaven; round and above all are boundless sea and sky, infinite space and a great silence. The dweller there is ever listening for he knows not what, feeling unconsciously that he is in the antechamber to something yet more vast which is just beyond his ken."

Katherine Routledge, *The Mystery of Easter Island*, 1919.

Thor Heyerdahl

Easter Island
The Mystery
Solved

Random House   New York

Contents

Going forward

Europeans run into a mystery

Copyright © 1989 by Thor Heyerdahl
All rights reserved under International and Pan-American Copyright Conventions. Published in the United States by Random House, Inc., New York. Published in Sweden as *Påskön, en gåta som fått svar* by Bokförlaget Bra Böcker, Höganäs. © Copyright acknowledgments for the photographs appear on p. 256.

Library of Congress Cataloging-in-Publication Data
Heyerdahl, Thor.
  Easter Island—the mystery solved.
  Bibliography: p.
  Includes index.
  1. Easter Island—Description and travel. 2. Easter Island—Antiquities. I. Title.
F3169.H4513 1989   996'.18   88-32204
ISBN 0-394-57906-2

Printed in Italy
First American Edition

The testimony of the islanders

Science comes to Easter Island

The circle is closed

Thrill of the unknown

Easter Island exists. Hidden in the blue. And it is, as you suspect, the hiding place of mysteries. Mention the name, and few people will be able to place it on a map. It is known, even famous, but more as a sort of dream island sailing above the clouds than as a piece of rock firmly planted on the ocean floor. Robinson Crusoe, the sunken continent of Mu, pyramid builders from space, the adventures of Sherlock Holmes—all these have a similar mysterious atmosphere, but are inventions of the human mind. Easter Island is *there*. And its mystery is reality.

Mysteries appeal to man. We like to be mystified, amazed, impressed. We like to solve riddles and crossword puzzles. We enjoy watching a good magician. We are drawn to the mysterious, the unknown, like wolves to their prey. The mystery is a teaser, an appetizer we like to savor. But satisfaction lies in the solution.

The more we learn, the clearer we see that we shall never run short of riddles. Dispose of one, and the curtain rises on the next. We live in a world of mysteries. Most follow us from cradle to grave, so close to our noses that we lose sight of them. We accept such mysteries as unsolvable, and satisfy ourselves by giving them names. Instinct. Gravity. Evolution. Why do all beavers build dams? How do migratory birds find their destinations? Instinct. Why does the ocean cling to all sides of a round planet? Gravity. Good answers. Why does one cell grow into an elephant and another into a daffodil? Evolution. Creation. Two answers. Your choice.

A generation ago there were still blank spaces on the map of earth to excite the curiosity of explorers and readers. Today there are none. Western culture is monopolizing our planet, threatening to make life monotonous for the venturesome traveler who is looking for something different and unusual. Worldwide tourism is increasing, but adventure is offered to the younger generation in the form of escapist interplanetary stories. Space age fairy-tales.

Until recently we visualized strange creatures and untold mysteries awaiting us on our neighboring planets Mars and Venus. Today we know better. We have seen televised images from the moon, where men from earth are the only moving things in a dead landscape of dust and rock. Unmanned space-craft have revealed that no planet but our own is habitable in this solar system, so we need not spend a year in a capsule to visit the rock deserts of Mars: we can have a similar sensation by walking into the Sahara wearing an oxygen mask and diver's suit. And today we know it is as uninviting to land on the fiery surface of Venus as to jump into the crater of Vesuvius.

Nonetheless, planets in other solar systems still retain their attraction. Some may be inhabited by living creatures and full of mysteries beyond our imagination, but they will retain their secrets perhaps forever, and be thousands of years remote from us, even if one day we are able to travel at the speed of light. We know that when we stare at the stars we are looking into the distant past. We see light that burned millennia ago. If telescopes could be made powerful enough, we might indeed witness life on planets in other solar systems; but life at a time when the pharaohs built the pyramids, or the Long-ears made stone giants walk out of the crater walls on Easter Island.

Travels through time

Here on our own planet, we need not wait for supertelescopes to be built in order for us to travel back through time. The past, with all its wonders and mysteries, is still with us here—and within our reach. This is the one planet where forgotten peoples and amazing cultures have indeed existed. Monsters weirder than any creature from outer space that movie makers can design have lumbered over our earth. If we search for it, we will find that all around us the past is mingled with the present. It is all part of a gigantic jigsaw puzzle that we have only just started to reconstruct from pieces preserved in rocks and ruins. Fossils and prehistoric monuments tell stories stranger than fiction. The past, we now begin to see, is as incredible as any fable. When scientists turn the time knob, fairy tales become reality. We see dragons begin to swim, then crawl and fly out of the ocean. We are shocked when we then turn the knob in the direction of our own era and see more monsters give birth to hairy creatures that slowly turn into men and women. If we turn back even further, the giant monsters shrivel up and become the microplankton of the sea. We must not turn too far back, however, for in the beginning there was nothing. Life began as a total mystery. Nothing became something, and in no modest quantity. A planet of rock and ocean waited like a virgin to be fertilized by the rays of the sun. The sun was the father of all life, the ocean the womb where all life began.

Today this is the accepted version of evolution, irrespective of the many varying hypotheses as to the driving force that produced it. Thus modern science has confirmed an old belief, for in the genealogies of the great ancient civilizations, the sun was honored as man's first ancestor. The sun is therefore an important part of the riddle we are going to tackle. As a divine ancestor, it tempted and guided men in westward movements across the oceans of the world. By accepting the sun as the father of all life, we give credit to the wisdom or intuition of the people we are about to follow across uncharted seas. The Incas believed that the sun-priest Kon-Tiki Viracocha abandoned his kingdom in Peru on a westward voyage into the Pacific in the wake of his father the sun. The last of the ruling Incas was beheaded by conquistadors from Europe because he maintained that the sun was to him and his people what Adam and Eve were to the foreign intruders.

One lesson modern man needs to learn is to be unprejudiced in his judgment of people of the past. Their abilities should not be underestimated. Beliefs and cultures have changed, and not always for the better, but the human brain has remained unaltered for many thousands of years. The average person at the time of Christ, or even five thousand years earlier, was as intelligent as the average person in our own day. The occasional genius existed then just as now, and so did the occasional imbecile. We have changed our attire and our environment, but our spirit, our needs, and our dreams are the same. For centuries people on this planet have looked down upon certain other branches of mankind as inferior to themselves. By now we should have learned that human qualities cannot be classified according to the shape of the nose or eyes or the color of the skin or hair. We have, in theory at least, accepted the equality of people living today, and we speak of a single human family. But we comfort ourselves with prejudice against people who lived before our own time—people who, of course, are unable to defend themselves against our chronological discrimination. This book is a modest attempt to learn one more lesson about human equality through the ages.

About the author

Thor Heyerdahl, born in Norway in 1914, first felt the easterly trade winds on his bare skin when he returned to nature on a South Sea island in 1937. Since early childhood he had been interested in animals and aboriginal cultures, and even opened a one-room museum in his parents' home. Fresh from Oslo University as a biologist, and having prepared for his experiment at the Kroepelien Polynesian library, Heyerdahl left with his young bride to live as Polynesians on the lonely island of Fatu-Hiva.

Although current theories assumed that the Polynesians' ancestors had sailed there from Asia, Heyerdahl found that the trade-wind clouds and ocean current were on the constant move from South America. The sweet potato and other native food crops were South American. Stone statues in the jungle and the legends of the islanders also pointed to a possible arrival from that direction, but the Polynesian language showed a relationship rooted in Southeast Asia, in the opposite direction. The young naturalist pieced parts of the puzzle together and presented a new theory. The Polynesians the European discoverers met had come from Southeast Asia with the Japan current by way of the extreme North Pacific and Northwest America, but before they had reached Polynesia by way of Hawaii the East Pacific had been settled by raft voyagers from South America.

The scientific world objected. It was said to be established that no South American people could have reached Polynesia with the primitive watercraft developed before European exploration began. But Heyerdahl refused to accept this unproven dogma, and in 1947 he built a balsa raft in the Incan pattern, and with five companions set out on one of the greatest sea adventures of all time, known as the *Kon-Tiki* expedition. Starting from Callao in Peru, the raft with the six men reached Raroia atoll in Polynesia after covering over five thousand miles in 101 days. A scientific dogma was proven wrong; Polynesia was well within the reach of aboriginal South American watercraft.

Forced to admit the seaworthiness of the Inca raft, the opposition stubbornly stuck to their view that the Incas had only used them for coastal traffic. Why else were the Galápagos Islands, closest to South America, still uninhabited? But by taking the first archaeologists on a survey of the Galápagos, Heyerdahl proved that this waterless group had been frequently visited before the time of European exploration, although the lack of fresh water had made a permanent settlement impossible. Numerous potsherds were excavated and identified at the United States National Museum as being of pre-Inca origin.

The success of the excavations encouraged Heyerdahl to take a step further out into the Pacific Ocean. He brought a team of archaeologists to Easter Island, where they made the first stratigraphic excavations ever done on that site. A wealth of discoveries were made underground, including strange statues hitherto only known in South America. The islanders also built small reed boats to show Heyerdahl how their ancestors went to sea. These were made in the same way and of the same reeds as those used by the Indians of South America.

The amazing qualities of the reed ships made Heyerdahl suspect that oceans had been highways used by the great early civilizations. The reed ships of Easter Island and of early Peru and Mexico were built like those of ancient Egypt and the Middle East. Could it be that they all had a common cradle, thus explaining the many parallels between the pre-Columbian civilizations on both sides of the Atlantic? So Heyerdahl built his second vessel, this time of papyrus reeds, and named it *Ra*, after the Egyptian sun god. He was helped in its construction by reed-boat builders from Lake Chad in Central Africa, and, in 1969, he embarked from the coast of Morocco with six companions and steered the almost fifty-foot-long reed ship in the direction of the setting sun. Although experts predicted that the papyrus reeds would become waterlogged and sink after two weeks, the reeds were still afloat after two months, when the ropes holding the bundles together burst. The crew was picked up by a boat a week short of the Caribbean islands.

The experiment had already proved what Heyerdahl had set out to prove— the mishap with the ropes was due to an oversight in the construction of the vessel. But Heyerdahl wished to complete his experiment, and immediately returned to Africa to build a second *Ra*, again from papyrus reeds, but this time with the help of South American Indians from Lake Titicaca, the only place in the world where this ancient shipbuilding technique is still in use. Just a year separated the launching of the two reed ships. *Ra II* was smaller than the first *Ra*—forty feet long—but with the same basic crew increased to eight. Again departing from Safi in Morocco, *Ra II* sailed 3,790 miles westward across the entire Atlantic, reaching Barbados after fifty-seven days without the loss of a single reed.

Heyerdahl sailed his reed ships under the United Nations flag and with a multinational crew to show that peaceful coexistence under extreme conditions was possible. He was also the first to warn the United Nations about the pollution of the world's oceans. *Ra II* is now in Norway, on permanent exhibition along with the original balsa or wood raft *Kon-Tiki*, at the Kon-Tiki Museum in Oslo.

Encouraged by his findings, Heyerdahl decided to tackle the third of the world's great oceans. The crossings with *Kon-Tiki* and the two *Ras* had been pure drift voyages, taking advantage of the winds and currents of the tropical belt on either side of America, which rotate like an escalator belt from east to west; but this does not happen in the Indian Ocean, where the elements change with the seasons. Determined to test the possibility of navigating a reed ship, and to test the claims of the marsh Arabs that reeds must be cut for the ships in August for maximum flotage, Heyerdahl went to Iraq, formerly Mesopotamia, where he built his largest reed ship. The *Tigris*, sixty feet long and named after the river from where it was launched, was built, as such craft had been in Sumerian times, from the local berdi reed. The international crew consisted of eleven men, who navigated the reed ship for five months, sailing from Iraq out of the Persian Gulf, then from Oman to Pakistan, with the final leg across the Indian Ocean from Asia to Africa, ending in Djibouti at the entrance to the Red Sea. The voyage showed that the three great civilizations of antiquity—Mesopotamia, Egypt and the Indus Valley—could have made overseas contact using the kind of vessel common to all three. In 1978, trapped in the middle of the African war

Fatu-Hiva 1937–38

Kon-Tiki 1947

zone, Heyerdahl burnt the reed ship and the crew jointly sent an appeal to the UN for the industrial nations to halt shipment of modern arms to the part of Africa where civilization first started.

The success of the *Tigris* expedition captured the attention of the nations around the Indian Ocean, and as a result Heyerdahl was invited by the president of the Republic of the Maldives to investigate the prehistory of his island country. A mysterious stone head had just been found on one of the Maldives' 1,200 coral islets. The Maldive nation had turned Moslem in 1153, and from then on religion forbade any depiction of human form, so here was tangible support of Heyerdahl's theory that early people had navigated in the open ocean. Since the Maldive archipelago lay far from any continent and the inhabitants had tried to conceal their pre-Moslem past, no archaeologist had hitherto been tempted to investigate the island. Heyerdahl realized the possibilities, and over a three-year period an archaeological expedition sponsored by the Maldive government and the Kon-Tiki Museum uncovered temple ruins and images hitherto hidden in the jungle. The excavation disclosed that the Maldive archipelago had been an important trading center since prehistoric times. It had been settled before the Arabs arrived, by both Buddhist and Hindu temple-builders, as well as by unknown architects who had left behind sun-oriented pyramidal structures.

By combining archaeology with ocean crossings, Heyerdahl had now proved the theory cen-

Galápagos 1952

Easter Island 1955–56

Ra I 1969

Ra II 1970

Tigris 1977–78

Maldives 1982–84

Back to Easter Island after thirty years. *From right:* Dr. Arne Skjølsvold, Pavel Pavel, the author, Governor Sergio Rapu with wife and daughter, and Gonzalo Figueroa.

Opposite page: A topknotted Easter Islander revives an ancestral custom by welcoming the returning author with chickens and bananas. *From left:* Arne Skjølsvold, Gonzalo Figueroa, Pavel Pavel, the author and the governor. Since the airport was opened in 1967, tourism has overtaken farming as Easter Island's most important industry. The tourists' undisguised admiration for the island's impressive antiquities has inspired a new respect in the younger islanders for the ancient arts and customs of their forefathers. They are keen to learn from the island's elders, not just to please the foreigners and give the island a good name, but to distinguish themselves in competition with their peers when no strangers are present.

tral to his thinking: the world oceans had served as highways for man ever since the first ships were built.

With the three main oceans conquered by prehistoric craft and his main theory proven, there was still one lonely spot in the world that Thor Heyerdahl could not get out of his mind: Easter Island. Thirty years after his first visit, he decided to return for a closer look into the island's past.

The lost islands of the Incas

Long before the time of Columbus, millennia before the Vikings hoisted sail, ships were navigating on all open seas and oceans. Deep-sea navigation did not start in Europe. Oceangoing vessels were first built in the Middle East. From West Asia and North Africa civilized man sailed on voyages of trade and exploration in early antiquity. Modern science has found that the stupendous megalithic temples on the island of Malta were constructed before the pharaohs built any of the pyramids in Egypt. And the Sumerians founded the first kingdom in Mesopotamia upon arrival from the island of Bahrain. Centuries before the birth of Christ, the merchant traffic in the open Indian Ocean was so busy that the Maldive Islands became an important trading nation. The navigators who settled these tiny atolls could afford the luxury of building pyramidal stupas and temples which in size and splendor could compete with those of powerful nations on the mainland.

Millennia before European history began, seafaring architects had sailed the Atlantic and built their megalithic structures on various islands around Great Britain. And when the Portuguese mariners finally ventured as far out as the Canary Islands, they found the white-skinned, bearded Guanches already there, descendants of unknown African seafarers.

Columbus and his followers found every inhabitable island off the American coast already discovered and settled. They were impressed by the maritime skill of the people in Mexico and Peru, who built watercraft that differed in principle from those made in Europe but were identical to those of the ancient Middle East.

But the prelude to the greatest mystery of any island began when the explorers from Europe first crossed the Isthmus of Panama and reached the Pacific shores. Only then did they find the wide-open gateway to the world's largest ocean. This same ocean had been known to Europeans from the coasts of the Philippines and China for two centuries, but it had remained impenetrable to them from that side due to the direction of winds and currents. Thus they did not yet know that this ocean was dotted with inhabitable islands, every single one of which had been settled by earlier voyagers.

From the moment the Spanish conquistadores encountered the tribes and nations of Panama and Peru, they heard about Inca sailing ventures in the unsheltered eastern Pacific Ocean. On the Isthmus of Panama, Pizarro and his men learned about the Inca empire and the large Incan sailing rafts that traveled up to the Isthmus to trade. On their way down the open coast to Ecuador, the advancing Spaniards were able to verify these reports for themselves: they captured and overhauled a number of Incan rafts. The first of these was described in detail as a balsa raft, with cotton sails and rigging in the manner of the Spanish caravels. On board were twenty men and women from Peru, with thirty tons of valuable merchandise.

On reaching Peru, the Spaniards were met out at sea by a whole flotilla of sailing rafts manned by Inca troops bound for Puná Island, off the coast. They had reached a nation where stories of maritime immigrants formed the basis of local history. A handful of Spaniards were able to march inland in peace and conquer the mighty military empire of the Incas, because they were mistaken for other seafarers supposed to have come down the coast before them. These traditional immigrants, the *Vira-cochas* (meaning "foam of the sea") were described as white and bearded like the Spaniards, and had once ruled the whole Inca territory. At the heart of Inca history was the belief that their empire had been founded by these seafarers, who, in the end, had left the continent, sailing westward into the open Pacific.

The Incas of Peru were so specific in their claims about the existence of inhabited islands far out in the ocean that their learned men, the *Amautas,* could relate the names of two of these islands, which had been visited by their late king, Inca Tupac Yupanqui. One was called *Ava Chumbi* and the other *Nina Chumbi,* the latter meaning "Fire Island." This seafaring Inca ruler was said to have manned a large fleet of balsa sailing rafts and sailed away for almost a year. He returned, bringing back with him dark-skinned prisoners from the islands. This sea voyage took place only three generations before the Spaniards arrived. Historians have speculated as to whether the Inca fleet visited the Galápagos Islands, which might have had active volcanoes at the time; this would have accounted for the islands' name. But the Galápagos group was uninhabited, and so close to the Inca empire that fishermen from that coast sailed there regularly; the Incas would not have needed to be away for an entire year in order to have visited it.

In the mid-sixteenth century, the historian Pedro Sarmiento de Gamboa gathered enough information about the closest of these two islands from the Inca historians and seafarers for him to pin down its position. It was estimated to lie about six hundred leagues (2,400 miles) west-southwest of the port of Callao in

Peru. This is exactly the right direction to our intriguing island, and also remarkably close to the right distance. The consistent claims of the aboriginal people of Peru prompted the Spanish viceroy to send out an expedition under the command of his nephew, Alvaro de Mendaña. With Sarmiento on board as advisor, Mendaña left in November 1567 with orders to steer for the islands mentioned by the Incas, and to form a settlement there. The expedition left Callao harbor in Peru following the right course obtained by Sarmiento from the Incas—west-southwest, but Mendaña refused to go along with the orders of the historian, and, after twenty-five days, altered his course to west-northwest. Thus they sailed past Easter Island and all of Polynesia without sighting land until they reached Melanesia. Melanesia, like Polynesia, had remained totally unknown to Europeans up until that time, although they had been familiar with Indonesia for two centuries. Mendaña was forced by the westbound winds and currents in the tropical belt to return to Peru by the long route through the extreme north Pacific, north of Hawaii. He later left Callao on a second expedition into the east Pacific, during which he became the European discoverer of Polynesia, landing on Fatu-Hiva in the Marquesas Islands in 1595. Thus the central coast of the former Inca empire became the embarkation point for the first European visitors to both Polynesia and Melanesia.

Two centuries were to pass before another Spanish expedition left the same port in Peru to rediscover the real mystery of the Pacific, but in the meantime a Dutch expedition had already found the island.

Europeans
run into
a mystery

What Roggeveen saw on Easter Day 1722

On Easter Sunday 1722, three Dutch sailing vessels under the command of Admiral Jacob Roggeveen ploughed into the shelter of an island not yet plotted on any map. Today it is shown on every map, and it bears the name of Easter Island.

Roggeveen had actually been sent by the Dutch West India Company to search for an island reported to have been sighted by the buccaneer Edward Davis in 1687. The Davis ship had left the pirates' cove in the Galápagos group to sail for southern Chile, but trade winds and the strong Humboldt Current had forced the ship westward, far out into the Pacific. The buccaneers had to steer their wind-driven vessel down into Antarctic waters to force it back to southern Chile, and during this detour they sighted a high, mountainous island with a low sandy atoll facing it. This could only be Mangareva, far to the west of Easter Island, the chief island in the Gambier Islands group in the east Pacific.

At the time Roggeveen was searching for Davis's island, all sailings into the Pacific had been from the American coast. Even though Europeans had colonized the Philippines four centuries earlier, no one had yet succeeded in forcing their way into the open Pacific from that side.

Roggeveen's ships were thousands of miles away from nowhere, in the empty

Meeting with the mystery.

The first time European eyes saw the monuments on the world's remotest inhabited island was on Easter Day 1722, when the Dutch Admiral Jacob Roggeveen made landfall and named the island. *Te-Pito-o-te-Henua* (The-Navel-of-the-World) was the name by which the natives themselves referred to this island in the midst of the mighty ocean halfway between South America and the nearest islands to the west.

wastes of the world's largest ocean, when the monotony of many weeks of rolling between blue sea and sky was broken. Several columns of smoke were rising from the indistinct contours of a tiny hilly island just coming into sight. The Dutch sailing ships had been discovered by the people ashore, who seemed to be sending up smoke signals to attract attention. As the three ships sailed closer, they were able to distinguish the fires that had been lit at intervals on the edge of black cliffs, and catch a glimpse of the rolling green landscape behind them. The Dutchmen realized they had accidentally put into a land that was the home of a completely unknown people—people who apparently wanted them ashore.

Evening approached and the officers held council on board. Not knowing who these strange people were, they decided to play it safe and stand offshore till daybreak. In the meantime, they celebrated Easter Day by proclaiming themselves discoverers, and they named the island in honor of the day.

Equally impatient were the people hidden in the darkness ashore. They already had their own name for the island, *Te-Pito-o-te-Henua* or "The-Navel-of-the-World." They must have marveled at the oil lamps flickering on the white sails as the three Dutch ships moved slowly through the starlit night, unable to find safe anchorage. The lamps on the ships and the fires on the cliffs vanished. Neither of the two peoples who had just discovered each other's existence and were now waiting to get better acquainted knew that the day marked an historic event—the birth of a riddle that was to puzzle laymen and scientists for more than two centuries.

Variable weather—thunder, unsteady winds and showers—prevented the Dutchmen from landing the following day. That night the stars reappeared and with them the constant trade wind from the east. The ships were able to move

At daybreak the first Europeans witnessed a strange ceremony. The islanders prostrated themselves to the rising sun and lit fires before giant statues. A group of islanders reenacted this rite when the Chilean training ship *Esmeralda* visted Easter Island recently.

in close enough to anchor in the moonlight off Anakena Bay on the northern coast.

By dawn, the Dutchmen were able to see the land in greater detail. To their surprise, they saw large numbers of people moving about among some colossal stone figures that rose high above their heads. The people ashore seemed more occupied with ceremonial rituals that appeared to honor their giant images and the rising sun than with the unknown visitors who had just arrived. The natives kindled fires in front of these images and prostrated themselves to the sun, then they squatted on their heels, heads bowed, and alternately raised and lowered their hands, palms held together as if in prayer.

Neither before or after were other Europeans to see what the Dutchmen witnessed this Easter morning, and as the visitors would remain for only a single day, they were unable to judge whether the rituals were in their honor or part of a daily routine.

The island was clearly well populated, and its inhabitants took the initiative. As the sun rose higher, they swam out to the visitors by the thousands, accompanied by small reed skiffs; others sat on the cliffs in large groups, staring, or ran up and down on the beach like deer.

Roggeveen's companion, Behrens, was the first to step ashore. Both of them left detailed records of what they observed. These records are of extreme importance, since fifty years would pass before this lonely island colony would again be visited by foreigners.

Much to their surprise, the Dutchmen observed that, the isolation of the island notwithstanding, its people were of mixed racial origin. They found some to be of a brownish hue, darker than Spaniards, yet they describe others as "quite white" and a few "of a reddish tint as if somewhat severely tanned by the sun."

The Dutch told the outside world of the ranks of enormous stone images erected with their backs to the sea on a hitherto unknown island far off the coast of Chile. The images were served by a priesthood whose skins were as pale as those of Europeans and who wore large wooden plugs in their artificially lengthened earlobes. The rest of the population were described as people of obviously mixed descent. Many of the pale-skinned ones had red hair.

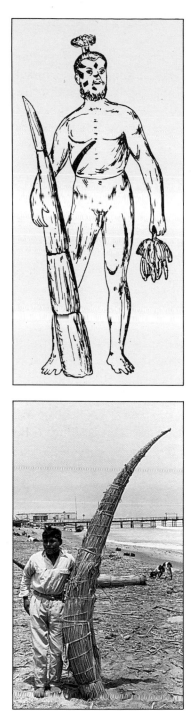

Roggeveen related how hundreds of islanders came out to his ship on little rafts. A later visitor, the Frenchman du Petit-Thouars, made a drawing of a man with such a raft. It was a reed raft of the kind used right up to the present day along the coast of Peru. In 1955 the islanders showed us how these *pora* rafts were fashioned and used for swimming out to sea. They are made of totora reeds, just as in Peru. This South American freshwater plant does not occur anywhere else in the Pacific, but grows in profusion in the crater lakes of Easter Island and on the desert west coast of South America, where it is cultivated by artificial irrigation. This un-Polynesian craft has been used since time immemorial by the coastal inhabitants of Peru, and ceramic figures of fisherman swimming on rafts are common in pre-Inca art.

Roggeveen and his crew made no drawings, but have left very detailed descriptions of the people they encountered ashore. The islanders of those days, however, portrayed themselves in wood, and Captain Cook brought home these lifelike figurines from his visit to the island later in the same century. They confirm the Dutchmen's testimony that some of the islanders had strikingly European features. The woman on the right clearly belongs to the Long-ears. The man with the goatee has portraits of his divine long-bearded ancestors carved in relief on his forehead, and a depression on his skull is suggestive of the early islanders' practice of trepanning.

Two shell-divers on totora rafts as depicted by a pre-Inca Mochican artist. Diving for Spondylus shells was an important occupation in ancient Peru.

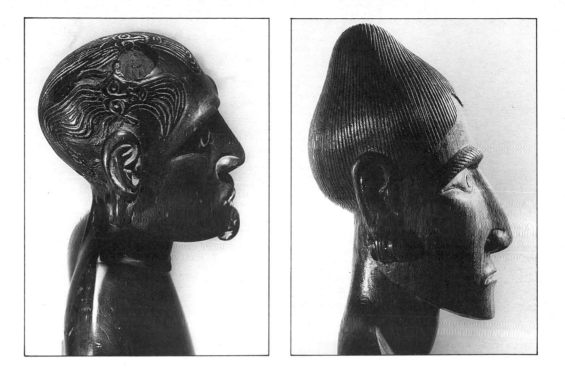

Different ethnic groups were clearly coexisting here. Both Roggeveen and Behrens mentioned how one specific class of islanders, those with fair skin, wore large chocks or disks in their artificially extended earlobes. Their ears were so long that, if they removed the disks, they had to hitch the rim of the lobe over the top of the ear to get it out of the way while they were working. Behrens stated that these long-eared individuals could easily be distinguished from those with normal ears not only by their appearance, but also because they displayed more reverence for the statues and were more devout in their ministrations. Some of the Long-ears wore feather headdresses. The islander Behrens described as the leader and assumed to be an idle priest, was "an entirely white man." Most of the men were nude, tattooed with strange birds and beasts. Many were bearded. Their hair was cut or plaited and coiled into a topknot. Roggeveen was amazed at the absence of women, and assumed that the men, out of jealousy, had hidden them inland. But Behrens observed a few, clothed with red and white wraps and with hats made of rushes. Some disrobed with laughing and inviting gestures. Roggeveen saw only a few houses behind the statues in Anakena Bay. They were shaped like an overturned reed boat, fifty feet long and fifteen feet wide, with a vaulted roof, and measuring nine feet high at the center. A solid thatch of reeds covered a framework of sticks. There were no windows, only a tunnel-shaped entranceway so low that the occupants had to enter on all fours. Nothing was found inside but reed mats and stone pillows. Roggeveen saw that food was baked in underground stone ovens, but Behrens walked to a village of about twenty houses, where he claimed to have seen that each household prepared meals in their own "pots made of clay or earth."

As far as the visitors could tell, the island appeared to be destitute of large trees, although some woodland was visible in the distance. But the soil was described as fertile, planted and bearing crops in neatly outlined fields. Three crops were identified by the visitors: the sweet potato, the banana, and sugar cane. The sweet potato was found to dominate the fields, and was described as the daily bread of the people. Subsistence was produced by soil cultivation, but

Red-headed men with long ears and goatees are known to have sailed off the northern coast of Peru in prehistoric times. They were portrayed by the pre-Inca Mochican coast dwellers on earthenware vessels found both in graves on the coast and on offshore islands in the Humboldt Current. They are often depicted as prisoners bound with ropes, and the coastal Indians always stressed their alien appearance by showing that, unlike the Indians themselves, their hair, beards, and pubic hair were red, and they were circumcised.

Kon-Tiki, the legendary bearded sun-king, reigned in Tiahuanaco and raised stone statues there before leading his long-eared followers to the coast and sailing away across the Pacific. On the northern coast he was always portrayed in pre-Inca times with large plugs in distended earlobes and a long beard. The Incas gave him the surname Viracocha, which means "foam of the sea" because he was white-skinned and went away across the sea. To this day, the locals in the Tiahuanaco area call all European visitors Viracocha.

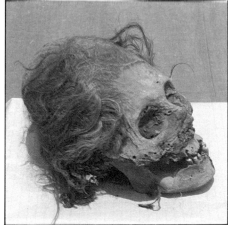

Mummy found in a pre-Inca grave on the desert coast of Peru. A large number of mummies with reddish or fair hair were buried among the black-haired aboriginal people in the oldest graves along the coast.

fishing seemed unimportant, and the boats of these singularly unmaritime island-ers were ridiculed by the Dutchmen. Other than the numerous reed floats used by the visitors swimming to the ships, only a few tiny canoes were seen, of which Roggeveen wrote with contempt. They were about ten feet long, flimsily made from small boards, and so narrow that even with their legs pressed together the sailors could barely squeeze themselves in. The seams leaked so much that the occupant had to divide his time equally between paddling and bailing.

Roggeveen's party had opened the door to a strange maritime puzzle: How could a people, expert in the tillage of the soil but ignorant of decent boat build-ing, have preceded Europeans to this island so totally hidden from the rest of the world? Who were these remarkably white people with barbarically elongated earlobes? Who were those among them with the red skins that seemed to have been burnt by the sun? Had they come at the same time as their brown-skinned companions, or on their own? And how had the enormous stone statues, which the white-skinned Long-ears seemed to venerate more than the other inhabi-tants, been carved and erected? The monumental images were found to be a good thirty feet tall, and on top of their heads they all carried an additional stone, a kind of crown.

At least the problem of the statues the Dutchmen believed to have solved to their own satisfaction. Roggeveen admitted that, at first, they had all been filled with wonder. But then he chopped off a piece from the weathered surface of one image and concluded that they were all patched together from clay, into which small stones had been stuck to make up the semblance of a human figure.

The visitors were disturbed at finding the islanders to be expert thieves, but

Roggeveen provisioned his ship with sweet potatoes, which are still the chief staple food of the Easter Islanders. Our foreman, Juan Haoa, who is of pure Easter Island ancestry, here shows one of the many local varieties. This important food plant is of American origin, and dried sweet potatoes and gourds, both cultivated on the island before the arrival of the Europeans, have been found in graves at Arica on the coast of northern Chile that date back to the seventeenth century BC. Both plants must have been introduced to Polynesia by prehistoric seafarers; the sweet potato is still called by its South American name, *kumara*.

to their delight they found their hosts to be otherwise friendly and without any kind of weapon. Behrens assumed that in case of need they relied on their long-eared idols, which he saw them falling down to invoke.

Before they set sail the same afternoon, to continue their downwind course toward Polynesia, these first foreign visitors recorded an incident. They happened to shoot one of the islanders by mistake. They also admitted that a dozen others had been killed as the result of a brawl—two of them had tried to steal from the sailors, and, when the other islanders had picked up stones and started to behave in a threatening manner, they were shot in the struggle that followed.

Fifty years were to pass before these lonely islanders saw any other Europeans.

The Dutch visitors in 1722 had discovered the Easter Island people and their monuments. They discovered the discoverers of the island. Their brief call sowed the seeds of a growing mystery, but their records also left us the first of the pieces required to solve the puzzle. An islander need not be very dark to be seen as darker than a Spaniard, but he must be very fair before a Dutchman will call him an entirely white man. It is not unusual for people to insert small plugs in their earlobes, or to make images of stone or clay. But it is indeed unusual for people to make their images as tall as three- or four-story houses and have to hang their earlobes over their ears in order to work. Yet it is not these bizarre customs but the products of the tillers of the soil that give us our first solid clue. Art and customs can be invented by man, but crops and plants cannot. Genetic evidence is as dependable as fingerprints. The staple food of the Easter Islanders, the sweet potato, is strictly an American plant. Only man could have brought it to the island, and he must have brought it by sea. An equally valid clue is the reference to bananas and sugar cane, plants that are native to Southeast Asia. Only men could have brought them, too, and those men must have traveled by way of Polynesia to distant Easter Island. Thus the mixed population discovered on the island by those first Europeans had an economy based on imported plants, proving that there must have been some contact with people on both sides of the Pacific during what we can call "pre-European" times.

The viceroy of Peru annexes the island

The memory of the Inca islands west of Chile and south-southwest of Callao harbor remained vivid in Peru, and was revived when Roggeveen's expedition reported to have seen an island in that very part of the ocean. In October 1770, the viceroy of Peru, Don Manuel de Amat, sent out an expedition of two ships under the command of Felipe Gonzalez y Haedo. Gonzalez was instructed to search for and annex an island believed to lie about six-hundred leagues off the coast of Chile, in the latitude of Copiapó, and to identify it, if possible, with Roggeveen's discovery. Roggeveen had estimated Easter Island's position to be about six-hundred leagues distant from Callao and about the same from mainland Chile.

Gonzalez' ships followed the given south-southwest course from Callao for two weeks. Unlike Mendaña's expedition from Peru, this one did not alter course until smoke signals were sighted on the horizons. Gonzalez' ships had been detected by the islanders, and again they had lit fires all along the coast, just as when they first discovered Roggeveen.

For the outside world, Gonzalez had rediscovered Easter Island. Records of what he and his sailors saw are preserved in his log and in the two journals kept by the pilots of his ships, Juan Hervé and Francisco Antonio de Agüera.

The Spaniards, like the Dutchmen before them, interpreted the fires along the coast as invitations to come ashore, and they were in fact received by an unarmed and friendly population. Their number, however, was estimated at less than one thousand, of which very few were women and children. The new visitors, like the earlier ones, suspected that some of the people and all the property were kept in hiding elsewhere. Agüera soon learned and stressed that the islanders were so fond of stealing that what one man obtained another would take from him, and he suggested that all possessions were probably concealed below ground, for the Spaniards never saw any of the stolen items again.

The Spaniards made the same reference to three distinct skin colors mentioned by the Dutchmen: white, swarthy and reddish. The hair of the former was described as chestnut colored and limp, sometimes tending to a red or cinnamon tint, and "if they wore clothing like ourselves they might very well pass for Europeans." The men were tall and well proportioned, often exceeding five feet nine inches in height. One measured six feet four inches, and another over six and a half feet.

The Spaniards remained at anchor for six days and had the opportunity to compile the first short word list of the contemporary Easter Island language, prior to any foreign influence. They were also the first to observe that these islanders had their own local form of script. But neither the written nor the spoken language was comprehensible to them.

These visitors, coming as they did from Peru, observed that the few men who were not naked were clothed in colored garments described to be "like a *poncho*."

The Poike peninsula. It was here that the Gonzalez expedition of 1770 officially annexed Easter Island to Peru by order of the Spanish viceroy of the former Inca empire. Gonzalez and his men marched in procession to this easterly cape and raised three crosses on the three peaks of the seaward ridge. Discovering that the people of Easter Island had a written language of their own, Gonzalez made them "sign" the instrument of annexation.

Poike are
[fr]ee from stones
[like] the rest of the
[s]urface, which is
[cover]ed with fragments of lava.
[Ac]cording to oral tradition,
Poike was the last refuge of
those of the islanders'
forefathers who were called
Long-ears because they
distended their pierced
earlobes with large plugs. The
other natives, the Short-ears,
helped the Long-ears to raise
the colossal statues, but
rebelled when they were forced
to clear the entire Poike
peninsula of stones. They
burned the Long-ears in a pyre
the Long-ears themselves had
lit in a defensive ditch running
across the width of the
peninsula.

The whole of Easter Island was
bare of trees when the
Europeans came. The island
was covered with loose stones
under a layer of grass and fern.
The first visitors tried in vain to
estimate the size of the island's
population, but, because of the
marked discrepancy in numbers
between men and women,
suspected that there were
secret hiding places inland. Nor
could they ever again find the
belongings that the islanders
stole from them.

Some of the island's plants were identified by the visitors. They added the
gourd, the *yuca* and the *achira* to the Dutchmen's list, and identified the local
reeds as the South American totora, the freshwater plant that was also used by
the Peruvian aborigines for making mats, houses and watercraft. They described
the boat shaped totora-reed huts precisely as the Dutch had, but added that such
houses were used only by powerful families; most of the natives lived in underground caves, the entrances to which were so narrow that it was necessary to
wriggle in feet first.

Hervé recorded that the islanders bred their chickens "in little runs scraped
out in the ground and thatched over." This seemingly unimportant remark later
assumes its own importance in the jigsaw puzzle that is Easter Island.

Although the Spaniards rowed all around the coast in their launch, they saw
neither boats nor mariners, only two very frail canoes, "so crank that they are
provided with an outrigger to prevent them from capsizing," each with two men
bringing bananas, chicken, and sweet potatoes to the visitors.

Agüera recorded that the giant statues were still greatly venerated, and he

A banana plant marks the entrance to one of the numerous open caves. The first Europeans to visit Easter Island were presented with gifts of bananas and chickens, a custom that continues today. Unlike the sweet potato and the gourd, the banana plant and the chicken could not have been introduced by seafarers from Peru, only from Polynesia. The observations of the first Europeans thus constitute genetic proof that Easter Island had been visited by seafarers from both east and west before the Europeans themselves discovered it.

The open landscape is rich in natural hiding places. Some of the caves were well known to all, while others had secret entrances. In a society where theft was a way of life, the latter often contained hidden family treasures. All that was needed was a boulder of suitable size to conceal the narrow entrance, which led into passages and vaults in the rock made by gas bubbles in the once-molten lava.

disproved the theory of the Dutchman, who had suggested that they were patched together from clay: "The material of the statue is very hard stone and therefore weighty; having tried it myself with a hoe it struck fire: a proof of its density." He marveled at the task of setting up such superb statues and keeping them balanced on a raised platform. How people lacking machinery, he said, could raise the colossal headpiece onto a monument of such height causes wonder. "Much remains to be worked out on this subject."

The records of these visitors from Peru in 1770 confirm in general the observations made by the Dutch almost fifty years earlier. The population appeared to have decreased, but, wary after their previous encounter with Europeans, perhaps more of the islanders preferred to stay in hiding. The mixture of physical types was clearly the same: some dark, some red-skinned, some resembling Europeans. The reference to the frail canoes with outriggers points to Polynesia, but in the fields the visitors from Peru recognized many plants from South America: the sweet potato, two varieties of gourd, totora reeds and even *yuca* and *achira*. Only the sweet potato and gourd had spread further out to other islands in Polynesia. Nevertheless, they, too, had come from either Peru or Chile, because sweet potatoes and gourds are among the most common plants found in pre-Inca tombs, dating back to periods long before Polynesia was settled.

Two hundred years would pass before the scientific world realized that the early Spanish visitors had repeatedly listed *yuca* and *achira* among the important Easter Island food crops. The word *yuca* is the term for manioc in various indigenous languages of Peru and other Central and South American countries, and this plant is a tropical American tuber propagated by stem cuttings. When the documents of the Gonzalez expedition were translated into English and published by the prominent British scholar Bolton G. Corney in 1908, he was so dumbfounded at finding a reference to South American *yuca* on Easter Island prior to European influence, that he concealed or obfuscated the evidence of manioc. In one instance he rendered the word *yuca* erroneously as "taro"; in three others he left it untranslated, adding erroneous footnotes confusing the readers. Not until 1986 did a Spanish scholar, Francisco Mellén Blanco, revise and bring together all the documents from the Gonzalez expedition, and in 1988 Robert Langdon of the Australian National University caused a sensation in the scientific world by publishing in *The Geographical Journal* a paper entitled "Manioc: A Long-Concealed Key to the Enigma of Easter Island." According to Langdon, Corney in his translation acted as he did because, in the climate of his times, he simply could not believe that manioc could have reached Easter Island prior to European influence. Langdon's conclusion was that the fact that manioc was clearly reported as cultivated on that Polynesian island in 1770 "greatly strengthens the case for prehistoric American Indian influence on Easter Island and other islands of eastern Polynesia."

The recorded vocabulary and the reference to a local form of script were also very significant new pieces in the puzzle. The Spaniards had no knowledge of any other Pacific island language, and thus the word list compiled by Agüera was based on a completely unbiased selection of random terms. The list includes words plainly of Polynesian origin, and others which are as clearly not. An example of the latter are the numerals, which differ totally from those of all Polynesian dialects. Nor do they have the slightest resemblance to Polynesian words with a different meaning. The Easter Island numbers recorded in 1770 (with their present Polynesian numbers of postmissionary origin in parentheses) were:

Left: Tapa figurine from Easter Island in the Belfast Museum of Art, Ireland. These figurines were made by the same technique as the large *paina* figures seen by the González expedition on the island. The art of handling the great stone statues was lost when the Long-ears were overthrown, and the much lighter *paina* figures were probably used as substitutes on the image *ahus* during latter-day ceremonies at the land witnessed by Spaniards from Peru in the eighteenth century.

In the later civil war period, tapa figures both large and small were carefully hidden away in caves—as indeed were other artifacts on Easter Island. Only a very few were preserved for posterity. During the nineteenth century, they found their way to museums in Boston and Belfast.

one: *coyana* (etahi), two: *corena* (erua), three: *cogujui* (etoru), four: *quiroqui* (eha), five: *majana* (erima), six: *feuto* (eono), seven: *fegea* (ehitu), eight: *moroqui* (evaru), nine: *vijoviri* (eiva), ten: *queromata* (etahi te anguhuru, and also etahi te kauatu).

Thus, in the eighteenth century, the language of the Easter Islanders clearly showed they were of mixed stock. We know today that many unrelated languages were spoken in pre-Inca time by the maritime peoples along the extensive coast from Ecuador to Chile, but we also know that, a few centuries before the Spaniards arrived, the highland Incas had conquered all those territories east of Easter Island and imposed their own Quechua language on every tribe and nation throughout their empire. The loss of the original language of the coastal cultures of western South America has deprived us of the basis for any comparison with the non-Polynesian words in Agüera's list.

The mixed population of Easter Island must have included at least one group with a rather advanced cultural inheritance. Their artist-engineers had carved statues of a stone so hard that they struck fire when hit with a hoe, and as high as three-story buildings. In addition, we learn that they had their own writing system. Script is a criterion of civilization. No one nation in Europe invented script. The art of writing reached Europe from the great Middle Eastern civilizations, and we can follow its spread from the early Sumerians up the Mesopotamian rivers to the Hittites and Phoenicians on the Mediterranean coast, and then on to Greece by way of Crete. Had the little community on lonely Easter Island invented a writing system on their own? Certainly those of them who had come from Polynesia had not brought it with them. No Polynesian tribe possessed the art of writing, and there was no script to be found westward in the entire Pacific closer than continental China on the opposite side of the planet. But a variety of distinct writing systems were in use in pre-Columbian America, in the culturally advanced territories nearest to Easter Island: Mexico, Central America, and, prior to the Inca period, apparently in Peru, as well. The casual reference by the chroniclers to a lost, pre-Inca script adds nothing to our knowledge apart from emphasizing the sparse global distribution of such writing.

The success of the Gonzalez expedition's itinerary may give us some information about feasible routes traveled prior to European exploration. By follow-

Headdress from Easter Island made of stuffed tapa in the shape of a feline head. There were no felines on any of the islands of Polynesia, but in pre-Inca Peru a puma's head was a symbol of chieftainship and often formed part of kings' headdresses. It is evident from the shape of the head, the cheeks and the spotted skin on the nose that the Easter Island artist tried to depict some kind of legendary feline figure. The museum in Boston acquired two such catlike headdresses from Easter Island during the nineteenth century.

ing the recollected itinerary of Inca Tupac Yupanqui to the nearest of the two islands described, the Spaniards from Peru found that one island lay just where Inca sailing directions had placed it. It was Easter Island. Both the Spaniards and, earlier, the Dutch, had found the island because they sighted smoke from fires lit along the coast.

Perhaps the Inca sailing fleet had had the same experience even earlier, and, because of the signals, named the place Fire Island. It is a Polynesian custom to send up columns of smoke to attract the attention of passing ships. When, in 1947, the raft *Kon-Tiki* drifted into Polynesia from Peru, we went past Pukapuka in the dark and discovered the island in the morning because of the smoke signals. A fire was next lit on the adjacent island of Angatau, in a futile attempt to make us turn and come ashore.

The probability that the Gonzalez expedition had discovered Nina Chumbi, Fire Island, and not Ava Chumbi is augmented by the fact that Ava Chumbi can now be identified as Mangareva, the next inhabited island further west. Mangareva was the island Roggeveen had been searching for in 1772, when he discovered Easter Island.

According to a tradition on Mangareva, the inhabitants believe that a legendary foreign ruler named Tupa had once come sailing from the east with a large fleet of rafts. The fleet remained afloat for a long time at the entrance to the lagoon on the east side of the reef. There, King Tupa camped on an island named Kava. The lagoon entrance was subsequently called Te-Ava-nui-o-Tupa, or "the great channel of Tupa." The legend was first reported by F. W. Christian, a British explorer who had not heard of Inca Tupac's voyage before. He wrote: "And the Mangarevans have a tradition of a chief called Tupa, a red man, who came from the east with a fleet of canoes of non-Polynesian model, more like rafts—surely a memory of some Peruvian *balsas* or raftships." The anthropologist Paul Rivet later suggested that it was Inca Tupac who had visited Mangareva, but later, when Sir Peter Buck published the Tupa tradition in his *Ethnology of Mangareva* Buck ignored the possibility that South American balsa rafts could have kept their buoyancy long enough to have visited Polynesia.

It seems safe enough to conclude that "The-Navel-of-the-World," called San Carlos by the Spaniards and Easter Island by the Dutchmen, was the Nina Chumbi of the Incas of Peru.

Captain Cook's island of misery

On the 11th of March 1774, only four years after the Spanish visit, Captain James Cook dropped anchor off the coast of Easter Island. It was Cook's second voyage of discovery in the South Seas, and the first time European sailing ships had managed to reach Polynesia from the direction of Asia. Cook had discovered that by sailing south from New Zealand he could avoid the tropical currents and trade winds, and take advantage of the westerly winds in the cold latitudes of the Antarctic drift ice. For most of the voyage he struggled with Antarctic blizzards and rough seas (between 60° and 70° south), but before reaching Chile he turned

Captain James Cook came to Easter Island in 1774, only four years after the Spaniards from Peru, and the expedition's artist, W. Hodges, made drawings of two of the Long-ears. When not filled out by plugs, the distended earlobes hung almost to their shoulders. The man wears a chieftain's feather bonnet, while the woman has a reed hat shaped like a reed boat. Roggeveen and González had found a mixed population, many of whom were tall, red-headed and pale-skinned. Cook, however, found a decimated population living in abject poverty, with the dark-skinned race in the majority.

north with the Humboldt Current, caught the easterly trade winds and, like the previous visitors, came upon Easter Island from the east. His trying voyage from New Zealand took him three-and-a-half months. Gonzalez had sailed to the island from Peru under pleasant conditions in five weeks.

With Cook on board the *Resolution* were two famous naturalists, George Forster and son. After the ordeal of their voyage through Antarctic waters, the Englishmen were in desperate need of fresh provisions. Having read the records of Roggeveen and Gonzalez, they arrived with great expectations, but upon landing made no effort to hide their disappointment. Both the island and its inhabitants seemed totally transformed in the four years since the Spanish visit. Cook's party found the islanders in a distressing condition and even the ground itself was described by them as dry and covered with stones. Forster wrote that the only

article of importance available was sweet potatoes, but after sharing out all they purchased it barely sufficed the sailors for a few scanty meals. He stressed that the other food crops scarcely deserved to be mentioned, and the fowl they obtained did not amount to fifty. Even water was scarce and had a bad taste. Less than thirty women were seen, and the entire population estimated at fewer than seven hundred; the natives were described as small, lean, timid and miserable. Cook did not see "anything which can induce ships that are not in the utmost distress to touch at this island." And added: "No nation need contend for the honour of the discovery of this island, as there can be few places which afford less convenience for shipping than it does."

Clearly, something drastic must have happened in the four years intervening between the voyages of Gonzalez and Cook. Here was a new mystery. Forster noticed abandoned plantations even on the summits of the hills, and postulated that perhaps a volcanic catastrophe might have reduced a formerly numerous and wealthy population to sudden misery.

In contrast to the previous visitors' accounts, the English found the poverty-stricken islanders to be armed. Cook recorded that they possessed offensive weapons in the form of short wooden clubs and spears. Forster described the latter as made of thin, crooked sticks with a sharp triangular piece of black glassy lava or flint forming a point at one end. He was puzzled by the fact that the friendly Easter Islanders now carried arms; he emphasized that they were too isolated for foreign wars, their numbers too inconsiderable, and their poverty too general to create great civil disturbances among them. "... we must add this circumstance to several others which are inexplicable to us in their kind."

To further the general impression of disaster, the English reported that many of the giants had now fallen and the elevated platforms on which they stood were visibly damaged. Forster uses the expression "overturned." On the west coast, where the *Resolution* anchored, the Englishmen could see several giants still standing, three of them on one huge platform and another, twenty feet tall, standing nearby balancing on a marvelously built wall, with a superimposed cylinder five feet in diameter on its crown. But an exploring party surveying the southeast coast reported the ruins of three platforms, each one of which had supported four stone giants. All had fallen from two of these platforms and one from the third, and each was broken in the fall or in some measure defaced.

Although the destruction seemed recent, Cook described the statues as "monuments of antiquity" and wrote: "... they must have been a work of immense time, and sufficiently show the ingenuity and perseverance of the islanders in the age in which they were built; for the present inhabitants have most certainly had no hand in them, as they do not even repair the foundations of those which are going to decay." Forster agreed. He said of the prehistoric vestiges: "... the most diligent enquiries on our part have not been sufficient to throw a clear light

Cook's Bay by the village of Hanga-roa, where Captain Cook's ship once lay at anchor.

Cook's expedition was the first to find many of the stone giants lying face-down. They had been tipped over, and the red cylinders that had crowned them were scattered over the temple court. Some had even rolled down to the water's edge, which gave rise to speculations that they had been shipped there from overseas. The misery and destruction that had fallen upon the islanders and their monuments in the four years that had passed since the visit from Peru made the British visitors wonder whether the island had suffered a natural disaster. Modern research has shown, however, that a series of tribal wars had raged on Easter Island during the period since the fall of the Long-ears a hundred years earlier. These wars continued to erupt periodically until the arrival of the missionaries in the second half of the nineteenth century.

on the surprising objects which struck our eyes in this island." About the gigantic monuments he said: "It is most reasonable to look upon them as the remains of better times. The nicest calculations which we could make never brought the number of inhabitants in this island beyond seven hundred, who, destitute of tools, of shelter, and clothing, are obliged to spend all their time in providing food to support their precarious existence."

The English found that the stone giants were no longer worshiped, although some islanders expressed their displeasure when the visitors walked across the stone platforms or examined the stones too closely. They observed that the platforms now seemed to be used as burying places for certain tribes or families. They saw a human skeleton lying inside one of them, covered with stones, and, looking around, they saw more human bones. They tried to get some information from the islanders, and from it concluded that the statues were monuments erected to the memory of some of their *ariki*, or kings. They learned that the statues had individual names, such as Gotomoara, Marapate, Kanaro, Gowaytoogoo, and Matta Matta, to which they sometimes prefixed the word *Moi* (actually

The *ahu* at Vinapu. The British expedition marveled at the precision of the masonry in the stone walls on Easter Island. Cook compared them to the best in England. He was particularly impressed by the huge wall of perfectly dressed megaliths at Hanga-roa, which unfortunately no longer exists—the blocks were used to build a new harbor. The dimensions of the structures and the perfect fit of the huge stone blocks were compared to the wall that can still be seen at Vinapu.

moai, the local term for image) and sometimes added the title *ariki.*

The technical achievement of the early generations who had erected the giant statues caused considerable speculation among the Englishmen. Forster admitted: "It was incomprehensible to me how such great masses could be formed by

What language did they speak, the people of the culture that depicted itself with such a tight-lipped expression? Cook managed with the help of a Tahitian interpreter to identify a few Polynesian words, but recorded that the language was incomprehensible even to his Tahitian helper. All Cook's interpreter could determine was that each statue had a specific name and had been raised in memory of a dead chieftain. The proud facial expressions and the long fingernails support this account, as such a manicure would have made any kind of manual labor impossible.

a set of people among whom we saw no tools; or raised and erected by them without machinery."

Cook and the members of his exploring party had different opinions as to the makeup of the statues. Cook examined a couple standing near the bay where he landed, and was convinced they were of stone, whereas the others, who had traveled further afield, were of the opinion that the material was fictitious. Captain Cook, a remarkably practical man, made the following entry in his own expedition report:

"We could hardly conceive how these islanders, wholly unacquainted with any mechanical power, could raise such stupendous figures, and afterwards place the large cylindric stones upon their heads. The only method I can conceive is by raising the upper end by little and little, supporting it by stones as it is raised, and building about it till they got it erect; thus a sort of mount, or scaffolding, would be made, on which they might roll the cylinder, and place it upon the head of the statue, and then the stones might be removed from about it. But if the stones are fictitious, the statues might have been put together on the place in their present position, and the cylinder put on by building a mount round them as above mentioned."

Nearly two centuries would pass before the seemingly casual descriptions and thoughts of Captain Cook became more than mere entertaining reading. Only today can we return to his and Forster's reports and fully understand the importance of comments that for a long time seemed to have little or no bearing on the solution of any problem. The Englishmen described statues nobody else had seen standing. Of particular interest is the mention of some standing here and there along a road, leading toward the Rano Raraku image quarry. The exploring party followed this road eastward from the great megalithic wall at Vinapu. Although they did not recognize the quarry for what it was, they must have come very close, to judge from a drawing by the expedition's artist. Forster described the road as a kind of cleared path through the stony terrain, on each side of

Cook's companions followed the ancient image road east from Vinapu and discovered individual stone giants left lying on the ground far from the *ahu* platforms. A few of them still stood erect, but were not firmly supported—they appeared to have been abandoned in haste. The largest of them shaded the whole party of nearly thirty men from the afternoon sun.

The members of Cook's expedition made no mention of the stone quarry at Rano Raraku, and historians have assumed that they never got that far. The assumption is wrong. The sides of the volcanic mountain may have been so overgrown with tall grass and shrubs before the introduction of sheep that nobody could see the quarry. The illustrations in Cook's own account of his voyage show that the expedition did reach Rano Raraku, where the quarry was. The statue beside the banana plant in Hodges's drawing is lying on its back with its head down the slope, and could only have been drawn from the foot of the volcano.

which grew a thin Jamaica grass so slippery that the Englishmen could not walk on it. Whereas the images on the burial platforms stood aloft on carefully built stone structures, those along the road were simply standing on the ground. Cook found it noteworthy that in general the latter were larger than those of the platforms. One which had fallen was measured, and found to be nearly twenty-seven-feet long with shoulders eight feet broad, and he wrote: "Yet this appeared considerably short of the size of one they saw standing: its shade, a little past two o'clock, being sufficient to shelter all the party, consisting of near thirty persons, from the rays of sun."

Returning toward their anchorage in Hanga-roa, the exploring party passed

The quarry in the Puna Pau crater, where the red topknots of the statues were made. Cook's party passed this crater on their way back across the island to Hanga-roa Bay. The British party found unfinished topknots lying abandoned in the extinct volcano, while finished cylinders lay up on the edge of the crater ready to be rolled to their respective destinations. The makers of the giant statues had picked a crater over four miles from the Rano Raraku quarry to get the special red scoria they wanted to decorate the heads of the images. The early European visitors, who could not speak the language, called these cylinders "hats." We now know that the local name for them was *pukao*, the native word for the traditional male topknot hairdo. A fair skin, European cast of feature, red hair and long ears combine to make up the first visitors' description of the priestly class that attended the images.

the volcanic cone of Puna Pau and looked into the crater of red volcanic scoria. There they found abandoned by the prehistoric sculptors a number of the large red stone cylinders which had never been transported to the statues they were designed for.

Cook was amazed by the design and workmanship of some of the megalithic platforms supporting the stone giants. He found them not inferior to the best stone facing in England. He noticed that although no cement was used, the joints were exceedingly tight and enormous stones mortised and tenoned one into another. The most impressive of these walls was in Hanga-roa. Forster wrote: "A remarkable circumstance was the junction of these stones, which were laid after the most excellent rules of art, fitting in such a manner as to make a durable piece of architecture."

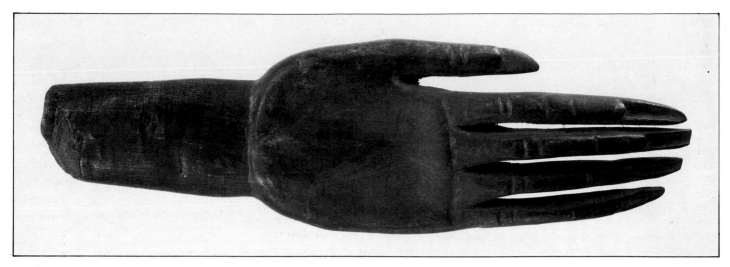

Wooden hand collected by members of Cook's expedition in 1774. Forster, a scientist with the expedition, took a great interest in this find. The long fingernails, similar to those found on the statues, indicate royal or high rank.

Subsequent European settlers broke this structure apart in a futile attempt to build a port, and we can only guess at its appearance by studying the now-famous wall in Vinapu. Visiting the image platform, where four out of seven statues were found standing, the Englishmen compared it to the one in Hanga-roa and found it to be "fitted exactly in the same manner."

Cook surprised the world by bringing back to Europe the strangest collection of small figurines. Hitherto the impression had been that no art had been produced on Easter Island except the colossal monoliths, which all followed a standard pattern. Suddenly the Englishmen returned with figurines carved in wood, testifying to a prolific imagination and unusual artistic ability. They were clearly not carved for the occasion, and must have been kept in hiding. Forster assumed that it was the poverty of the islanders and their desire to obtain some cloth from the English travelers that prompted them to expose such articles for sale—articles they would not have parted with under other circumstances.

The previous visitors had found nothing but mats and stone pillows inside the huts, and the Englishmen saw nothing but containers made from gourds, so where could these art objects have been hidden? Forster pointed out that there were so few of the boat-shaped reed-houses that they must be crammed full at night unless most of the people slept in the open. He was admitted through the funnel-shaped opening of one of them, and wrote: "We crept on all fours into this opening, and found the inside of the hut perfectly naked and empty, there being not so much as a wisp of straw to lie down upon." Cook observed, however, that some of the islanders had "a kind of vaulted houses built of stone," but he never went inside any of them. He suspected that some of the stone structures might communicate with natural caverns, and wished he could have pursued this suspicion, but was prevented by the islanders, who always denied him admittance.

The need for hiding places was as apparent as ever. Cook wrote: "It was with some difficulty we could keep the hats on our heads, but hardly possible to keep anything in our pockets, not even what [they] themselves had sold us; for they would watch every opportunity to snatch it from us, so that we sometimes bought the same thing two or three times over, and after all did not get it."

Articles that the Spaniards before them had lost and never seen again were now openly displayed. The Englishmen noticed a broad-brimmed Spanish hat, a

grego jacket and several handkerchiefs clearly lost by the Gonzalez expedition.

Cook's party saw only small, lean and miserable people on Easter Island, but Cook, the first known foreign visitor with any previous knowledge of Polynesia, recognized Polynesian features in some of them. Where were the white, red-haired giants with European traits the Dutchmen had discovered and the Spaniards described only four years earlier? Were they in hiding or had they been massacred? Cook had brought with him from his previous visit to Polynesia a native of Tahiti named Oededee (properly Otiti). He noted that the first Easter Islander who boarded the *Resolution* fathomed the ships' length while calling the numbers in Tahitian. Still, Cook added, "his language was, in a manner, wholly unintelligible to all of us." This is an important statement. The Englishmen tried to communicate with the islanders through the aid of Otiti, but with scant success. Even the simple effort of obtaining the name of the island failed. They recorded three different names, but none made sense. The one suggested by Otiti was Teapy, which was obviously a mistake and showed, to Cook, Otiti's inability to communicate. Cook, however, with the aid of Otiti, was able to assemble a list of seventeen carefully selected words that were clearly Polynesian. He published only these, and omitted samples of the local word list, which, in his words, were "wholly unintelligible," even to Otiti. He therefore unintentionally gave subsequent linguistic researchers a misleading impression of the Easter Island language.

Cook is generally quoted to show that the Easter Islanders of his time spoke Polynesian. The local language was in fact so remarkably *non*-Polynesian that Cook was unable to make use of his Polynesian interpreter. His word list tells us no more about the ethnic composition of the Easter Island community than what we have already seen in Agüera's unselective word list: that clearly a Polynesian element existed among the aboriginal settlers of Easter Island.

Resolution rode at anchor off Hanga-roa, subsequently known as Cook's Bay, for five days, but the visitors only made two trips ashore. The expedition then hoisted sail for the usual easy downwind passage into tropical Polynesia.

Bizarre but artistic figures, finely carved in red toromiro wood, began to emerge from their hiding places during Cook's stay. In 1774, the British visitors came to the conclusion that the poverty that had fallen upon the island since the Spaniards' previous visit had induced the natives to barter away heirlooms with which they would not otherwise have parted willingly.

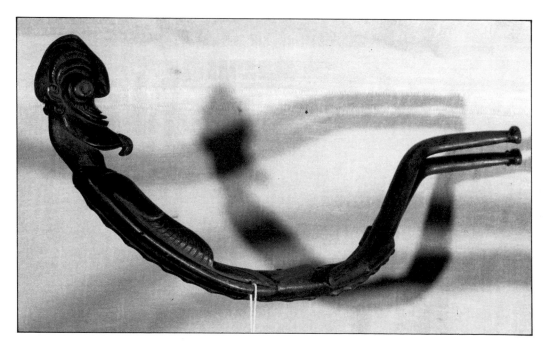

The *moai kavakava*, or ribbed image, was a common motif of woodcarvings from Easter Island. They were first seen in Europe when Captain Cook's expedition returned home. These figurines always depict a tall, thin, stooped man with long ears, goatee, hooked nose, prominent ribs, short legs and circumcised genitals. Island tradition tells of two kings who came to Easter Island independently of each other, bringing distinct groups of settlers with them: first Hotu Matua from the east, and later Tuu-ko-ihu from the west. It was Tuu-ko-ihu who carved the first *moai kavakava* portraying two wretched *aku-aku* whom he found hiding in the topknot quarry. Tuu-ko-ihu was probably a Short-ear, while the long-eared figurines he carved represented the folk from the east who were already on the island.

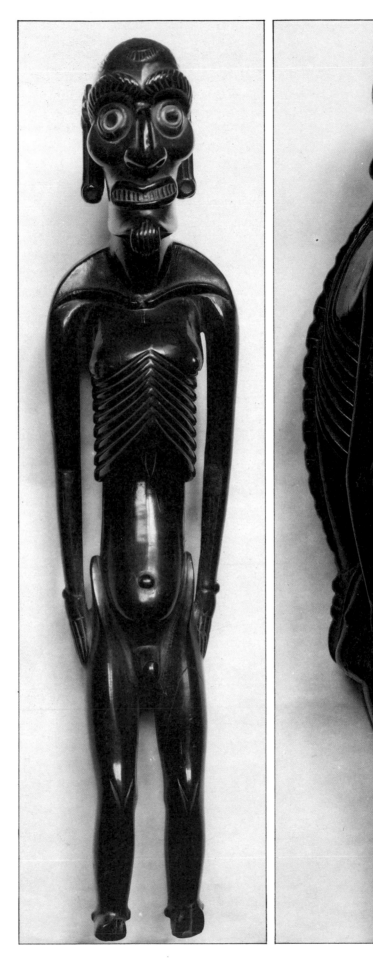

Top: The *moai papa,* or flat image, was another common type of woodcarving that Cook and his crew were the first to collect. There is no legend to explain the significance or origin of these wooden sculptures, but great pains were always taken to make them as flat as possible, even if it wasted a great deal of wood.

Bottom: Flat female figures of this type also occurred widely in ancient Peru, where they are believed to have symbolized a flat "Mother Earth" (*pampa,* meaning flat or a plain). Such flat female figurines have often been found in pre-Inca graves on the coast of Peru, and are always equally flat, whether they are carved in wood or molded in gold or clay. Their kinship to the *moai papa* of Easter Island is underlined by the fact that they were sometimes attached to strings so that they could be worn or jiggled like their Easter Island counterparts. Statuettes of this kind are not found on any other islands in the Pacific.

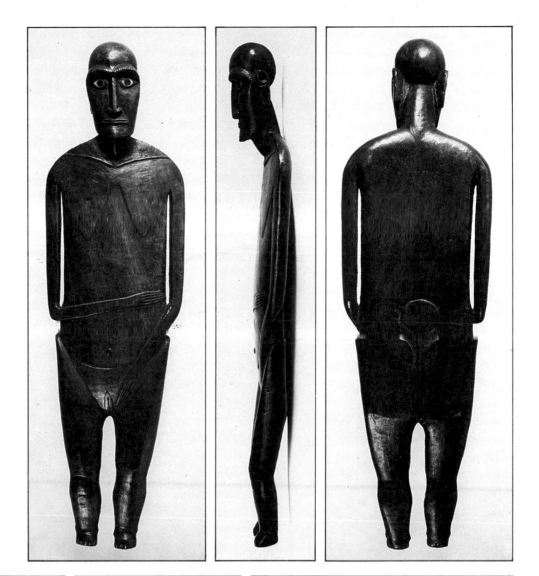

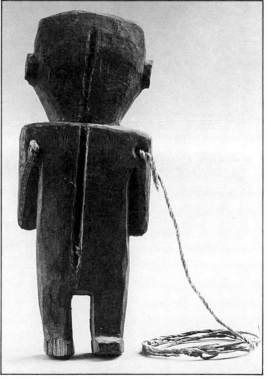

Most deductions from Cook and Forster's observations in 1774 will follow the development of subsequent events. What immediately emerges, obviously, is the fact that some drama had taken place on the navel of the world in the four-year period since Gonzalez' visit. Easter Island is not in the earthquake zone, and volcanoes had not been active since man opened quarries in the crater walls and planted reeds in the lakes at their bottom. A tidal wave could have hit one coast, but not overthrown statues at random all around the island. Human hostilities seem to be the only remaining explanation, the more so since the miserable survivors were now armed with clubs and spears. These islanders had no neighbors, but were themselves a mixed lot, so it could have been a civil war that forced them to abandon their fields and spurred them on to tear down the statues their ancestors had set up. According to what Cook's men learned, these stone colossi were funeral monuments erected in honor of deceased chiefs, and since all were carved with long ears, it would seem reasonable to ascribe their presence to the specific ethnic group that practiced ear extension. According to the earlier Dutch voyagers, these had been the ones who showed most care for the statues.

That the mysterious little island concealed secrets which the heirs to the giant images kept to themselves became more apparent when a new form of art emerged, out of a landscape so barren that everything seemed to be immediately obvious to the eye.

Forth from hiding to meet the Frenchmen

So far as is recorded, the people of Easter Island were to receive foreign visitors only once more in the eighteenth century. In 1786, Admiral J.F.G. de la Pérouse sailed two French frigates on a direct downwind voyage from the central coast of Chile.

Easter Island had again changed face. The twelve years that had passed since Cook's visit had sufficed to re-establish the island's normal economy, but did not, however, explain the sudden reappearance of a proportionate number of women. When the Frenchmen landed in Hanga-roa, or Cook's Bay, they counted some twelve hundred natives assembled ashore, out of which about three hundred were women. A great many more women with their children were seen in the interior of the island, and La Pérouse estimated the population to be at least two thousand, equally divided between both sexes. The great majority of women must therefore have been hidden during Cook's visit, as the Englishmen saw fewer than thirty. Oddly, the French visitors did not see a single old man on the island. La Pérouse wrote:

"We all entered into those caverns in which Mr. Forster and some officers of Captain Cook had first supposed the women might have been concealed. They are subterranean dwelling places. . . . That the inhabitants, however, concealed their women when Captain Cook visited them in 1772 [actually 1774], there can be no doubt; but it is impossible for me to ascertain the cause. It is probable, that to his generous conduct with regard to this people we were indebted for the confidence they showed us, which enabled us to judge more accurately of the state of their population."

Even the men seemed to have changed. Rollin, surgeon-major of the expedition, wrote:

"Instead of meeting with men exhausted by famine . . . I found, on the contrary, a considerable population, with more beauty and grace than I afterwards met with in any other island; and a soil, which, with very little labour, furnished excellent provisions, and in abundance more than sufficient for the consumption of the inhabitants. . . ."

La Pérouse felt that three days of labor by each native would be sufficient to procure subsistence for a year. Scarcely one tenth of the island was cultivated at that time, but what had been done showed great skill and was tidily arranged in regular strips. The Frenchmen described the islanders as agriculturalists, their subsistence came from the land, not from the sea. The crop was the same as that recorded by the previous visitors, but La Pérouse made the first attempt to introduce new species. The expedition gardener went about the island sowing maize and a variety of other crops, and the Frenchmen also planted fruit trees and sent ashore a pair of hogs, a pair of goats, and three sheep as gifts to the people.

Planting new crops all over the island enabled La Pérouse to form an opinion of the local soil, and he advanced the theory that barren Easter Island had once been densely wooded, and that the disappearance of the forest was the cause of the decline of the ancient civilization. Both La Pérouse and de Langle, captain of the accompanying vessel, agreed with Cook and his companions in considering the great monuments to be vestiges of antiquity. De Langle observed some statues on the edge of the Rano Kao crater which were so visibly eroded that he saw in them the proof that the volcano had been inactive for many centuries. The hypothesis advanced by La Pérouse was that the original civilization bloomed while the island was still wooded and thus rich in springs and brooks, which later vanished when man destroyed the forest. With the trees gone, the soil was exposed to the burning heat of the sun. The ruling classes disappeared; in the arid landscape that arose, everybody became equally poor and could not persuade others to help erect monuments. He concluded:

"Thus the wonder disappears; . . . if there are no other more modern monuments on the island, it is because all conditions are equal; because a man finds little temptation to become a king of a people almost naked, and who lives upon potatoes and yams; and because, as these Indians cannot make war from the want of neighbors they have no need of a chief."

The possibility that the island had been ravaged by civil wars did not occur to La Pérouse, as he stated that the people were without arms with the exception of three or four, each of whom carried a long wooden club that might have been a chieftain's symbol.

The expedition engineer, M. Bernizet, made the first careful study of the various forms of Easter Island dwellings. He described and illustrated with detailed drawings three different types of houses—and thereby deepened the Easter Island mystery. All three were completely unlike usual Polynesian house forms, and each type was so unique that there must have been a special reason for their existence on the island.

An important type, obviously, were the boat-shaped reed huts already described by previous visitors. One measured by the engineer was found to be three hundred and ten feet long, but only ten feet wide at center, narrowing to

The next expedition landed on Easter Island in 1786, led by the Frenchman La Pérouse. This time the women emerged from their hiding places, a change of attitude which the Frenchmen ascribed to the gentlemanly behavior of the British twelve years earlier. The expedition's artist here shows the visitors measuring images that still stood erect on their stone platforms, crowned with topknots in place. The islanders' admiration for theft as a fine art was something that Europeans found hard to understand. The artist has drawn a man in the act of stealing a French hat lying on the *ahu*, while a woman hiding behind a fallen stone topknot picks a Frenchman's pocket. Two women are admiring a mirror brought by a Frenchman; one of them is wearing a boat-shaped reed hat of the same type as the one drawn by Cook's artist.

The first architectural drawings of an Easter Island *ahu* were made in 1786 by M. Bernizet, the engineer of the French expedition. The stone-clad structure falls away steeply on the seaward side, while the side facing the open temple court takes the form of a flight of steps, giving the *ahu* the shape of a stepped semi-pyramid. The foundation contains a burial chamber of later date.

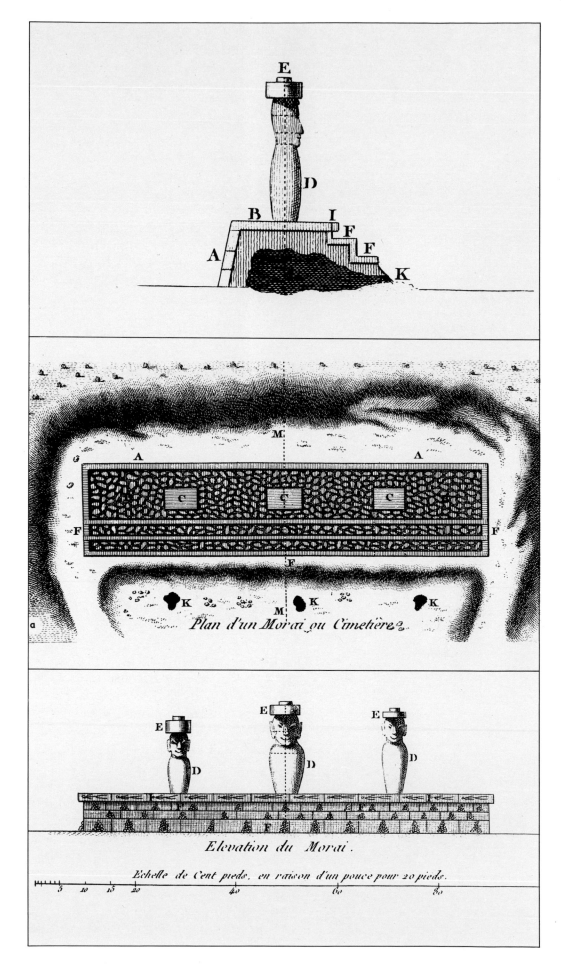

Plan d'un Morai ou Cimetière.

Elevation du Morai.

Echelle de Cent pieds, en raison d'un pouce pour 20 pieds.

a point at each end. La Pérouse saw one of them in Hanga-roa which he said was large enough to contain upward of two hundred persons. Given this dimension and the lack of furniture, he concluded that it might have been the home of a chief. With the addition of two or three other small houses a little distance apart, it formed a village by itself. Cooking was done outside in a stone-lined earth oven.

The second type of house was built entirely from stone. The ground plan was rounded or ellipsoid, with extremely thick walls, and the vaulted roof was built from slabs placed horizontally to form a false arch. No mortar was used in the construction.

The third type was an entirely underground structure, and thus as non-Polynesian as the two others. A stone-lined ramp, terminating in steps of cut stone, led to an underground door, the uprights, cornice and architrave of which were formed of large cut stones neatly joined together. The dwelling itself was a rounded or oval cell cut out of the rock, with the same form and dimensions as the stone houses on the surface.

Although the Frenchmen entered all three types of houses, they saw none of the wood carvings the islanders had brought forth from hiding and sold to the Englishmen in their time of distress.

The religious structures were also studied by the Frenchmen, who discovered that some of the image platforms had large plazas on the inland side, surrounded by parapets. One such enclosure was measured to be over three hundred and twenty-eight feet long and almost square, and the visitors were unable to determine whether it was an unfinished reservoir for water or the commencement of a fortress. Some of these walled enclosures were partly, and others completely, obliterated by silt.

The expedition engineer examined equally attentively the elevated masonry platforms on which some of the statues were still standing, their cylinders on their heads, and discovered three irregular caves had been dug into the core of one of them. They were filled with a great quantity of human bones. La Pérouse agreed that the image platforms were used as burial places, but said that in recent years the islanders had reduced their efforts by simply building small pyramidal heaps of stones with a whitewashed boulder on top. He vividly described how an islander lay down on the ground by the side of one of these little heaps, pretending to be dead, explaining that they covered a grave. And by raising his hands toward heaven he appeared to be trying to say that the spirit had escaped to the sky. La Pérouse said that at first he was cautious about acknowledging that the native believed in another life, but when de Langle and others reported that they had seen the same thing, he and all the officers of his ships came to the conclusion that the Easter Islanders did believe in an afterlife.

The French expedition accomplished all this during a ten-hour visit, and in the evening of the day of their arrival they continued downwind into Polynesia proper. The Easter Islanders were to again remain undisturbed by European visitors—until the beginning of the next century.

The precise studies of Easter Island architecture published by the French make us pause for reflection. The word lists collected by the Spaniards and the Englishmen had shown the presence of a Polynesian element on the island. But why were none of the houses built in the Polynesian manner? There are neither boat-shaped houses, stone houses, nor subterranean dwellings in Polynesia, and the presence of three distinct non-Polynesian house forms calls for a reasonable

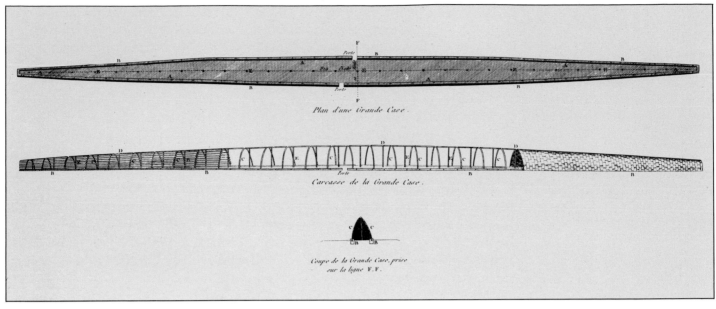

Plan d'une Grande Case.

Carcasse de la Grande Case.

Coupe de la Grande Case, prise sur la ligne F.F.

The various types of dwelling on Easter Island were carefully studied by the La Pérouse expedition. Bernizet made measurements and drawings of three quite distinct types, all clearly un-Polynesian. One type was extremely elongated, built of bent branches and totora reeds and shaped like an upturned canoe. One such house was nearly 328 feet long and could hold two hundred people, but the entrance was so low that one had to wriggle in feet-first *(above)*.

The second type was built entirely of stone, with thick masonry walls rising to an arched roof *(right)*. The third was an underground dwelling, invisible from ground level except for the square entrance leading to a sloping tunnel that ended in steps before a stone doorway *(bottom)*. None of them were of Polynesian design. Stone buildings were totally alien to Polynesian culture, though they were characteristic of pre-Inca settlements on the nearest part of the mainland.

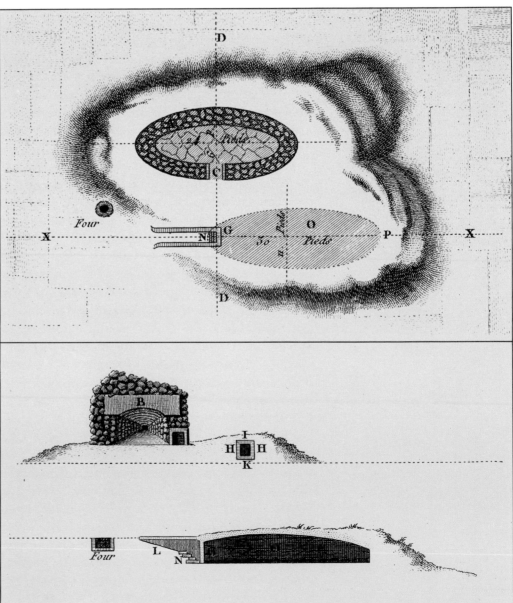

Round stone tower with square entrance as drawn by the French visitors to Easter Island. The tower is a *tupa*, a mysterious structure that was common in the area known today as La Pérouse Bay, after its French discoverer. The present-day islanders cannot explain the original purpose of these buildings, but the un-Polynesian *tupa* is strongly reminiscent of the *chullpa* often found among the pre-Inca ruins on the arid slopes from Lake Titicaca down to the Pacific coast. In both regions, these prehistoric towers are presumably the remains of plundered mausoleums from an earlier period.

explanation. Reed houses, stone houses, and underground dwellings occur on the timberless Pacific slopes of South America, but the absence of forested land on Easter Island can hardly be considered an excuse, for the Easter Islanders could still have built Polynesian houses from twigs, cane and braided mats, as on the other islands. The Easter Islanders had access to American totora reeds, which did not grow in the rest of Polynesia, and they could have used this reed to build in Polynesian style, using full-size doorways, if this idea had been brought from the west. So why did they prefer to build dwellings resembling overturned boats, with funnel-shaped, creep-in entrances like those of a dog-house? And if this seemingly awkward structure did in fact have advantages over normal Pacific Island house forms, why then also bother to invent corbel-vaulted stone houses, and in addition build dwellings underground?

The reference to the very old statues on the rim of the volcano Rano Kao in 1786 does tell us something. These statues are no longer there. In subsequent centuries the continuously roaring surf undermined the tall cliffs on the seaward side of the volcano, causing the monuments to tumble into the advancing ocean. These continuous inroads of the ocean into the tuff of the volcanic cones that formed the corners of the triangular island thus visibly altered the landscape in historic times. We shall see later that there are reasons to suspect that some of the oldest buildings have been lost to the sea, too.

The maize and other plants brought by the French also disappeared. Neither they nor the domestic animals set ashore were ever seen again by subsequent visitors. Even this teaches us a lesson. There are those who have argued that Easter Island could not have been reached from South America in pre-European times, because of the absence of maize in the aboriginal island agriculture. Were this a valid argument, one could ask: Would the disappearance of the maize the Frenchmen planted prove that they had, in fact, never landed? Plants are like fingerprints: missing ones tell us nothing. But those present, like the sweet potato, the manioc, and the gourd, can be decisive in revealing, among other things, the sailing routes of early explorers.

Paenga, the foundation stones of Easter Island reed houses, still dot the landscape. The stones were laid in the soil in the shape of a reed boat. It must have taken much patient labor to shape the hard basalt rock and bore deep holes in it. To make the pointed ends the right shape, special *paenga* were hewn to the correct curvature. The holes were bored to hold branches as supports for the arched reed roof.

A prelude to Christian civilization

By the nineteenth century, the net of spiritual and economic interests from the Christian world had ensnared all the aboriginal communities around Easter Island. The only reason why this one island kept its freedom was its unique geo-

Old *paenga* stones were often dug out of earlier foundations and reused in the Middle Period of the island's history as building blocks in *ahu* walls. This suggests that the first boat-shaped houses with *paenga* foundations date back to the early period of habitation.

Excavation of the pre-Inca image platforms at Tiahuanaco in what is now Bolivia has uncovered stones remarkably like the *paenga* of Easter Island. We do not know what they were originally used for, only that they were reused in walls of a later period—just as on Easter Island.

graphical position outside all commercial sailing routes. Formally it belonged to Peru, but the people on the island were blissfully ignorant of this. As the traffic of foreign sailing vessels in the Pacific increased, Easter Island, in spite of Cook's dim assessment, became a much more frequented port of call. A chronological summary of foreign contact may serve to clarify later events on the island, and explain the behavior of the islanders during this period of acculturation.

1804: A Russian ship under the command of U. F. Lisjanskij sailed straight down to Easter Island from Chile. Lisjanskij recorded that the people ashore lit fires in different places along the coast as soon as they spotted the ship. He, too, took the fires as an invitation to land, but bad weather prevented him from doing so. He barely managed to send a lieutenant ashore with some trading goods; he then sailed close inshore around the island for five days and made a number of observations.

He counted only twenty-three houses near the shoreline, most of them in Hanga-roa, where Cook had landed, and in Hotu-iti, the bay near the image quarries. The Russians also made a count of all the large statues they could see still standing around the coast. The total number was now reduced to twenty.

1805: A year after Lisjanskij's visit, the Easter Islanders were to suffer the first of a series of slave raids, which resulted in a deadly blow to their culture. For half a century, Easter Island experienced a period of unrest and turmoil, for the most part caused by foreign visitors. These visitors put little on record that can help us answer the riddles of the island, yet they cannot be ignored if we want to understand the changing mentality and now savage behavior exhibited by the people by the time the missionaries ventured ashore to re-establish peace and order.

The slave raid of 1805 was led by the American captain of the New London schooner *Nancy*. He sailed to Easter Island from the Juan Fernández Islands off Chile and landed in Hanga-roa Bay with the intention of kidnapping native labor. His plan was to carry them back to the Chilean island of Más Afuera to work for a colony of seal hunters he wanted to establish there. After a bloody assault, he managed to capture twelve men and ten women. When, three days after leaving the island, he removed their chains, all the men immediately jumped overboard and swam in the direction of their long-since invisible home. The sailors prevented the women from doing the same. Failing to catch the men, who dove under water each time the boat approached them, the captain left with the women only, but later returned for another slave raid.

1806: Captain Alexander Adams of Hawaii sailed to Easter Island on his brig, having received a personal report from the master of the *Nancy* about his experiences there. Adams reported that the islanders' attitude was so hostile that he was unable to land.

1808: Captain Amasa Delano reached Easter Island, but reported that the high surf prevented him from even attempting a landing.

1809: Captain Windship of the *Albatross* reached Easter Island and tried to get ashore. But, like Adams, he was prevented by the visibly hostile reception of the population.

1816: A second Russian expedition arrived, led by O. E. Kotzebue. Ignorant of recent events, although he too had come from Chile, his intention was to investigate the now-famous monuments of the Island. The Russians were met by two patched-together canoes, less than seven feet long and correspondingly slim, but the natives paddling them kept at a gunshot's distance. They displayed some roots, as if selling them, but refused to come any nearer. When Kotzebue and seventeen of his men attempted to land, they were met with a shower of stones thrown at them by a multitude of islanders, who laughed and shouted and wriggled their bodies in an apparent war dance. The Russians fired warning shots

A row of overturned statues lying nose down, their topknots rolled inland. After Captain Cook's visit in 1774, European ships sailing round the coast found more and more fallen statues. When the Russian expedition led by Lisjanskij came in 1804, there were only twenty statues still standing. Four of the them were at Hanga-roa, and seven more were discovered after the Russian ship had rounded the southern headland. When the next Russian expedition under Kotzebue arrived in 1816, not a single statue remained standing at Hanga-roa, and only two on the south coast. By the time the missionaries settled on the island in 1864, the last statue had been overthrown in the intertribal wars. All lay face-down, their heads pointing inland.

and finally managed to force their way ashore for a short visit. Amidst stone throwing and much roaring from the natives they obtained some vegetable products in exchange for scraps of iron and knives.

The Russians did not see a single woman on the island, and any advance inland from their landing place in Hanga-roa was prevented by the men ashore. Kotzebue finally decided to return to his ship, his farewell hastened by a further hail of stones. He recorded that in spite of careful search he did not find the statues seen by Cook and La Pérouse. The four statues his compatriot Lisjanskij had seen standing in Hanga-roa twelve years earlier had been overthrown in the tumultuous intervening period. Of the seven monuments Lisjanskij had seen immediately after rounding the south cape, Kotzebue now saw two, and these were the only ones observed by his expedition. His ship did not, however, circumnavigate the whole island.

The Russians noted no houses, except a seven-foot-tall building constructed from small stones, into which people entered by crawling through an opening on the side.

Kotzebue looked in vain for vestiges of the plants and animals left by La Pérouse, and came to the conclusion that the only change since the French visit was the continued destruction of the monuments.

1822: A number of whaling masters had by now begun hunting in the vicinity of Easter Island. It is known that the skipper of one American whaling ship called at Easter Island and took a number of women on board. They were thrown overboard the following day and forced to swim back to the coast, while an officer, apparently merely for entertainment, shot one of the islanders.

1825: Captain F. W. Beechey, accompanied by Admiral E. Belcher, sailed to Easter Island from Chile and attempted to land in Hanga-roa Bay. As they approached the island, they found that the men ashore "followed along the coast and lighted fires in different directions, the largest of which was opposite the landing place." Multitudes of women were crowded on the rocks in the bay, singing or beating their bare breasts with inviting gestures.

It appears that the islanders attempted to lure these Englishmen ashore to catch them in a trap. At first all went well. When some of the crew rowed in, the islanders, apparently friendly, brought some of their food crops as well as nets and "idols," which were thrown into the boats without bargaining. Once well ashore, the Englishmen were exposed to lively trading, mixed with the usual stealing. Then suddenly one of the islanders, presumed to be a chief as he was wearing a cloak and headdress of feathers, came hurrying from the huts, attended by men with short clubs. A conch-shell trumpet was blown, and all the women disappeared. Immediately the men, armed with clubs and sticks, started open plunder. As the visitors withdrew to their boats, they were the target of a heavy shower of large stones thrown with such precision that several men were knocked under the thwarts and every person wounded. In self-defense, the English sailors finally shot the chief and possibly one other islander.

Upon sailing around the coast to visit Hotu-iti Bay at the foot of the Rano Raraku image quarries, Beechey wrote:

"The greatest attention appeared to be paid to the cultivation of the soil. Such places as were not immediately exposed to the scorching rays of the sun were laid out in oblong strips, taking the direction of the ravines; and furrows were ploughed at right angles to them for the purpose of intercepting the streams of water in their descent." He added that the islanders availed themselves of the crater lake inside the Rano Raraku volcano as a natural reservoir for watering their cultivations.

1828: J.-A. Moerenhout visited Easter Island for the first time. He returned for a second visit in 1834, each time sailing from the coast of Chile. He devoted much of his report to a description of the strong southern branch of the Humboldt Current from South America, which, he stressed, hastens sailing ships from the coast of northern Chile and southern Peru toward Easter Island, even in uncertain winds. He recommended all navigators follow this particular track if they wanted to reach Easter Island and the islands further west.

Moerenhout saw statues still standing on the north coast. He sailed near enough to the shore to be greeted by a swimming islander about six feet tall, with extended ear lobes, who tried to persuade him to come ashore. But Moerenhout refrained from the temptation, as venereal diseases brought by visiting whalers were now reported to have become a plague on the island.

1831: The schooner *Discoverer* lay to for a day, and H. Cunning recorded that a number of natives came on board, described as lively and good-natured; they were inclined to take anything portable, but seemed willing to give anything in exchange for the merest trifle. They brought bananas, yams, sweet potatoes and "a root called cocos in the West Indies." Cunning wrote that the sides of the hills were extremely well cultivated, laid out in squares in great numbers. But he

The author sitting on a driftwood log from South America in Anakena Bay, where Hotu Matua, the first king of Easter Island, landed. According to tradition he came from the east after being defeated in battle in a vast land where it was so hot that the sun caused plants to wither at certain seasons of the year. The navigator Moerenhout made two voyages from Chile to Easter Island in 1828 and 1834. Much of his report was devoted to describing the local ocean current, and he advised other navigators to choose northern Chile as the starting point for voyages to Easter Island, because they could then take advantage of the southern branch of the Humboldt Current. That way they would get there quicker, even with a feeble wind. This great stump of a Chilean pine, washed ashore in the very spot where Hotu Matua landed, is proof that the current still follows the same path.

did not dare go ashore for botanical specimens for fear of the numerous inhabitants who lined the shore.

1838: Admiral du Petit-Thouars reached Easter Island from Mexico. He was still a great distance from shore when shouts were heard from two Easter Islanders they thought to be swimming, ". . . but we were much surprised to perceive that these natives were each riding astride a reed roller in the form of a sheaf of corn. To be sure of a favourable reception they brought us bananas, sweet potatoes and yams enveloped in their reeds." The swimmers also brought Petit-Thouars a most peculiar wooden image representing a double head without body. The eyes were inlaid with black obsidian inserted as pupils into white bone. Although he did not land, Petit-Thouars sailed close enough along the coast to notice two types of dwellings. He described the boat-shaped reed houses as large and bright when seen from the sea, and added: "One could also distinguish a very great number of small houses, black and round like ovens."

1843: The French missionary Monseigneur E. Rouchouze attempted to sail to Easter Island from Polynesia, bringing with him a group of religious followers of both sexes. No further news arrived from this Catholic mission, and when J. Hamilton visited Easter Island with his barque twelve years later, the islanders appeared to be as savage as ever. His party landed, intending to trade, but the natives capsized the boat and tried to take the clothes off the crew. He lost his second officer in the fight ashore. Hamilton observed that the islanders themselves were in possession of some European boats. "I do not think," he remarked, "they came honestly by them . . ." The existence of these boats probably explain why nothing more had been heard from the Catholic mission.

1859: Some slave raiders arriving from Peru succeeded in kidnapping a number of Easter Islanders, whom, this time, they managed to sell for labor back in the former Inca empire.

The great Peruvian slave raid

History repeats itself. It also, of course, repeats prehistory. The geography, the elements, and the interplay between man and nature in the Pacific did not change with the arrival of Europeans or the introduction of script with recorded history.

South America played the dominant role during an entire historic period of Easter Island, with Chile and Peru as the constantly repeated jumping-off points. It was no coincidence, therefore, that it was slave raiders under Captain Aiguirre who, in 1862, sailed from Callao in Peru and put an end to the aboriginal Easter Island culture. Aiguirre followed the course familiar since Incan times and recorded by Mendaña and Gonzalez. The purpose of his voyage was to "recruit labor" on an island supposedly belonging to Peru.

On his arrival, Aiguirre found no less than seven other Peruvian ships already there. They had all sailed to Easter Island for the same purpose. The captains of all the ships agreed to collaborate, and eighty armed men were sent ashore, spreading trade goods on the ground to attract the islanders. When about five hundred of the Easter Islanders gathered and started to examine the articles, mostly on their knees, the slave raiders fell on them. They captured two hundred; nearly a dozen were shot dead. The rest escaped by climbing up the steep rocks or diving into the ocean. The captives were chained and carried on board the various ships, where they met many more of their relatives, captured in secrecy when bartering with the foreign vessels.

Among the Easter Islanders carried off for the slave market in Peru were the island king, Kaimakoi, and his sons and daughters. With them were nearly all the principal personalities and learned men of the community, who were to die in South America. They are often referred to as having ended their days as guano workers on the Chincha Islands off the coast of Peru, but recent research has shown that the Easter Islanders worked as slaves only on the Peruvian mainland.

The Catholic bishop of Tahiti, Tepano Jaussen, protested the continuing Peruvian slave raids on Easter Island, and following pressure put on them by the French minister in Lima, the Peruvian authorities ordered the return of the surviving enslaved Easter Islanders—about one thousand in all. They were to be returned by way of Bishop Jaussen on Tahiti. But before the long return voyage, disease and travail had taken a toll of about nine hundred persons in less than a year. Of the remaining hundred, the majority died of smallpox on the voyage back. Only fifteen survived to be repatriated to Easter Island. And these fifteen brought with them a smallpox epidemic. By this time the terror-stricken population had fled from their houses to secret underground hideouts, but were unable to escape the contagious new disease. The cultivated land was abandoned, and famine followed. Soon the total population was reduced to a hundred and eleven souls. But prior to this, one lonely European, full of honest intentions, had settled ashore.

The testimony of the islanders

Lay Brother Eyraud's wild adventure

Lay Brother Eugène Eyraud (from an oil painting). Few men have risked their lives so bravely to preach peace and brotherhood. Eyraud took up residence as the only foreigner on Easter Island in 1864, at the height of the savagery. A hatred toward foreigners had been whipped to fever pitch two years earlier, when slave raiders from Peru had carried off most of the island's population—by then a sorry remnant of a once-proud civilization that had reverted to barbarism and cannibalism after two centuries of tribal warfare and cultural collapse.

A lonely schooner was tacking slowly into sight of Easter Island two years after the disastrous slave raid from Peru. The little vessel was beating stubbornly into the wind, coming from Tahiti in the wake of the lost missionaries. On board was a pious Frenchman who came with the best motives with a burden of guilt as a representative of the "Christian" world—a world that had brought so much crime and brutality to the formerly unarmed and hospitable island population. Lay Brother Eugène Eyraud had been sent on a mission from Polynesia by the Congrégation des Sacrés-Coeurs in Belgium.

Fires were no longer lit along the coast by the people who saw the sails. Foreign visitors were no longer desired. Nobody prostrated themselves toward the rising sun. No rows of standing stone giants were there to protect the heirs of those they represented. All lay nose to the ground, unable to help or hurt human beings. The sun scorched the scraggy grass and fern that had conquered the once orderly irrigated fields.

Easter Island, the former home of an organized society with skilled artists and master masons and engineers, was by 1864 the barren hideout of a few bewildered cave dwellers. The survivors, adults and children, struggled to safeguard scarce plots of sweet potatoes. On constant guard against theft. Alert to the arrival of sails. Always ready to escape underground and leave the open grassland empty between sea and sky. The secret caves were their only security, their only means of escape.

This was the situation when a sunlit sail was sighted in the wrong direction. To the west. Not to the east, from where all other visitors, and most recently the slave raiders, had appeared. The little sailing vessel came from the Catholic mission on Tahiti. It was January, and the surviving Easter Islanders had just observed the sun marking the second midsummer since the last slave raid. They could expect new raiders any time.

Lay Brother Eyraud must have had some fear of what awaited him ashore. With him were six Easter Islanders, being repatriated from the slave raids. He knew well that nobody had set foot ashore in peace since the turn of the eighteenth century, yet he came alone, with his Bible and his crates and enough building material for a little house. He was intent on settling down with the islanders.

Wisely, he did not go ashore in the first boatload, along with the repatriated slaves. They were accompanied by Daniel, a young Mangarevan who reported back to him. In a letter to his superiors in Chile, Eyraud repeated Daniel's words:

"The people are horrible to look at. They are menacing, armed with lances, and most of them are nude. The feathers they wear as ornaments, the tattoos, their savage cries, give altogether a dreadful appearance."

Yet Eyraud himself ventured ashore, and watched the schooner hoisting sail to return downwind to Tahiti. He remained ashore, unarmed and alone on the beach, and was probably the first foreigner to see every single individual coming out of hiding. He wrote:

"Daniel must certainly be pardoned for getting afraid. A multitude of men, women, and children, that could amount to about twelve hundred, had nothing reassuring about them. The men were armed with a kind of lance formed by a stick at the end of which were fixed a sharp stone."

Eyraud described the savage-looking crowd that came toward him as wearing little or nothing but body paint and feathers. Many had their hair standing up in a topknot, and their earlobes pierced and extended. He noted that the custom of extending the earlobes was now most common among the women, whereas the early explorers had noted it among the men.

He found no chief on the island. No authority. Complete anarchy. The strongest individuals held sway over the others, and over peace and war. There was no thought of celebrating the return of the repatriated islanders. They and Eyraud had their hands full guarding their belongings from theft by everybody present.

Eyraud followed the crowd up to a few small reed huts. As evening approached, he managed to join a family and crept in through the low entrance tunnel. He slept on reed mats with his hosts and noted: "The inventory is very simple: it consists of a bottle-gourd for bringing water, and a small plaited reed-bag for fetching sweet potatoes. . . . When the day came, the first object I observed was a small house idol, to which they seemed to pay but little attention."

Eyraud quickly set up his own little hut, built from the planks he had brought ashore, and locked up his crates inside. In the coming months he constantly struggled to protect himself against violence and theft. He reported that all the natives were thieves and that if some stole less than others, it was due merely to lack of opportunity.

Eyraud lived alone with the Easter Islanders for nine months, in close contact with every household. In spite of the decimation of the original population, most children and many women had kept in hiding during the raids, and thus saved the various families from total annihilation. As Eyraud had come straight from Polynesia, his opinion of the local people is important:

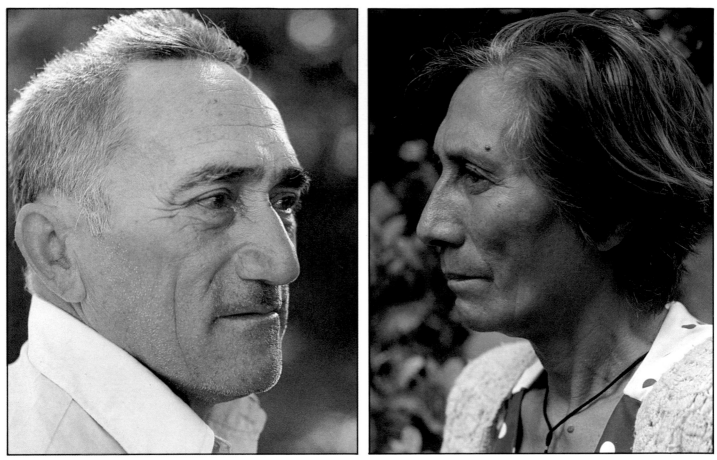

The last full-blooded descendants of the Long-ears. *Left:* Adan Atan, brother of the former mayor, Pedro Atan, is the twelfth-generation direct descendant of Ororoine, the last Long-ear to survive the massacre in the Poike trench. *Right:* Maria Atan is Pedro's daughter. According to Father Sebastian's genealogy, after the recent death of her father, she and her uncle Adan are the only remaining full-blooded descendants of the Long-ears.

Right: Easter Islanders of unmixed descent. Careful genealogical records have been kept on Easter Island, where it has never been counted a disgrace for a woman to bear a child fathered by a visiting foreigner. This attitude is mutual, so there are ever fewer who consider themselves, or are acknowledged by the church's birth records and their fellow-islanders, to be pure representatives of the aboriginal population of Easter

"These savages are tall, strong, and well built. Their features resemble far more the European type than those of the other islanders of Oceania. Among all the Polynesians the Marquesans are those to which they display the greatest resemblance. Their complexion, although a little copper-colored, does neither differ much from the hue of the European, and a great number are even completely white."

Eyraud came to Easter Island as a teacher. The books he used were the Bible and various religious texts in Polynesian. He benefited in his contact with the natives by the little he had learned of their language in advance from the repatriated islanders, as well as from the Polynesian words that were part of local speech. To judge from Eyraud's reports to his superiors, he learned little from his hosts about themselves except their cult, which he was striving to eliminate. He found no surviving interest in the fallen images, but noted that the islanders recalled one supreme god called Make-Make. He stressed that though he always associated with them in the greatest familiarity, he never discovered any formal religious practice:

"In all the houses many statuettes are seen, about thirty centimeters high, representing male figures, fishes, birds, etc. They are undoubtedly idols, but I have not noticed that they have been attributed any kinds of honors. I have occasionally seen the natives taking these statues, lifting them into the air, making some gestures, and accompanying all of it with a sort of dance and an insignificant

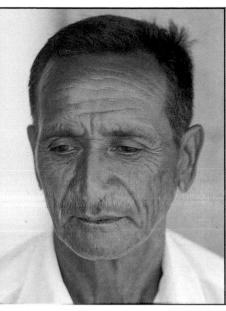

Island. Whereas Adan and Maria Atan are believed to be the last full-blooded descendants of the Long-ears, these chosen few can lay claim to pedigrees counting exclusively members of the island's aboriginal population: Juan Haoa, his son Leonardo Haoa Pakomio, Pedro Pate, Amelia Tepano Ika, Simón Teao Hereveri, his brother Tadeo, their mother Maria Hereveri Pakomio, and Maria Tepano Ika. Presumably counting both Long-ears and Short-ears among their ancestors, the European-like physiognomies with thin lips and sharp noses are still marked.

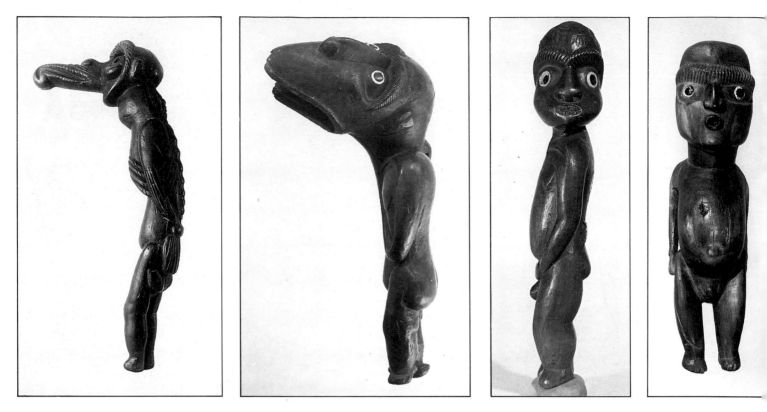

When Eyraud awoke in a dark native hut upon his first night ashore, his eyes beheld a spooky collection of grotesque wooden figures of monsters and creatures out of a nightmare. In contrast to the standardized ribbed male and flat female figures, these bizarre carvings were all different and bespoke the unbridled imagination and creativity of the carver. The well-known Easter Island archaeologist Lavachery has pointed out that this phenomenon stands in sharp contrast to the rest of Polynesia, where the art of woodcarving adheres slavishly to stylized forms such as the Tiki figurines of the Marquesas.

song. What do they mean with that? I believe they do not know much about it. They do quite simply what they have seen their fathers do, without offering it any further thought. If you ask them what it means, they answer you as about their games, that such is the custom of the country."

These were the figurines so highly valued by the outside world when first brought out for barter during the time of Cook's visit. Now, seen by the missionary in every hut, they became the target of Eyraud's obsession. He collected none, but made it his first priority to have all such carvings obliterated. For the first time since the early Spaniards, we also hear of the existence of a local script:

"In all their houses one can find tablets of wood or sticks covered with many kinds of hieroglyphic signs: figures of animals unknown on the island, which the natives trace by means of sharp stones. Each figure has its own name; but the little they make of these tablets makes me inclined to think that these signs, the remains of a primitive script, are for them at present a custom which they preserve without searching the meaning. The natives do neither know how to read nor write . . ."

The lay brother passionately desired to destroy this pagan script as well as the wooden figurines. They tied their owners to heathen ancestral beliefs and customs. He did his utmost to have the written tablets burnt or otherwise destroyed, and they quickly disappeared. The Easter Islanders, who had lost confidence in their own faith, had no reason to resist a new religion. To them, Eyraud's god was easily substituted for Make-Make. Indeed to them the Supreme God preferred by the foreigner was probably the same as theirs, only with another name and a different form of worship.

Clear evidence of the earlier sun worship was noted by Eyraud, who wrote that

when he spoke of the calendar and the rising of the sun, the natives showed an extreme interest and even the aged moved closer to take their place among his pupils. The reason for this interest soon became plain when Eyraud discovered that the position of the sun set the date for a truly pagan event. Torometi, his island assistant, warned him in advance: trouble would begin when the position of the sun called for the "bird-man" competition. The celebrations started when the sun reached its equinox in September, the austral, or southern, spring. The entire population would first assemble at Mataveri, at the foot of the volcano Rano Kao. After a peaceful period during which foot races and other sports took place, the competitors for the "bird-man" title would move up to a ceremonial stone-house village on top of the volcano. Once the bird-man was selected, he and his followers would immediately descend to the lowland, to fall upon the houses and rob and plunder all the chickens and sweet potatoes they could find.

Eyraud's problems reached their climax when this so-called Mataveri period began, on the ninth month of his stay. His native protector, Torometi, had already stolen most of his possessions and little was left locked up in the planked cabin:

"The time of *Mataveri* approached, and there was a little agitation. Torometi above all became increasingly distrustful. He requested from me the rest of my effects, 'to hide them,' he said, as if someone was planning to steal from us. As these people always distrust each other mutually, and with good reason, they are always on guard to defend and hide the little they possess. The hiding places were indeed abundant. The entire island is perforated by deep caves, some natural and others artificial, which do not communicate with the outside but through a very narrow opening. Some stones suffice to close and conceal the entrance. The entire population of the island could, at a moment's notice, disappear by hiding in these subterranean places. There it was that Torometi insisted on placing and safeguarding the rest of my belongings. I refused blankly. But Torometi, his brother, and his wife, reinforced by neighbours, caught hold of me and made all resistance impossible. They took possession of my keys, carried away the property they found, and left me with hardly anything but my mattress and locked-up tool boxes. When this operation was terminated they gave me the keys back."

When the bird-man descended from the mountain, Eyraud fled to another part of the island. But he was soon found and literally carried back. In the quarrels that followed, Torometi's house was burnt to the ground, as was that of his brother. Eyraud was dragged along by the crowd toward Mataveri. During this march, he was stripped of the clothes and shoes he was wearing. The crowd tore up his catechism and prayer book and tried to attach the pages to their own personal apparel. From then on Eyraud was forced to follow Torometi about the island like a slave. The lay brother finally managed to flee the island on a visiting schooner.

Defeated and humiliated, Eyraud escaped, but he had lost the first round. The bird-man was left ashore with his kin, the sole master of religious ceremonies. Nobody suspected that the peaceful foreigner would dare to settle among them again, perhaps not even Eyraud himself. Nevertheless, he had been the first foreigner to get a real foothold within the community. He alone had been in all the houses, seen their sacred tablets and the dances of the wooden figures, shared their meals, their strifes, their cave secrets. Their fear of the bird-man. He had also been the first visitor to really talk with them, take part in their conversations and detect their intelligence, their human affections, their sense of humor. Even physically many of them were indistinguishable from Europeans. When Eyraud later returned to these islanders who had treated him so badly, it was with the conviction that they were people like himself, made savage by unfortunate circumstances.

Famine and massacres had clearly altered the inheritable gene pool on this island but little since the visits of Roggeveen and the early Spaniards. Ignorant of their observations, Eyraud noted independently that many of the Easter Islanders were remarkably white and with features more European than Polynesian. Those who were of Polynesian type he found to resemble the inhabitants of the Marquesas Islands.

Apart from religious matters, Eyraud took little interest in the Easter Island culture. Coming as he did from the Society Islands he was familiar with the gods Tiki, Tane, and Tangaroa, who were common to all Polynesia and in every group reckoned as progenitors of the royal lines of divine descent. None of these principal Polynesian gods were known to the Easter Islanders. Their god, Make-Make, was a deity unknown in Polynesia. His representative on earth was not a hereditary king, but an annually selected bird-man, feared and hated by the population. There must have been a very dominant non-Polynesian element in the Easter Island culture to make the Polynesian immigrants abandon their ancestral gods. Nowhere within their own territory did the conservative Polynesians invent new gods simply because they sailed from one island to another.

According to Eyraud, the great variety of wooden figurines found in all the houses were idols, remnants of a former religion. The islanders were merely doing what their fathers had done when they lifted these into the air, accompanying the gesture with dance and song. It was said to be the custom of the country. If so, it was certainly not a custom in Polynesia. Wherever idols were found in Polynesia, they were always of one standard, stereotyped and unvarying form. In the Marquesas, where small house images were most common, they all represented the god Tiki. And one Tiki was a slavish repetition of all the others. They had the same goggle-shaped eyes, huge mouths, and broad, flat noses, whether miniatures or life-size statues, and whether carved from wood, stone, or bone.

Eyraud's most important discovery was the inscribed tablets found with the images in all the houses. That discovery confirmed the statement by the early Spaniards that the people on this island had a script indigenous to themselves. Eyraud recognized what he saw on the tablets as the remnants of a primitive form of writing, but, because the present population could neither read nor write, they treasured these tablets as ceremonial objects of a forgotten past, without searching for their meaning. Eyraud ordered all the tablets burnt, because it was clear to him that they were remnants of some inherited pagan rite. Whatever their origins, they were certainly not heirlooms from Polynesia. But the conquistadores of Peru reported that the Incas painted their history on certain boards that the Spaniards burned when they found them stored in the Temple of the Sun. Earlier, the Cuna Indians of Panama incised religious texts on wooded tablets like those of Easter Island. But if Eyraud's attempts to obliterate every trace of the script had been as successful as that of the conquistadores in Peru, the sadly sparse record of what he saw would have left us with no idea of what they looked like.

Make-Make goes underground

History is full of unsung heroes. Lay Brother Eyraud is one of them. He was set ashore again on the same beach only a year and a half after his dramatic escape from the island. With him this time was a Catholic priest from Tahiti, Father Hippolyte Roussel, and three native Mangarevans. Later, Father Gaspard Zumbohm and Brother Théodule Escolan joined them. They were all received without hostility. The islanders understood from Eyraud that these foreigners had been sent by Bishop Tepano Jaussen in Tahiti, whom they all respected, as it was he who had stopped the slave raids.

This little immigrant group from French Oceania set up European-type houses and built small plank churches both in Hanga-roa and Vaihu. During the five years in which they managed to maintain a foothold ashore, they made a lasting impact on the aboriginal culture, most particularly on the language. Teachings and conversation were and continued to be in Tahitian. They now also succeeded in introducing oranges, figs, peaches, pumpkins, beans and maize. They took ashore sheep, pigs, horses, cattle, donkeys, cats and rabbits. All made a profound impression on the local people. Not the least of their amazements was their first sight of a wheel, on a wheelbarrow.

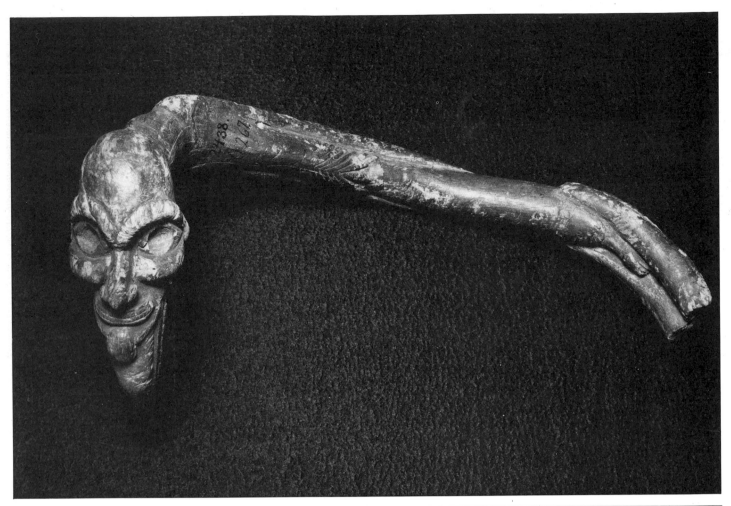

This gnarled stick, taken home to Oslo by a Norwegian sea-captain and now in the Ethnographic Museum there, was one of the first wood-carvings to leave Easter Island in the days of the early missionaries. It has a head with a long beard at one end. Seen from the front, the head is obviously that of a bearded man. But if the stick is turned and viewed in profile, the beard becomes a beak with protuberances like those of a turkey, and the magic stick is thus transformed into the sacred bird-man of Easter Island. There was no bird like a turkey in Oceania; the turkey was indigenous to South America in pre-European time, and was widely domesticated in ancient Peru.

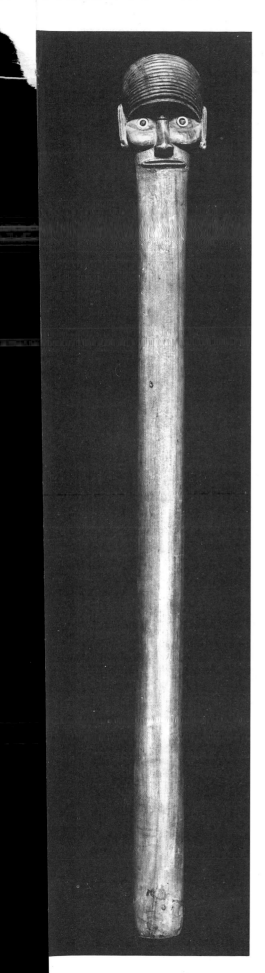

A ceremonial club, the *ua*, also obtained in 1868 and brought to the Ethnographic Museum in Oslo by the Norwegian Captain Arup. The *ua*, evidently a symbol of power, was modeled on a standardized prototype invariably surmounted by a two-faced Janus head with inlaid eyes of seashells and obsidian. The only weapons used on Easter Island were clubs, slingshots and obsidian spearheads fixed to shafts. Archaeological excavations show that no weapons were manufactured during the first two periods of the island's culture. But with the onset of the tribal wars and subsequent cultural decline, obsidian spearheads *(mataa)* suddenly began to be mass produced.

Since Eyraud and his companions were the first to introduce the new faith, they were also the last to put on record details about the former faith before it could be influenced by European teachings. Zumbohm wrote:

"Among the gods and godesses of their mythology, our Indians acknowledge one they call the Great God, *Etua,* who they say is superior to all the others. *Ko Make-Make* was his name; he rewarded the good and punished the bad. . . . Make-Make manifested his anger by thunder. . . . Through the will and work of the supreme god, the first man and the first woman came forth from the earth, almost like the plant that germinates from the soil; they had immortal souls as had all their descendants . . . the souls of bad people stay near their corpses suffering hunger and thirst in proportion to their wickedness. From there they occasionally come to beg food from their relatives and friends, and one must give food to them to get rid of their importunity. I had many opportunities to fight against this superstition. . . . Very often . . . they were induced to put food in the grave of a relative . . ."

Roussel recorded that the former society on the island had been divided into four different classes: kings, priests, warriors, and commoners. Easter Island had always had a king, ever since the first one, Hotu, landed, until the last one was carried away with his sons to die in slavery in Peru. In the final period of civil wars, when the last of the *moai,* the great statues, were overturned from their *ahu,* or platforms, the king had no real power and the warriors waged war without consulting him. Yet he had nothing to fear, for nobody would disturb him. But in ancient times, when the *moai* were still being carved and respected, the kings were divine; they had absolute command over men and *moai* alike. The first fruits of the country were brought to them with great ceremony. Their heads were *tapu,* forbidden, and their hair must be allowed to grow and could never be cut. Their hands, too, were *tapu*, and the only work they were alowed to do was to twist fishing lines or make nets as a form of recreation. Their entire persons, their dwellings, their food and anything they used were *tapu* to people of both sexes.

Zumbohm recorded that in former times the high priests ate children in the name of Make-Make.

The missionaries arrived too late to see a single statue still standing on its platform. Once war had been declared, all valuable objects were carried away and hidden in caves. After the battle, the losers themselves disappeared for a time, while the victors burned their houses and fields and overturned their enemy's statues. Chickens and fish had formerly been offered on the *ahu*, but now the platforms were only used for burials.

Roussel was the first to visit and recognize the image quarries in the crater walls of Rano Raraku. He was also the first to assume that the statues—now fallen—seen standing along what Cook's party called "the image roads" had been abandoned during transportation. He was puzzled by the technical problem of getting the stone giants from the quarries to the distant *ahu*, and did not take the local explanation seriously:

"The means of their erection and transportation have remained unknown. It survives as a fable: The great chief at that time, who was omnipotent like his predecessors, had commanded them to walk; on his command they had all begun to move while choosing sites to the best of their own liking."

The ability of the omnipotent chiefs of the past to make the statues walk could hardly be taken as anything but a fable by the missionaries. On the other hand, Roussel accepted another claim by the islanders:

"What tradition has been able to transmit is that the enormous cylinder which rests on their head has been superimposed by elevations of stones."

Zumbohm, too, marveled at the way the statues were transported:

"Here is a mystery which seems to me will long remain unsolved. I must admit, however, that our Indians do not let themselves be embarrassed by this problem; they present the following solution: 'Formerly' they say, 'all these *moai* were assembled in one and the same place. One day Make-Make gave them the signal to depart, and immediately they began marching and came to the places they occupy today!'"

Time would show that it was easier to make the Easter Islanders change the name for their omnipotent god than to deprive them of the firm tradition that their ancestors had made the statues "walk." After two years of combined effort, the four missionaries succeeded in converting the last of the Easter Islanders to Christianity. It seemed as if, at least on the surface, Make-Make and all his pagan paraphernalia had been driven away. Then Eyraud died and was buried on the island. Soon afterwards Zumbohm left, seriously ill. Hostilities now broke out once more, so severe that Roussel and Escolan were forced to close the mission and escape. They left the island for good in 1871.

These missionaries and their Polynesian companions from French Oceania began to refer to Easter Island as Rapa-nui, and thus added another name and another mystery to an island which already seemed to have enough of both. Rapa-nui means Great Rapa, as distinct from Rapa-iti or Little Rapa, an island about the same size southeast of Tahiti. The possible origin of this name might have arrived with the missionaries from French Oceania, for on Rapa-iti a tradition survived claiming that island had been settled by pregnant women escaping from massacres on Easter Island, to them known as Rapa-nui. This tradition is in agreement with the possibility of a downwind voyage from east to west, and furthermore gives sense to the epithets Great and Little for two islands that are actually of similar size. If a new place is renamed after a former habitat, it is a common custom among emigrants to distinguish between them by adding "little" to the new settlement, and only then does the former one get the affix "great." There is only one other island in the world with the same name—Rapa—and it happens to be about the same distance from Easter Island, but in the opposite direction: Rapa Island in Lake Titicaca, Peru. There are no stone statues on Rapa-iti, but there are many in the area around Lake Titicaca, and the one on Rapa Island in the lake depicts a man with long ears.

Perhaps Rapa was the early name for Easter Island, which Cook's Tahitian interpreter was unable to obtain. The two other aboriginal names are purely poetic and descriptive: *Te-Pito-o-te-Henua,* or "The Navel-of-the-World," and *Mata-Kite-Rangi,* "Eyes-Looking-at-Heaven." Both names are also worthy of analysis.

The navel is, naturally, associated with birth. As a geographical term for an extremely lonely island, "Navel-of-the-World" can only refer to the link at birth between the ancestral country and the later settlements. Easter Island lies halfway between the ancient South American continent and the numerous more recently settled Polynesian islands. The idea of using this very same geographical term had also occurred to the Incas, who named their own capital, Cuzco, "The Navel."

The word *Rangi* for "heaven" reappears elsewhere in Polynesia as *Rani* and *Ani,* commonly used also as a poetic reference to the legendary Polynesian fatherland. Whereas Mata-Kite-Rangi, "Eyes-Looking-at-Heaven" is another name for Easter Island, *Mata-Rani,* or "Eyes-of-Heaven," is the name of an ancient aboriginal port on the south coast of Peru, just below Lake Titicaca. Once a harbor for the Tiahuanaco kingdom, it remains the best natural harbor in all the southern part of Peru.

It appears that the aboriginal names for Easter Island, from Fire Island to Rapa, have something to tell us about the local puzzle.

Although the missionaries stressed that they found no chief on Easter Island, the local people told them that in ancient times there had been a marked class distinction. Before the civil war, their ancestors had been ruled by a hereditary hierarchy of sacred priest kings. Their hereditary line continued uninterrupted until the final slave raid, but by then they had long since lost their totalitarian power and omnipotence. During the last generations of kings, the warriors decided questions of war and peace, and the annual bird-man was left to harass the population as he pleased. The collapse of the totalitarian hierarchy must have taken place before the arrival of the first Europeans. No supreme sovereign ceremonially received Roggeveen or the Spaniards when they landed. The fact that the Dutch found that peace and apparent equality had been reestablished appears to indicate that the collapse of the organized monarchy must have taken place well before 1722. When Cook arrived in 1774, a civil war must have once again ravaged the island, and part of the impoverished population was in hiding.

A divine hierarchy of priest-kings is a trait common to the great civilizations of antiquity, and it has been pointed out that this was a custom all Polynesian tribes shared with the advanced cultures of ancient America. The eating of children as a priestly offering to the gods seems savage in the extreme, and in marked contrast to the otherwise high degree of Easter Island culture, with its script and megalithic architecture. Yet other great civilizations, like those of the Aztecs and the Phoenicians, maintained the same horrible practice of offering and eating children as part of their religious rites.

There seemed to be a strange anomaly in the Easter Island tribal recollections of the movements of the statues and the cylinders placed on their heads: The statues, they said, "walked" from the quarries to the *ahu,* but it required manual labor for the cylinders to be placed in position. Why could not the omnipotent chiefs of that time have used the same magic system for the cylinders as for the *moai?* In searching for the answer, Father Roussel examined the surfaces of the statues found abandoned in transit along the roads. All surfaces were found to be polished and undamaged by friction, and he concluded that they must have been pulled, protected, on top of some sort of sledge.

Why did Easter Island's traditional memory recall the period of the omnipotent kings and how they got the cylinders up on their *moai,* and yet resort to fables about statues walking?

The shepherds of Mammon expel the shepherds of Christ

There was little for the outside world to harvest on Easter Island once the trade in human beings had been forbidden by the church, and the church had collected the local souls. Yet the missionaries were still there when a French captain, Dutroux-Bornier, landed, intent on utilizing the barren landscape.

Dutroux-Bornier had been the master on the ship that brought Eyraud back from Tahiti in 1866. On that occasion he wrote the missionaries a letter expressing his admiration for their noble intention to improve the native morals and living conditions. But on that occasion, after seeing the grassy landscape that had claimed the former plantations, he also made his own plans. And in 1870 he came back to settle as a sheep rancher.

By now the missionaries had pacified the Easter Islanders, and it was no longer in the interest of the sheep rancher to have them around. He had no sooner established himself on the island than he began to cause trouble for the two missionaries who remained, Father Roussel and Brother Escolan. The majority of the Easter Islanders had been assembled by the missionaries in the plank-built houses around the two small churches in Hanga-roa and Vaihu. They were no longer scattered all over the island in stone houses and reed huts, nor hiding in their secret caves. The ownership of land was nevertheless maintained according to tribal inheritance.

In exchange for some pieces of cloth, Dutroux-Bornier managed to buy the islanders' most fertile land at Mataveri, the former site of the spring festivals. He next persuaded a number of families to leave the Hanga-roa mission center and move to his own land. With their aid he began open raids on the remaining settlements in Hanga-roa and Vaihu. A few families who had remained in Anakena, on the opposite side of the island, also joined him. Soon Easter Island was

Top: A wooden *rei-miro,* a crescent-shaped ornament worn as a pectoral by men of high rank. The pointed ends are usually adorned with crescent-shaped male heads with goatees, but sometimes with conches or birds' heads. Specimens were sent to Bishop Jaussen on Tahiti by his missionaries on Easter Island, and he was the first to make a systematic study of the various standard designs of figures and symbols. He also recorded the names of the pieces, including the *tahonga,* an egg-shaped pendant with one or two human heads at the blunt end.

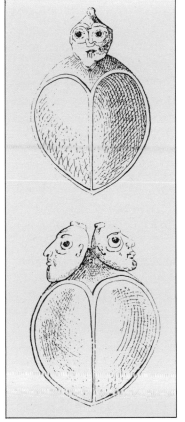

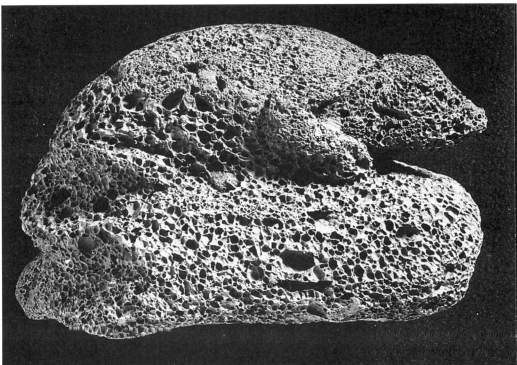

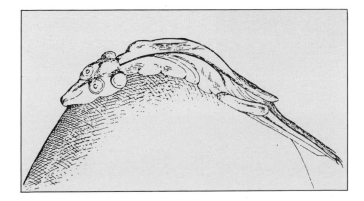

Bottom: A *moai maea.* This type of small, unclassifiable stone sculpture was held to have magic powers and was first depicted by Bishop Jaussen in this sketch from the early missionary period. No two were alike, and unlike the wood-carvings, they were not worn on ceremonial occasions—in fact they were never displayed in public. Each family kept its own collection hidden from the rest of the community. Jaussen's sketch shows a winged quadruped carved in relief on top of a stone. Nearly a century later, several Easter Island families showed their secret collections to the author. The specimens included both quadrupeds and winged creatures carved in relief on stones, like the one shown at center right.

involved in a new civil war. There was shooting and casualties. Houses on both sides were again set on fire. The two unfortunate missionaries lost control.

Before leaving Tahiti, Dutroux-Bornier had associated with J. Brander, an equally unscrupulous trader and the owner of a copra plantation on that island. The two had agreed to move most of the remaining Easter Islanders to Tahiti. Brander needed labor on his plantation, and Dutroux-Bornier wanted all the land on Easter Island for himself and for raising sheep. After burning the islanders' huts, Dutroux-Bornier had their sweet potatoes pulled out of the ground. He did this on three separate occasions. The purpose was to make life on the island intolerable for the surviving population.

Conditions also became impossible for the two missionaries, and they left permanently in 1871, settling in Mangareva. They took with them about fifty Easter Islanders, while many more volunteered to leave for Brander's copra plantation on Tahiti. This exodus to eastern Polynesia of the native landowners freed Dutroux-Bornier to tear down their dwellings all over the island. He used the stones from the thick walls to build miles of fences for his sheep.

Three months after the missionaries left, the Russian corvette *Vitjazj* anchored for two hours in Hanga-roa Bay. It was visited by Dutroux-Bornier, who was now accompanied by one American and one German assistant. These three reported that there were only two hundred and thirty natives left on their island, and a schooner was expected to return from Tahiti to fetch another load.

When a French warship called in 1877, the three foreigners were no longer there. The inhabitants of Hanga-roa said that a few months earlier Dutroux-Bornier had fallen from a horse while drunk, and been killed. It later appeared that he had been murdered by the same aborigines whose return to barbarism he had fostered. They had killed him when he tried to declare his native wife queen of the island. His murderers had also killed his wife, and intended to kill his two young daughters, but the children suddenly dropped from sight. An old man hid them in his cave, and the rage of their pursuers, unable to find them, ultimately diminished. The old man brought them out as imperceptibly as he had made them disappear.

With both the missionaries and the shepherds gone, the remaining original inhabitants of the Navel-of-the-World were again left to themselves, now in the company of a few imported horses, rabbits—and several thousand sheep.

The riddle of the written tablets

Before the missionaries left the island they presented the world with one of the most baffling problems in the history of written language. Eyraud had made the original discovery when he had found the inscribed tablets in all the huts, but to him they were the work of the devil and he ordered them destroyed. Although he reported what he had seen in a letter to his superiors in Valparaiso, he did not say a word to the three companions who came with him when he returned to the island. Nor did he collect a single written board to show to Bishop Jaussen when he fled back to Tahiti. When he died on August 20, 1868, his three com-

A *rongo-rongo* tablet. The González expedition of 1770 was the first to discover that the islanders had a written language of their own, but Brother Eyraud was the first to report, in 1864, that they inscribed their hieroglyphs on wooden tablets. Because these tablets were used in what he called heathen rites, he ordered them burned and never told his fellow missionaries of his discovery. He did, however, write to his superiors in Valparaiso telling them what he had seen. A few tablets were saved for posterity; the islanders hid them in secret family caves, and Father Zumbohm rediscovered the existence of the *rongo-rongo* tablets after Eyraud's death.

panions had no idea that inscribed tablets had ever existed on Easter Island. Eyraud's forays during his first visit to the island had been so thorough that none were found by the other missionaries in the plank houses of the new villages.

The existence of an Easter Island script was brought to the attention of the world by pure coincidence. A casual discovery was made by Father Zumbohm after the death of Eyraud. He wrote to his superiors:

"Sometimes we have happened to find on the seashore certain stones with traces of incisions; but seeing that the local natives made no importance of it, we thought there was no reason for us to be concerned. However, a certain day when I made an excursion with the school children, of whom I shall speak shortly, I saw in the hands of a young boy a rather curious object which he had just found on a cliff. It was a piece of wood, about fourteen inches long and about twelve inches wide, but somewhat rounded on one side. One could detect the characters, in regular lines, which the weathering had unfortunately altered. Seeing how attentively I observed his find, the child presented it to me, and I preserved it carefully. The next day an Indian, who had noted the importance I attached to this discovery, brought me a similar object, but of a greater dimension and very well preserved, which he let me have for a piece of cloth. On it were incised miniature fishes, birds, and other things known in the country, as well as imaginary figures. I gathered together the most learned of our Indians, to interrogate them on the meaning of these characters, which had every appearance of a hieroglyphic script. All appeared to be content to see this object, and they told me its name, which I have forgotten, whereupon some of them started to read the text by singing. But others shouted: 'No, it is not like that!' The disagreement among my teachers was so great that, in spite of my effort, I was not much more informed after their lesson than beforehand. Later, on a journey, I showed this curiosity to Monseigneur of Axiéri [as Bishop Jaussen was called in Tahiti] who regarded it with a very great interest, while regretting strongly that I was not able to explain to him the meaning of all these figures. 'It is,' he told me, 'the first trace of script which has been found in all the islands of Oceania.' Seeing how this object was precious in the eyes of our beloved prelate, I hasted to present it to him. His Excellency recommended me to instantly get in touch with Father Hippolyte Roussel in order to decipher, if possible, the other writing which I had left behind on Easter Island. Subsequently I found another one, which was about 4.4 feet long and 1.3 feet wide, and I purchased it immediately in exchange for some clothing. But as I did not at that moment have means for taking care of this exchange, the owner of the little memento would not at all hand it over before he received the price agreed upon. He accordingly was to come to my residence, but I waited in vain for him. Meeting him some days later, I asked him why he had not brought me what I had bought from him. He answered me that he had it no more, but he would not tell me what he had done with it. Afterwards, I was assured that a mischievous individ-

Rongo-rongo tablets, here being shown to Figueroa, Skjølsvold, and the author, are preserved as priceless treasures in the Museo Nacional de Historia Natural in Santiago, Chile. Only a score or so specimens have been recovered piecemeal from underground caches. Erroneous reports to the contrary, nobody has yet succeeded in deciphering the *rongo-rongo* characters. Computer experiments by Soviet scientists suggest that they are written in a forgotten language.

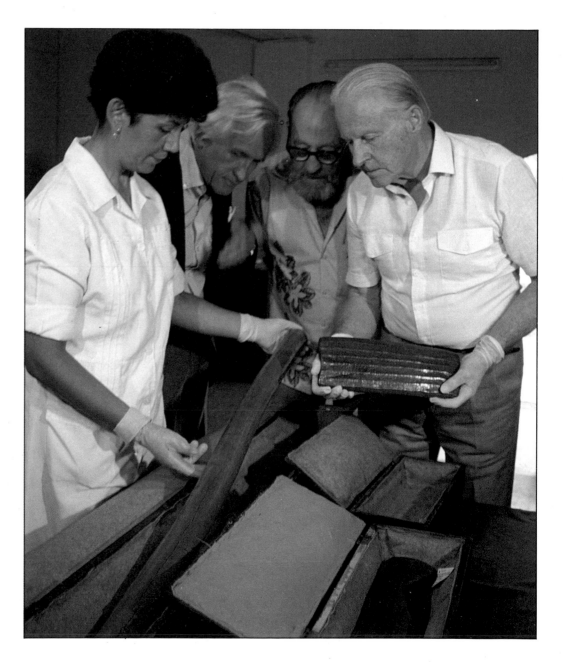

Of the three *rongo-rongo* tablets preserved in the National Museum in Chile, one shows distinct signs of having been rescued from the fanatical missionary's bonfire. The *rongo-rongo* characters have been incised in parallel lines with a rat's tooth, several of them recurring at irregular intervals. Alternate lines are written upside-down, with the end of one line running into the beginning of the next according to a system known as boustrophedon. When the missionaries quizzed the natives, they found that none of the latter could interpret a single character. A couple of young islanders who had been taken to Tahiti later claimed to be able to read the inscriptions, but their claims proved false.

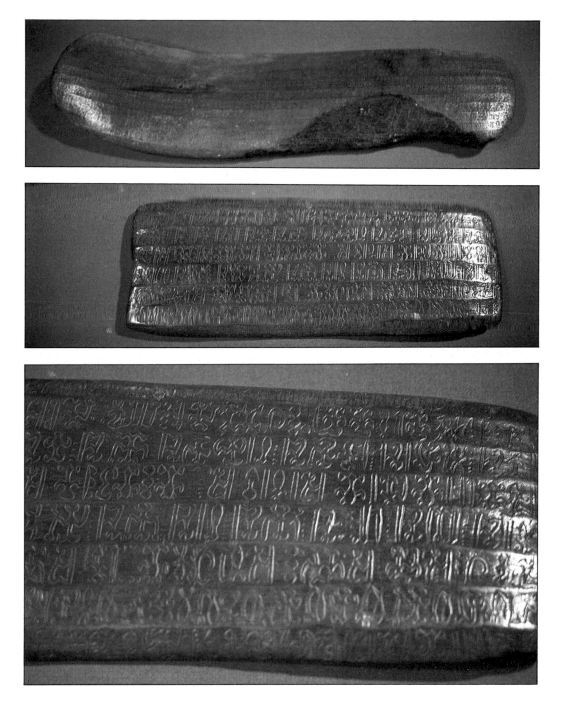

ual, due to jealousy or offense, had possessed himself of this object and burned it. I have deeply regretted this loss, which I have not been able to repair with any other discovery of the same nature. I certainly have no doubt that this Indian script is of real interest to science."

In Tahiti Bishop Jaussen was so excited about the written tablet he had received from Father Zumbohm that he sent a message to Easter Island:

"At the first opportunity I begged Father Roussel to gather together for me what he could find of these tablets, which are inutile to the natives hereafter. 'They use them to light their kitchen fires,' said an Easter Islander who accompanied Father Zumbohm. In spite of Father Roussel's appeal, nobody, and I do not know why, presented themselves to explain to him these tablets."

In the meantime Roussel had already made his own observations:

"They have some songs accompanied by rhythmic motions, very monotonous and very indecent. They pretend to have had a certain script, by means of which they let pass to posterity the important facts of their country. I have seen this script imprinted on a piece of polished wood more or less long; it very much resembles the Egyptian hieroglyphics. Personally I do not believe that they have ever got any sense out of these characters. The few Indians who pretended to understand them, when put to a test, recited nothing but ridiculous and unintelligible tales."

Father Roussel did his best to obtain further tablets for the bishop. None were left. The islanders said that all those Eyraud had seen in their houses had been burnt according to his orders. If any were hidden, the owners would not admit it to Father Roussel, as it would show that they had disobeyed the orders of the church.

That same year, in 1868, a Norwegian merchant captain, Petter Arup, called at Easter Island. He did not represent the church. An amazing variety of ancient images and even an inscribed tablet were brought to him for barter by the recent converts. The captain showed all these objects to Father Roussel, who became so excited about the tablet filled with signs the islanders called *rongo-rongo* that he received it as a gift. The tablet was sent to the bishop in Tahiti, while the captain took the images with him back to Norway, where they are now in the Ethnographic Museum in Oslo.

The missionaries were still on the island in 1870 when the Chilean Captain I. L. Gana visited it. He managed to obtain three more *rongo-rongo* tablets, which he took back to Chile. They, too, were visibly old. These tablets were said to have been hidden in a stone house at Orongo. Up there, in the bird-man village, the lay visitors also witnessed a quite heathen-seeming performance in which men and women danced in the nude, with "improper and immoral movements."

Before he left, even Father Roussel succeeded in obtaining a total of five inscribed tablets. He sent them to the bishop, who recorded that all the others had "gone up in smoke."

Although his missionaries on Easter Island had failed, Bishop Jaussen was determined to find someone who could read the hieroglyphics. He decided to test some of the young men working on Brander's plantation in Tahiti. When, during his first visit, Eyraud had asked all the families there about the tablets, none of them had been able to read them nor understand a single sign. But now a young man named Metoro claimed to be an expert, and Brander gave him leave to visit the bishop for the time needed to read the tablets. Metoro used his time well. For fifteen days he continued to chant endless texts from the five tablets the bishop possessed, while enjoying the bishop's food and hospitality to the full. Finally the good bishop got suspicious and stopped Metoro's recital. According to him, Metoro had an explanation: only some of the words were carved on the tablets; the reader had to memorize by heart all the invisible texts missing in between. The patient bishop had halted Metoro's performance because "the words added in the chant would have given it a length of more than two hundred pages, the reading of which would not have been bearable."

To his disappointment, the bishop discovered that the texts chanted by Metoro made no sense at all. And when asked for the meaning of a single sign Metoro had no reply, or gave a different meaning each time. Yet in reciting his own concocted texts Metoro was at least performing in the same way he had seen the tablets used on Easter Island. The recital was done in a monotonous chant—

and the tablets were turned upside down at the end of each line. This confirmed what the bishop suspected from looking at the characters: In every second line the figures of men, quadrupeds, birdmen, birds and fishes were carved upside down. The script was written in boustrophedon, that is, having alternate lines written in opposite directions. (The word literally means "turning like oxen in plowing.")

Impressed by this, Bishop Jaussen refused to ignore Metoro's recitals altogether. He realized that Metoro had invented much of his long song, but nevertheless the bishop tried to work out a short list of signs whose meanings he had gleaned from these monologues. He found that Metoro had given many different meanings to the same sign, and many different signs for the same word. Thus he listed six different signs for "rat" and nine for "water." There was a special sign for "three wise kings," another for "crustacean cut in two"; one for "bird with three eyes," and other meaningless phrases—all of which clearly demonstrated their obvious, spur-of-the-moment fakery.

Nothing was published until after Bishop Jaussen's death. Then Father Ildefonse found the bishop's handwritten copy of Metoro's "translations," which he ridiculed in a sample he published;

"Man, go away. I will remain on my earth. Father, you who sit on your throne, go to your child. He enjoyed himself in the sky. The bird has flown from the earth, coming to the man who eats on earth. The man feeds the hen, he has put the hen under water, he has taken its feathers. Hen, take care of the spear, go to the good place, go right up to the king, to his house, fly: it is flown to the good place, far from the spear: flying, towards the children of the earth it is flown into safety."

Unfortunately, the nonsense produced by Metoro on the spur of the moment was in one way or another to have an impact on science for a century. Bishop Jaussen's confrère de Harlez also attempted a word list, and in 1895 compared the meanings to the sequences of signs on the five tablets, finding absolutely no consistency. The immediate result was a new theory: the *rongo-rongo* signs did not represent a script at all. To de Harlez they were just "a succession of mutually independent images."

It made sense to many that the savage, uncultivated "Polynesian-speaking" Easter Islanders could not have possessed any form of script. Nevertheless the mysterious *rongo-rongo* board continued to intrigue scholars all over the world. The California Academy of Sciences had already tried to procure one of the Bishop Jaussen's tablets through Thomas Croft, an American resident in Tahiti. Croft obtained photographs from the bishop, but no tablets. He then located a compatriot of Metoro who, like him, professed to be versed in the reading of *rongo-rongo*. Croft reported to the Academy in California.

"In reference to my translation of the inscriptions, I am sorry to inform you that I was cruelly disappointed in my interpreter. On the day on which he was brought to my residence by his countryman, who had recommended him as competent to give me a translation of the characters, I wrote down part of what he pretended to interpret for me, and my hopes were raised to the highest pitch. This day was Sunday, the only day when he was at leisure to attend to such things. During the following week I had mislaid the manuscripts, and when he came again on the succeeding Sunday, I thought it best to begin anew with the translation, and I proceeded to again write down his interpretation, both in his own dialect and in the Tahitian dialect of the Malay language. As I proceeded, however, it struck me that the second translation of the same characters differed materially from the first. This thought kept growing upon me more and more as I advanced, until at last I became convinced that he was deceiving me, and that he did not or could not truly interpret the characters. I concluded, however, not to be too hasty in the matter; and so I gently told him to go away for the present, and to come back again on the following Sunday. He did not come again on that day, and not until the next Sunday. In the meantime, however, I had found the first manuscript, and having compared it with the second, I found that they differed very greatly. When he finally came again, I requested him to again go over his former translation, so that I might correct the errors and omissions in my manuscript. He did so, and I found that his third pretended interpretation again differed from either of his former translations. I then called his attention to these facts—told him that it was impossible that the same characters should have three different meanings on three different Sundays; that he knew nothing, probably, of the meaning of the characters; that he was trying to deceive me, and that he had better leave. He left."

Jaussen never followed Croft's advice and put Metoro to a similar test. Metoro's recitals and Jaussen's *rongo-rongo* vocabulary, together with his tablets, ended up after Jaussen's death at the headquarters of the Congrégation des Sacrès-Coeurs in Europe. Here they were re-examined in the 1950s by a German researcher and his followers, who for a while impressed and confused the scientific world by the sensational claim that *rongo-rongo* was at last deciphered, thanks to Metoro's system. Some parts of the bishop's false word list was also secretly copied by Easter Islanders on Tahiti and found their way back to their home island, where they were put into hiding with the other sacred possessions in the caves. Here they were found by our Norwegian expedition, when we finally managed to break the secrets of the family caves. But all this happened generations later.

In the meantime, the mystery of Easter Island's written tablets came to fascinate the world at large as much as the riddle of the giant statues.

Observations of an English surgeon

The missionaries were still on the island when the English battleship *Topaz* visited it in 1868. We learn from the ship's surgeon, J. L. Palmer, that the religious teachers and their Mangarevan helpers from French Polynesia had altered the Easter Island language so much that it was "impossible to say what it was originally."

The missionaries had come to teach, not to learn. Their intensive efforts had affected the local faith, manners, and language. But the people themselves were obviously still the same. Palmer confirmed once more that they had "features more resembling European than ordinary Polynesian. They were fairer, some almost white. Some had red hair."

When the British battleship *Topaz* called at Easter Island in 1868, the ship's surgeon, J. L. Palmer, made the first attempt to draw a group of gigantic heads sticking up out of the ground below the quarry at Rano Raraku. This drawing appears to have been made inside the crater itself. Palmer also copied pictures of some weird monsters that figured frequently in native art; the bearded heads of three Long-ears are depicted as sea-monsters with the bodies of whales. A quadrupedal Long-ear with a human mask resembles a short-tailed feline with claws and whiskers.

The four missionaries were concerned only about the future of the Easter Islanders, and their interest in the island's past was restricted to the pagan beliefs and practices they had come to Easter Island to abolish. Yet they willingly helped Palmer obtain the first fragments of Easter Island's traditional history, which Palmer in turn presented in his scholarly reports to the Ethnological Society and the Royal Geographic Society in London.

Palmer was able to report that, according to the conviction of the Easter Islanders prior to the missionary influence, two different peoples had settled their island in ancient times. The ancestors of the present population had found, on arrival, an earlier people in possession of the land. These earlier settlers were given credit for the statues: "These were the work of a former race; the present one came here more recently, banished, it is said, from *Oparo* . . ."

Top: The *Topaz* expedition visited the ceremonial village of stone houses at Orongo and examined the interiors of the houses. These were the only buildings not destroyed in the tribal wars, because this village was the only religious shrine held sacred by all the tribes on the island. This was where the people gathered to greet the sun at each vernal equinox, and where all adult males participated in the annual bird-man contest.

Bottom: Inside one of the centrally located houses at Orongo the members of the *Topaz* expedition found a statuette that followed the traditional model, though carved from basalt instead of the softer tuff stone from Rano Raraku. This statuette, which was taken to the British Museum in London, was the only one of its kind to have escaped the ravages of the tribal wars. The great reverence that all the islanders showed for it may indicate that it represented their common ancestor, the supreme and only real god, Make-Make. This sacred statue may have been the prototype of all the ancestral images of the Middle Period. The descendants of the Long-ears interpreted the triple bow with a circle above it and an M-shaped design below it as representing a rainbow with the sun above and rain beneath. The bird-men, the double-bladed *ao* paddles, and the vulva signs appear to be secondary carvings, however, which would suggest that the people of the Middle Period inherited this sculpture from the Early Period.

An ornate statue from Tiahuanaco, where megalithic sculptors erected numerous images out in the open. Monolithic images are found from Colombia and Ecuador to Peru and Bolivia, wherever the sculptors had access to suitable raw material. The megalithic platforms and gigantic images of Tiahuanaco were first compared to the Easter Island statues in 1870, when Palmer presented his observations to the Royal Geographical Society in London. Sir Clements Markham, the noted authority on Andean culture, held that it was impossible not to be struck by the resemblance between the statues from the two places, though he had to admit that those on the mainland were more lavishly decorated than their counterparts on Easter Island. Such ornate statues, however, have been proven to belong to a secondary period in the Andes, and our Norwegian expedition subsequently excavated images that appear to be the missing link.

The missionaries at first assumed that Oparo must have been Rapa-iti and that Great Rapa was named after Little Rapa. Father Roussel later abandoned this theory and, inspired by his companions from Mangareva, proposed that Oparo must have been Mangareva, where he himself later went to live.

Roussel had already recorded that *Hotu* (actually *Hotu Matua*) was the first king on Easter Island. In 1868, Palmer learned that the subsequent immigration was led by *Tu-ku-i-u* (actually *Tuu-ko-ihu*). A most important piece of information was that the newcomers "adopted the religion which they found upon the island."

Although the missionaries had forbidden the pagan house images, and accordingly were shown no more of them, the islanders willingly let Palmer inspect them. They were back in the houses, but swathed in native *tapa* cloth and kept in niches or suspended from ridgepoles. Some were judged by Palmer to be of great antiquity, others seemed to be quite new. Some were images in human form, others were described as grotesque figures of sharks, lizards, distorted fowls, a man with a toucan's bill for a nose, and purely imaginary creatures— "and from their decay, these must have been of extreme age."

Palmer put on record that the various families also had their own small images carved from stone. These were apparently not in the houses, however—at least he was not shown any—and he did not learn why.

Inside one of the largest ceremonial stone houses of Orongo, on top of Rana Kao, the Englishmen discovered an exceptionally beautiful small-scale statue, buried to its shoulders in the ground. Unlike the other *moai*, which were carved from yellowish Rano Raraku tuff, this statue was made of hard, dark basalt and its back was covered with reliefs of bird-men, double-bladed paddles, and vulva symbols. Remains of paint still covered the statue, the face and body having been painted white, the reliefs red. The name of the ceremonial house was *Tau-ra-renga, ra* meaning "sun," and the image was known as *Hoa-haka-nana-ia*. The little statue was removed and taken to the British Museum. Although it was only 8.2 feet tall, and weighed about four tons, the missionaries reported that three hundred sailors and two hundred islanders were required to bring the statue down the slopes of the volcano to Cook's Bay.

Palmer noticed the large, sickle-shaped ships cut into the red cylinders left in the Puna Pau quarries, which contrasted so totally with the straight, patched-together canoes of the islanders. He recognized such curves on the local reed floats still in use, which he described as somewhat like a huge elephant's tusks. "They resemble much the 'caballitos' which are used on the Peruvian coast . . ."

Back in England, Palmer was invited to lecture on Easter Island before the Royal Geographical Society. The result was the first of the scholarly polemics on the origin of the Easter Island population. We learn from the proceedings of the Society in 1870 that the noted contemporary authority on Inca history and Andean culture, Sir Clements Markham, joined in the discussion. Markham was struck by the Easter Island analogies to the prehistoric remains he himself had seen in southern Peru and around Lake Titicaca:

"When the Spaniards conquered the country there were at Tiahuanaco ruins of platforms similar to those on Easter Island, upon which were statues also resembling, to a certain extent, those of Easter Island. They represented giants with enormous ears, and with crowns on their heads, or conical caps. There, however, the resemblance appeared to end, for the Aymara images were very ornate. . . . It was impossible not to be struck with the resemblance between those remains and those on Easter Island."

Markham assumed that no South American craft could have reached Easter Island, and he therefore proposed that the presumably maritime Easter Islanders could have inspired the pre-Inca culture. Admiral Belcher was also present at Palmer's lecture. He had been to Easter Island in 1825 with Beechey, and although he did not go ashore he was so impressed by Captain Cook's list of Rapanui words that he rejected the concept of Easter Island's contact with people other than the Polynesians.

In the learned discussion for and against contact between the ancient sculptors of Peru and Easter Island, nobody took into account what the Easter Islanders themselves had told Palmer: that their island had been settled twice. Their ancestors, they said, had found the statue makers on the island and had accepted the religion of their predecessors.

But no Easter Islanders were present at the learned discussion, and their oral history was ignored. The linguistic argument was considered conclusive. Palmer's observations of analogies between Peruvian and Easter Island reed boats, and Markham's claim that the giant statues on stone platforms in both areas looked alike, were noted down and then forgotten.

In retrospect there are important lessons to learn from what the original inhabitants of Easter Island told the first foreigners, those who were able to converse with them for the very first time and put on record what the islanders could tell before the outside world began to affect and alter Easter Island's inherited beliefs and memories. The minds of the islanders were wide open to the lessons taught by the foreigners, but these visitors in turn did not to the same extent trust what the islanders told them. Europeans have always been more eager to teach than to learn. It seems to have been particularly difficult to learn from unfortunate people in miserable living conditions, such as the Easter Islanders were at the time of Eyraud's arrival.

No sooner had Palmer's dialogue started than the missionaries told him that the Easter Islanders claimed to have descended from a mixed race. Their ancestors had told them that their island had been peopled twice. The striking mixture of physical types had been stressed by foreigners since the time of European discovery, but when the islanders tried to offer the reason, which was in fact the highlight of local history, the Europeans felt they had nothing to learn. How could naked savages know anything about their distant past? In Europe most people knew little about their own families beyond the names of their grandparents. Yet the Easter Islanders professed to know the names of kings who had arrived ages before Roggeveen.

The essence of what the residents of the country tried to share with the foreigners was simple: an earlier people were already on the island when their ancestors arrived. These ancestors abandoned their own religion upon arrival, and learned from the statue makers to worship Make-Make. This was the history of the country. And history was the basis of Easter Island religion. The Easter Islanders were ancestor worshipers. Their *moai* were ancestral monuments.

Polynesian gods were not worshiped on Easter Island. Make-Make was worshiped, and he was not a Polynesian deity. From this it may be inferred that the newcomers, those who abandoned their ancestral religion, were the Polynesians.

The word *moai* is not a Polynesian word. The word for statues in the Marquesas and Raivavae, the only islands in Polynesia where statues appear, is *tiki*, the name of the principal Polynesian god. The word *moai*, then, must pertain to the language of the first settlers.

The beautifully carved and fitted megalithic walls seen by Cook's party in Hanga-roa and Vinapu supported the statues, and, like the *moai* they held, had to be the design of the early settlers also. There are no such masonry walls anywhere in Polynesia, and none in the Marquesas and Raivavae, where the few stone *tiki* stand. Markham was the first to point out that there are indeed such walls in Tiahuanaco. They, too, were built to support giant stone men and, to his mind, it was impossible not to be struck with the resemblance between these remains and those on Easter Island.

Return of the idols and a new shepherd

When the French warship *La Flore* called at Easter Island in 1872, the missionaries were gone. The artist Pierre Loti, alias Julien Viaud, was on board as a midshipman, and made drawings of the visit. One of these shows that some islanders had already moved back into their reed huts. Small stone images were openly set up as guardians on either side of the door.

When another warship, the *Seignelay,* anchored off the coast in 1877, the island was still without foreigners and had a population of one hundred and eleven. A. Pinart, one of the passengers, went ashore to explore. He found about thirty native huts at Mataveri, where Dutroux-Bornier's residence had been. Some were of planks, some of reeds as shown in Loti's drawings. A native queen pretended to have certain powers over the population.

Pinart went as far as to the Hotu-iti plains at the foot of the Rano Raraku quarries, where he found the ruins of an abandoned village of stone houses. He noted other ruins of stone houses scattered along the south coast. Some had been circular, others rectangular. The walls were of dry stone masonry, slightly more than 3.3 feet high: "They were constructed from fragments of lava; the roofs, probably made from vegetable materials, had completely disappeared."

These ruins were not to remain for very long, either, and with their disappearance the existence of non-Polynesian stone dwellings was completely overlooked by later scientific investigators. Since the time of Dutroux-Bornier, the walls of the stone houses had provided convenient building material for the many miles of sheep fences that were gradually to be built across the landscape.

In the year of the *Seignelay*'s visit, when the Easter Island population was at the lowest in its turbulent history, a sheep ranger from Tahiti was again set ashore. In contrast to his infamous predecessor, this new representative of Maison Brander, Alexander P. Salmon, would prove to be a blessing for the abandoned community. He was a humane and intelligent half-Tahitian, sent to replace the assassinated Dutroux-Bornier. His family had intermarried with the royal family in Tahiti. In addition to his Tahitian mother tongue, he had learned to communicate with the Easter Islanders in their own language, because he had worked with those employed on Brander's plantation. A considerable number of Easter Islanders returned home with Salmon.

Top: The French artist and writer Julien Viaud (Pierre Loti) visited Easter Island in 1872, two years after renewed intertribal feuds had driven out the missionaries. If we compare his drawing of the hillside below Rano Raraku with the photograph taken on the same spot by our expedition in 1956 (p. 186), we see that hardly any silt from the quarry uphill has been deposited in the past century. While the quarry was being worked, well-organized gangs of workers carried the rubble down the mountain in baskets and dumped it on large refuse piles on the plain below. When operations suddenly stopped, heavy rainfall washed all the remaining debris from the quarry down the mountainside in the course of a few years, half burying the unfinished images that were temporarily parked at the mountain's foot. That was the way the first Europeans found them.

Bottom: After the departure of the missionaries, the Easter Islanders reverted to paganism, as Loti observed during his visit in 1872. Before they were expelled in 1870, the missionaries had assured the bishop of Tahiti that there were no works of heathen art left on the island, but Loti found stone images that had been retrieved from temporary caches and re-erected as guardian totems outside the boat-shaped reed houses. The illustration also shows a chieftain with feather bonnet and ceremonial *ua* club. (Reproduced from Julien Viaud's original drawing by permission of the Association International des Amis de Pierre Loti.)

In the absence of missionaries, Salmon set about doing all he could to improve the sad condition of the remaining population. He also took great interest in the island's past and devoted much effort to the gathering of surviving tribal memories. Only fifteen years had passed since the Peruvian slave raid, so he was able to obtain the original and as yet unmuddled versions of these stories from the elders, who were of advanced years at the time of the raid. Salmon thus became not only an indispensable informant but also an interpreter for the researchers who were soon to make their way to Easter Island, intent on unraveling the mysteries of the monuments and written tablets.

Salmon and the colonists from Tahiti were still the only foreigners ashore when Commander B. F. Clark arrived on HMS *Sappho* in 1882. The British com-

Loti found that the pagan rites with fire offerings had been resumed once all the foreigners had been expelled from the island. He called his drawing "Idolatrous Festival on Easter Island." While the women were once more free to dance naked, the men adorned themselves with feather bonnets and other status symbols, such as the double-bladed *ao* paddle. (*Harpers Weekly,* April 26, 1873.)

Like Bernizet before him, Loti drew an *ahu* as a stepped pyramid steeper at the back than at the front. This is interesting, because latter-day visitors have found the fronts covered with ramps that often contain graves dating from the intertribal wars. When the Spaniards conquered the Inca empire in Peru, they discovered that the natives worshiped the sun god at stepped pyramids, most of which have since been destroyed. The large adobe pyramid (*right*) at Eten on the coast of Peru, now badly eroded but drawn by Leicht in 1944, follows the same architectural design as the Easter Island *ahu,* even to the addition of a frontal ramp. The *huaca,* the commonest type of religious structure in the Andean region of South America, was an altarlike outdoor platform with a flight of steps. In the highlands, where workable stone was available, the *huacas* were faced with dressed and fitted stones and filled with stone rubble, whereas those on the desert coast where workable stone was missing, were built of adobe, blocks of sun-baked clay. Stone images, often of gigantic proportions, have been found on such raised temple platforms everywhere from Tula in Mexico to Huaraz in Peru and Tiahuanaco in Bolivia—just as on Easter Island.

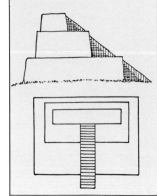

mander took a personal interest in the island and its population. As Peru had never followed up on the annexation by Gonzalez in 1770, Clark made an official appeal to his own government for British protection, but got no response. There happened to be an important piece of information in his letter to the British Admiralty. He first stressed that Mr. Salmon spoke the native language thoroughly, and that therefore all the information he got about native names and traditions could be relied upon. He then reported:

"Mr. Salmon says that, after long talks with the natives on the subject, they all say they originally landed on the north side of the island, at Anakena, and came from the *East* in two canoes, . . ."

The British commander underlined the *direction* from which the first settlers had come, according to the unanimous claim of the islanders. He now also gave the full name of the first king, Hotu, as *Hotometua,* said to mean "The Prolific Father." The king and queen were said to have been in separate vessels, and on finding the island they parted and circumnavigated the coast in both directions. Then they joined up and made their first landing on the beach in Anakena Bay. They went to settle in the plains of Hotu-iti, at the foot of what would become the image quarries: " . . . they there built the stone houses the remains of which still exist and made the statues with which the hill is covered." But, he added, "the first statue was not made till some fifty years after they landed."

Thus the testimony of the islanders, before their ancestral history was confused by European theories, was that their royal line commenced with an organized settlement of a king and his queen, who came from the *east*, from the direction of South America, and built the village of stone houses, the ruins of which were still there in the time of the missionaries. Some fifty years after their landing, these original settlers of Easter Island began to carve the first stone statue. This makes sense, for if the statues were ancestral monuments, as recorded by Captain Cook, there would have been no need of any *moai* . . . until the first king died.

Commander Geiseler and the magic stones

One of the strange stone structures that are peculiar to Easter Island and have no counterpart anywhere else in Polynesia. There are two types; both look alike from the outside, where only two small openings can be seen. The openings lead into the interior, but are too small to admit a human head. One type is almost entirely solid, fitted with large and small stones that leave only a narrow longitudinal shaft in the interior. The other type has a slightly wider chamber.

When Captain Geiseler of the German battleship *Hyäne* visited the island in 1882, he made a sketch of one of the these structures (*bottom*). He asked the islanders what it was, and was told that it was the tomb of an old-time chieftain. Geiseler confirmed this story by opening the tomb and finding human bones in the central chamber. The Germans then opened several other similar structures, and found human remains in all of them.

The Easter Islanders of today have forgotten the original purpose of these prehistoric buildings, and give the same explanation that a subtle young islander offered when asked about them by a visiting scholar in this century: "It's just a *hare moa*" (henhouse). The name has stuck in spite of Geiseler's observations.

The German battleship *Hyäne* under the command of Geiseler also anchored off the island in 1882, a few months after the departure of the *Sappho*. This German man-of-war called in for a week en route from Chile to Polynesia. The purpose

In 1883 Geiseler published his account of his visit to Easter Island. He was the first to illustrate the characteristic "weeping eye" ornament from the religious paintings in the stone houses of Orongo. It later turned out that this stylized motif was very widespread on Easter Island, though totally unknown in the rest of Oceania. It was, on the other hand, common in many parts of the Americas, and was specially characteristic of the pre-Inca cultural center of Tiahuanaco and regions directly influenced by that area.

There were carved stone heads solidly embedded in the masonry and projecting from the walls of the Orongo houses. Some of them were so ancient that they crumbled at a touch. Geiseler drew one of them. Architectural ornaments of this kind are unknown in Polynesia, but typical of ancient Tiahuanaco and other regions in the Andes, including Chavín.

of the visit to Easter Island was to conduct research on the local culture for the Ethnographic Department of the Kaiserliches Museum in Berlin. Investigations were carried out under the direction of Paymaster Weisser, who collaborated closely with Salmon. With Salmon's aid, a large ethnographic collection was obtained and taken to various German museums.

The Germans counted a hundred and fifty Easter Islanders now living on the island with Salmon. They were divided between two neighboring villages, Hangaroa and Mataveri. Geiseler found that the influence of the missionaries had disappeared, "leaving almost no traces among the remaining population." But an old man made the sign of the cross each time the Germans offered him food, even though he appeared to revere and show honor to his own images. Some of these were of stone.

The Easter Islanders, as we have seen, had not readily exposed their little stone

images to the view of foreigners. Palmer had referred to the existence of such small sculptures, but the islanders had refused to display them. As the Germans had come expressly to collect artifacts, they managed, with a certain degree of persistence, to see a number of them and even to take several away.

Although stone figurines were never mentioned by name by any of the missionaries, they must have been aware of their existence, for Bishop Jaussen published a drawing of one representing a winged quadruped in high relief on an arched stone. The bishop had also received photographs of several stone specimens obtained by the Chilean Gana expedition. Geiseler now learnt that these art objects were known as *moai maea,* which simply means "stone image," as opposed to the *moai toromiro,* the "wooden images." The latter followed standard prototypes known to all, and there was no secrecy about them. But the little figurines of stone were different.

"These images always remain in the huts, they are a kind of family images, of which each family possesses at least one, whereas the wooden images were brought along to the feasts."

Geiseler probably referred to the doorway images seen by Pierre Loti when he described stone images two to three feet tall, sometimes with a red miniature cylinder on top. He wrote that in most cases the *moai maea* inside the dwellings were simply stone heads with faces carved on them. One was described as being double-faced and carved from red scoria with the mouth painted white.

The most remarkable sculpture obtained by the Germans was carved from a large boulder of extremely hard and heavy basalt. It represented a grotesque, froglike monster with upturned human head and beard. The bulky body had a short tail, was without arms but had enormous hind limbs flexed forward, ending in clawlike, three-finger hands. The sculpture was taken to the Imperial Museum in Dresden with a note from Paymaster Weisser stating that all the Easter Islanders knew this image and considered it to be as old as the oldest statue on the island.

The Germans also investigated Orongo on top of Rano Kao. When they excavated the floor in one of the cermonial stone houses, they found a small and very eroded *moai maea.* They also discovered stone heads inserted in the walls, too eroded to remove. They learnt what actually happened in this bird-man village during the rites of Mataveri times: From the stone houses up on the rim of the crater the competitors for the bird-man title had a spectacular view over the ocean. Below them lay the three rocky bird islets, which they watched while keeping a constant eye on the eastern horizon. They were expecting the first of the sooty terns to arrive on their annual migration from the bird islet of Sala y Gomez, which lay in the direction of South America. These wide-ranging birds from the east symbolically represented Make-Make to the Easter Islanders. As soon as they arrived and alighted on the rock islets to lay their eggs, the participants in the religious competition rushed down the sixteen-hundred-foot high cliff to the sea and threw themselves into their tusk-shaped reed skiffs to go out in search of the first egg. The one who returned safely with that egg became the sacred bird-man of the year, and was favored with almost unlimited privileges until the next year's competition.

The Germans made a thorough, if rather rough-and-ready, archaeological examination of some strange stone structures of non-Polynesian type on Easter Island. What they discovered is noteworthy because in modern times they have simply been dismissed as *hare moa,* or "chicken houses" (although the early Spaniards had recorded that the chickens were merely kept in runs scraped out in the

Left: Geiseler was also the first to distinguish between *moai toromiro* and *moai maea*—figurines of wood and stone respectively. He determined that the latter type were never publicly displayed, but were regarded as secret, private family images. With the help of Salmon, a recently arrived shepherd who spoke the native language, the German expedition nevertheless succeeded in procuring specimens of both types of figurines. These were taken back to Germany and distributed among several museums. The wooden figurines included an artistically carved quadruped that could not have represented any known speciies to be found on the island, where there were few four-legged beasts. With its round head and lack of a tail, it could not be either a lizard or a rat, the only four-legged animals on Easter Island, and it is tempting to assume that it was an effigy of that mysterious creature so typical of Easter Island religious art, the short-tailed feline, symbolizing royalty and the supreme god.

ground and thatched over). The Germans opened up several of these stone structures, and found heavy roof slabs topping thick masonry walls. Inside, there was only enough room for a very narrow trough. Two small holes led through a frame of carved stone arches to the inside. Before opening the first of these impressive structures, Geiseler obtained this information:

"A native, whose property it was, showed through pantomime that a dead chief (ariki) was buried inside. When his consent was duly purchased, part of the roof was uncovered, to obtain a view of the interior, and here we found, in addition to a human skull and some bones, also various skeletons of birds. When the native was shown the bird bones . . . he pointed to the round holes on the outside to demonstrate that the birds had only flown in accidentally, and died when not finding the exit. When asked about the purpose of the two holes in the tomb, he made us understand that the soul of the dead thus had an exit, and that two holes were present because, when the god *Make-Make* wanted to pursue the soul to kill it, it had an opportunity to escape through the other hole."

The Germans dismantled a number of these stone structures, all of which were found to contain a single body, presumably those of a chief. The owners of the land willingly let the visitors open these mausoleums, apparently having no ties of kinship to the deceased. Obviously these structures were tombs of former times that just happened to be on their land. The chickens were too common to require such structures. Geiseler speaks of about ten thousand living all over the landscape and in the ruins of the former settlements.

The Germans visited the Rano Raraku image quarries, and were informed that the carving of the *moai* had been done by a professional-class group of image sculptors. Some of the islanders claimed to be their descendants. There was no secrecy about the procedures, and the Germans were taken up to the rim of the crater above the quarries and shown some large cylindrical holes, clearly manmade. Here, said the islanders, their ancestors had inserted colossal tree trunks, which held the cables used in lowering the *moai* down to the plains below, once they had been detached from the rock up on the mountainside. Once maneuvered to the foot of the volcano, the stone men were set up on end, to enable the sculptors to complete work on the backs before they "walked" to their destinations. The old islanders were even able to recall the names of most of the statues, or the chiefs they represented.

More impressed by what he saw of prehistoric remains than in what he heard from the living, Geiseler did not attempt an explanation of why the Easter Islanders divided into two groups when testifying to the origins of their ancestors. He simply recorded that one group insisted that their forefathers had come from the east, the others that theirs had come from the west.

Geiseler did record, however, that these islanders had a second god, Haua, who also received first-fruit offerings, although he seemed to have been just a companion or assistant to the great god Make-Make.

From what Geiseler learned with the aid of Salmon, no family or population group could have been completely exterminated in the civil wars. Men were killed in battle, or captured and then fed in special houses in front of the *ahu* images until they were eaten in honor of the gods at the feasts. But the women and their children were spared; they were awarded to the warriors as booty, and formed new branches on old family trees. After the feasting, the islanders would all dance and sing. Geiseler witnessed one musical performance, and was impressed by the high standards and beautiful harmonies of the choir. "The dance differs from what is customary in other parts of Polynesia," he wrote, ". . .

Unlike the realistic figurines worn on festive occasions, an almost infinite variety of grotesque *moai toromiro* carvings gradually began to emerge from their secret hiding places. The chief function of their repulsive appearance seems to have been to frighten off strangers and protect their owners. Some of these figurines had obsidian eyes.

here they stand on one leg and stretch the other by thrusting it out in jerks in the rhythm of the song. . . . During the singing, a carved figure of a woman is usually moved by the leader of the choir, also on one leg in time with the dance.''

An old chief named Hangeto had a tablet, but refused to part with it. He said the *rongo-rongo* had enabled his ancestors to preserve records of the past. *Rongo-rongo* was also used so that runners could deliver messages without knowing their contents, because not everyone possessed the skill of reading *rongo-rongo*.

Geiseler saw fishing tackle unlike anything found elsewhere in Polynesia—enormous nets made from strings and ropes of totora fibers over six hundred feet long. He was also shown a large fishhook made of hard basalt, beautifully carved and polished, and so treasured as an ancestral heirloom that the owners refused to part with it. But if fishing had once been important, it had died out. He wrote:

"Canoes no longer exist on the island, and even the swimming on reed bundles seems to have fallen into disuse."

Geiseler noticed some large circular pits, evidently manmade, on the rim of the Rano Raraku volcano immediately above the quarry. The islanders stated positively that their ancestors had dug them as sockets for poles to support the ropes by which the immense stone images were lowered from the quarry down to the plain. The natives still held to this traditional belief when we visited the island a hundred years later. But nobody believed them, because the holes were bigger than any tree known to have grown on the island.

The visitors from the *Hyäne* had thrown new light on the obscure existence of a special class of family images, the *moai maea,* which had no functional relation to the wooden figurines known since the time of Captain Cook. The antiquity of these heterogenous stone images was borne out by the native claim that the frog-like boulder was as old as the oldest *moai,* and by the excavations at Orongo of one stone figurine so eroded that it broke upon touch. If the native claim could be taken literally, the froglike sculpture would have dated from the first settlers and reflect an imported concept. There are no frogs nor any sculptures remotely resembling this old Easter Island carving in any part of Polynesia. But in ancient Peru frogs and toads were well known and commonly depicted in local art as a sacred animal. It is relevant in retrospect that in 1770 the early Spaniards had recorded that a common tattoo motif on Easter Island was a collar traced around the neck, "and depending from it the figure of a small animal resembling a toad, or frog, which they call *cogé.*" *Cogé* is not a Polynesian word.

The German expedition conducted the first archaeological operations on Easter Island, though their methods were in the rough-and-ready manner typical of the period. They tore apart a number of *Hare moa* which, according to the owners, were mausoleums for ancient chiefs. Human bones were found inside a trough so narrow that birds had been trapped there, unable to get out. Throughout the recent period on Easter Island, corpses were simply placed under a loose pile of stones on the *ahu* or out in the fields. The important people found worthy of being placed in the mausoleums opened by the Geisler expedition must therefore have lived in an earlier period, when elaborate stoneworks flourished, and followed funeral practices brought from somewhere other than Polynesia. In ancient South America, masonry mausoleums were common. In Polynesia the chicken was common, but no Polynesians built chicken houses of stone. Geiseler was told that there were no chickens on Easter Island in the early period, and that, until the chicken was introduced, the eggs of seabirds were important. It would make sense, then, that the stone mausoleums were early South American elements in the Easter Island culture, abandoned and forgotten in the later period when the Polynesians came with their chickens.

Perhaps the Germans did not believe the islanders, who told them that the circular holes on the rim above the quarries had served as postholes for some kind of cable railway or funicular that eased the descent of the detached *moai.* Neither, perhaps, did they believe the islanders' claims that the statues were set up below the quarries so that their backs could be refinished and retouched before the final walk. But fortunately the Germans did put these traditions on record. Today we have proof of the ability of the island's population to pass on unwritten memories, for Geiseler recorded that *"Ko-Pilo-Pilo"* was the name of one of the tallest *moai* standing heads appearing above the silt at the foot of the quarries. In 1919, Mrs. Routledge was given its name as Piro-Piro. It was still recalled as Piro-Piro when it was excavated by us in 1956. We found the total height to be almost forty feet, but the part visible above the ground from the shoulders up was the same as that observed by Geiseler. This gives us the additional information that the descent of loose material from the abandoned quarries above had in fact ended long before the Germans arrived. The Easter Islanders must have retained details of their traditions about working on statues since a time before the silt buried and concealed the images up to their necks—for they said that the statues had to be erected to have their backs finished. Since first seen by Europeans, the *moai* at the foot of the quarries were thought by all foreign visitors to be nothing but colossal heads without bodies.

Paymaster Thomson obtains the sacred history

Four years after the German visit, in the winter of 1886, an American team of investigators arrived with the U.S.S. *Mohican*. The paymaster on board, William J. Thomson, was set ashore in a new effort to unveil the mysteries still shrouding Easter Island's past. The ship's surgeon, G. H. Cooke, accompanied Thomson on his field explorations, which were to become the most extensive so far.

The amount of work accomplished by the American visitors during their eleven-day survey was almost incredible. They measured and described one hundred and thirteen masonry *ahu,* and recorded their names. Five hundred and fifty-five statues were examined, all of a standard type, differing mainly in size. All but one were males. All had long ears, except three eroded ones with short ears at *ahu* Motu-opopo. Four hundred of them had been transported from the quarry to different parts of the island.

The Americans were the first to detect an oddity: many of the prehistoric *ahu* or temple platforms had been rebuilt. Thomson noted that broken heads and body fragments of older statues had been used in the walls as casual building

According to information the islanders gave orally to their German guests in 1882, the images below the quarry at Rano Raraku had been erected there only long enough to allow the rough-hewn backs to be polished, after which they were to have been walked upright to their appointed *ahu* platforms. This unlikely story was dismissed as sheer fantasy by most observers from the outside world, although strange shapes of the neck were noted.

When Paymaster Thomson came to Easter Island with the USS *Mohican* four years after Geiseler, he, too, confirmed that there was a special type of portable stone statuette called *moai maea*. He managed to secure a particularly weird specimen (*left*) for the National Museum in Washington, D.C. The mask of a flat human face looks up from a lumpy, ungainly body with stunted limbs that conform to the natural shape of the stone. Thomson also found a head of unusual shape broken off at the neck (*right*). It differs from the typical statuettes in both its proportions and the shape of the face. As this head was later lost, nobody seems to have noticed that it evidently had inlaid eyes, probably discs of black obsidian. Had this been previously noted, there might have been less resistance to the theory that the stone statues had once had inlaid eyes—a resistance that lasted until the theory was proven by actual discoveries.

blocks. These older images were of a somewhat different type and sometimes carved from a rock distinct from that of the Rano Raraku quarries. Some were of dark basalt, some of red scoria. A large broken head of red tufa was noted among the colossal foundation stones of *ahu* Tongariki in Hotu-iti, the largest *ahu* on the island. From his survey of the various *ahu*, Thomson drew the conclusion that they had been "erected and destroyed by succeeding generations."

Some of the *ahu* Thomson saw and described are no more. In 1960 an enormous tidal wave entered Hotu-iti Bay and hit *ahu* Tongariki full force. The fifteen fallen *moai* that lay on top were thrown inland and the megalithic blocks and image fragments of the wall were scattered in total chaos. Thomson's records tell us that this impressive structure was not alone in falling victim to the waves. He described an *ahu* with a record number of sixteen fallen statues that lay on an inaccessible terrace halfway up the cliffs east of Rano Kao: "It is hardly probable that the images were lowered from the top by ropes, and the natural conclusion is that a roadway once existed which has been undermined by the waves and has fallen into the sea."

Since the time of Thomson's visit, this entire *ahu* has indeed fallen into the sea. When our expedition searched for that site in 1955, it found nothing but a naked rock wall almost a thousand feet high. Part of a *moai* was detected in the talus below, where the roaring surf hit the foot of the rocks.

Another *ahu* subsequently lost to the sea was seen by the American survey party on the north coast. This *ahu*, referred to as Ahu Ahau by Thomson, impressed him so much that he made a drawing which he published to show the style of stone fitting. The prehistoric architects of this megalithic structure had used the same masonry technique so admired by Captain Cook's party in Hangaroa and Vinapu. The drawing shows that, here too, the perfectly fitted blocks of the original structure had been reorganized and its original esthetic design destroyed to fit a different function in a late reconstruction period. Ahu Ahau was still there half a century later, and was visited by the French ethnologist A. Métraux, who wrote:

". . . when we visited it in 1934 a gaping fissure had already detached its right wing, and a few rainstorms would have been enough to send the mausoleum crashing down six hundred feet into the sea."

When our Norwegian expedition visited this same area in 1955, the ocean had indeed swallowed up Ahu Ahau, and with it had gone a neighboring *ahu,* also seen and admired by Thomson, who described it as an exceedingly fine platform of igneous rock, containing some remarkably large stones decorated with reliefs of faces and figures.

It was close to these two fine *ahu* that Thomson's exploring party made what was probably their most important discovery, and the loss of what they found there means the loss of a significant key to the island's mystery:

"On the high bluff west of Kotatake Mountain we discovered the ruins of a settlement extending more than a mile along the coastline and inland to the base of the hill. These remains bear unmistakable evidences of being the oldest habitations on the island. The houses are elliptical in shape, with doorways facing the sea, and were built of uncut stone. Some of the walls are standing, but the majority are scattered about in the utmost confusion. An extremely interesting feature of these ancient ruins is the fact that each dwelling was provided with a small cave or niche at the rear end, built of loose lava stones, which was in a number of instances covered by an arch supported by a fairly shaped keystone. The recesses were undoubtedly designed to contain the household gods, and the keystone, although extremely rough in construction, is unmistakable in its application. Our guides had no knowledge of this locality and knew no distinctive name for it.

"Messrs. Salmon and Brander had not visited the spot, because the location is bleak and desolate and, as far as they had heard, was a trackless waste, devoid of all interest."

Since Thomson's party walked through these extensive village ruins, the whole area, dwellings as well as *ahu,* have been lost to the never-resting ocean. Our archaeological expedition of 1955–56 ascertained this, and it was confirmed later by the Chilean archaeologists Claudio Christino and Patricia Vargas, when they systematically mapped all prehistoric sites on the island. The cliffs of this high northern coastal region are as dangerously subject to the elements as those of Rano Kao and the peninsula of Poike. These three areas, formed by the three main volcanoes on the island, are composed of tuff that is less resistant to the erosion of the surf than the harder lava of the intermittent lowland coasts.

The lowland plains of Anakena and La Pérouse Bay were also found by Thomson to be full of ruins of houses, but of a different type, "built of loose stones, nearly circular in shape." They were estimated to be from a period later than the elliptical slab houses seen on the north coast, as they were built from crude lava fragments mixed with artificially shaped basalt blocks taken from demolished buildings: "Any sort of material that came handy appears to have been freely used by the builders of these houses. In several we found well-cut heads that had formerly ornamented image platforms, built in the walls, some facing inside and others in the opposite direction."

At the time of Thomson's visit, the islanders had just invented a new use for these abandoned relics of the past. With their fields threatened by the eighteen thousand sheep and the six hundred head of cattle which Salmon now had grazing all over the island, they used the walls of the old houses as fences for small garden plots. Thomson called it "a happy expedient to escape the ravages of the animals lately imported by the foreign residents," and says the only disadvantage was the small confined area available for each plot. His companion Cooke made the same observation. Forced to fence in their crops against the herds, the

Thomson made a drawing of Ahu Oahu on the high plateau of the north coast. The drawing shows the curious way the stones are fashioned and fitted together. He estimated the weight of the central stone at six tons, and measured the diameter of a round block lying on its side as over five feet. This *ahu* later fell into the sea in a landslide that also carried away the ground it stood on and a whole nearby village of stone houses, which Thomson believed to be the oldest structures on the island. The masonry of this lost *ahu* must have dated from the Early Period. The upper row of stones on the front wall has been turned over sideways to lie flat and thus make a firm horizontal support for a Middle Period *ahu* image. Since this fine *ahu* later fell into the sea, it seems likely that the ceaseless pounding of the surf at the bottom of the cliffs may also have caused the total loss of other walls from the Early Period.

Rapanui preferred a ready-made fence to building one, and therefore had begun to use the walls of former stone houses:

"There are many of these scattered over the island, particularly on the eastern half. These require but little repair to put them in order and secure against the entrance of the sheep, and although small, they amply suffice to supply the needs of the native husbandman."

The stone-house villages were clearly vestiges from the days of organized community life, when peace and order prevailed. The people of post-missionary times had not seen them inhabited. They recalled the period of constant feuds and slave raids when everybody lived in darkness underground. The American exploring party visited several such prehistoric living caves, and found that some had also been used as depositories for the dead. One had recesses and angles walled up and filled with human bones, while carvings of boats, men and fishes decorated the walls. Thomson wrote: "The feeble rays of our candles were quickly absorbed by the somber surroundings, heightening the apparent extent and gloom of the recesses. Careful investigation proved that all of the caves visited had been used as dwelling-places by the early inhabitants." He added:

"It is reported that small images, inscribed tablets, and other objects of interest have been hidden away in such caves and finally lost through landslides."

One such cavern was found accidentally. It had a narrow entrance covered by loose rocks and intentionally concealed. "It contained a small image about 3 feet high, carved out of hard gray rock. It was a splendid specimen of the work . . ."

No wonder, with such surroundings, that Thomson found the surviving population to be superstitious to an extraordinary extent.

"Deified spirits were believed to be constantly wandering about the earth and to have more or less influence over the human affairs. Spirits were supposed to appear to sleeping persons and to communicate with them through visions or dreams. Gnomes, ghouls, and goblins were believed to inhabit inaccessible caves and niches in the rock and to have the power of prowling about after dark. The small wooden and stone images known as 'household gods' were made to represent certain spirits and belong to a different order from the gods, though accredited with many of the same attributes. They occupied a prominent place in every dwelling and were regarded as the medium through which communications might be made with the spirits, but were never worshipped."

Thomson took some of the wooden household images, as well as one *moai maea,* to the Smithsonian Institution in Washington. The *moai maea* was a crude

boulder about fourteen-and-a-half inches long, carved into a hunchbacked monster with distorted arms and anthropomorphic head. It had no resemblance whatsoever to the *moai* on the *ahu* platforms. The islanders made it clear to Thomson that there was no relationship between the large outdoor and the small indoor stone images. The *moai* of the *ahu* were intended as monuments to important persons. The *moai maea* were protective spirits. Neither type of carving depicted the supreme god, Make-Make, lord of sea and sky. He was symbolically carved on the rocks of Orongo, amongst the reliefs of his servants, the bird-men and his messengers, the sooty terns. Thomson was shown the figures of Make-Make:

"The most important sculptured rocks on this island are in the immediate vicinity of the stone houses at Orongo. . . . The apparent age of some of the rock carvings antedates the neighboring stone houses, the images, and other relics on the island except the ruined village on the bluff west of Kotatake Mountain. Fishes and turtles appear frequently among these sculptures, but the most common figure is a mythical animal, half human in form, with bowed back and long claw-like legs and arms. According to the natives, this symbol was intended to represent the god 'Meke-Meke,' the great spirit of the sea. The general outline of this figure rudely carved upon the rocks bore a striking resemblance to the decoration on a piece of pottery which I once dug up in Peru, while making excavations among the graves of the Incas."

Left: Thomson and his companions arrived just in time to see the immigrant shepherds from Tahiti demolish the prehistoric stone houses to build miles of drystone walls with which to fence in their herds of sheep and other imported livestock. The islanders themselves managed to save only a few of the foundation walls of round huts that once had conical reed roofs. They began to use them as barriers to protect their own tiny gardens from the ravages of the grazing animals. When the first ethnologists came to Easter Island after the turn of the century, the new generation of islanders had forgotten the original purpose of the little round walls. The records left by eighteenth- and nineteenth-century visitors were overlooked by scholars, whose preconceptions excluded the possibility of finding stone houses of non-Polynesian-type on Easter Island. It was sufficiently difficult to explain why the Easter Islanders at the time of the missionaries' arrival lived in the un-Polynesian boat-shaped houses built of totora reeds.

Thomson also saw another most peculiar symbol, painted on a slab inside one of the adjacent stone houses. It depicted the bust of a person with huge eyes, with stripes to indicate tear marks running down the cheeks. The tears were the most prominent features in this representation of someone who was clearly of religious importance.

Though Geiseler had failed four years earlier, Thomson succeeded in obtaining two of the hidden *rongo-rongo* tablets. His greatest contribution to science was probably his tenacious effort to save, with Salmon's aid, whatever memory the island elders still had of the incised tablets, their origins and significance. Thomson recorded:

"The native traditions in regard to the incised tablets simply assert that Hotu Matua, the first king, possessed the knowledge of this written language, and brought with him to the island sixty-seven tablets containing allegories, traditions, genealogical tables, and proverbs relating to the land from which he had migrated. A knowledge of the written characters was confined to the royal family, the chiefs of the six districts into which the island was divided, sons of those chiefs, and certain priests or teachers, but the people were assembled at Anakena Bay once each year to hear all the tablets read. The feast of the tablets was regarded as their most important fete day, and not even war was allowed to interfere with it."

Thomson interviewed Ure Vaeiko, an old man who had been the cook for King Ngaara, the leader whose death came just before the last Peruvian slave raid. Ure Vaeiko, now aged eighty-three, was one of the patriarchs of the island and professed to have been under instruction in the art of the *rongo-rongo* at the time of the slave raid. Thomson assumed that this old man must have heard the tablets read so many times that he ought to know the short texts by heart, even if he did not understand the characters. He and Salmon approached the old man:

"Negotiations were opened with him for a translation of the two tablets purchased; but he declined to furnish any information, on the ground that it had been forbidden by the priests. Presents of money and valuables were sent him from time to time, but he invariably replied to all overtures that he was now old and feeble and had but a short time to live, and declined most positively to ruin his chances for salvation by doing what his Christian instructors had forbidden. Finally the old fellow, to avoid temptation, took to the hills with the determination to remain in hiding until after the departure of the *Mochican*. . . ."

One evening, Thomson and his party came upon this old native unexpectedly; he had returned to his home during a heavy downpour of rain. "When he found escape impossible he became sullen, and refused to look at or touch a tablet. As a compromise it was proposed that he should relate some of the ancient traditions. This was readily acceded to . . . During the recital certain stimulants that had been provided for such an emergency were produced. . . . A judicious indulgence in the present comforts dispelled all fears in regard to the future state, and at an auspicious moment the photographs of the tablets owned by the bishop were produced for inspection. Old Ure Vaeiko had never seen a photograph before, and was surprised to find how faithfully they reproduced the tablets which he had known in his young days. A tablet would have met with opposition, but no objection could be urged against a photograph, especially something possessed by the good bishop, whom he had been instructed to reverence. The photographs were recognized immediately, and the appropriate legend related with fluency and without hesitation from beginning to end. The story of all the tablets of which we had knowledge was finally obtained, the words of the native being written down by Mr. Salmon as they were uttered, and afterwards translated into English. . . . Ure Vaeiko's fluent interpretation of the tablet was not interrupted, though it became evident that he was not actually reading the characters. It was noticed that the shifting position did not accord with the number of symbols on the lines, and afterwards when the photograph of another tablet was substituted, the same story was continued without the change being discovered. The old fellow was quite discomposed when charged with fraud at the close of an all-night session, and at first maintained that the characters were all understood, but he could not give the signification of hieroglyphics copied indiscriminately from tablets already marked. He explained at great length that the actual value and significance of the symbols had been forgotten, but the tablets were recognized by unmistakable features and the interpretation of them was beyond question; just as a person might recognize a book in a foreign language and be perfectly sure of the contents without being able to actually read it."

Thomson recorded that during the recital of text from one of the tablets, translation was stopped at a section where the text was supposed "to have been written in some ancient language, the key to which has long ago been lost. After this unknown section the translation is continued . . ." But a bit further ahead the translation was again interrupted, due to one more section being written in the forgotten language.

Thomson, Cooke, and Salmon spent an entire night interviewing old Ure Vaeiko, who had been nearly sixty when aboriginal life on Easter Island was interrupted by the slave raiders. Wary because of the fraud of the two young men on Tahiti, Thomson had Ure Vaeiko's recitals put to a test by next calling upon another of the elders:

"An old man called Kaitae, who claims relationship to the last king, Maurata, afterwards recognized several of the tablets from the photographs and related the same story exactly as that given previously by Ure Vaeiko."

It appeared that each of the tablets had its own name, and Thomson and Cooke concluded that a reference to those names would bring to mind the specific text associated with that tablet, even among those who no longer understood the signs. The texts they obtained from the two old men were considered by Cooke as "traditions which otherwise, perhaps, would in a few years have perished with the people to whose ancestors it relates . . ."

Undoubtedly the most important text obtained independently from the two old men was one that related, in the usual allegorical form, the tradition concerning King Hotu Matua's arrival: Hotu Matua had been a powerful chief in a large country to the east that was much ravaged by great wars. His kingship followed the short and disrupted reign of his father, and he himself was also involved in family wars. His brother, Machaa, had fallen in love with a beautiful maiden desired by Oroi, the great chief of a neighboring clan, and desperate conflict was imminent. Machaa decided to escape. The great god Make-Make had told him that "by steering toward the setting sun" he would find an uninhabited island. Machaa embarked with the girl and a crew, and Easter Island was sighted after two months at sea. Upon landing, one of Machaa's men was killed by a large turtle, and buried in Anakena.

Oroi, still in the former fatherland, was furious, and sought revenge by attacking Machaa's brother, Hotu Matua. War to the death was carried on until Hotu Matua, defeated in three great battles, determined to flee. He embarked with three hundred chosen followers in two large vessels, each ninety feet long and six feet deep, provisioned for a long voyage:

"In the night, and on the eve of another battle, they sailed away, with the understanding that the setting sun was to be their compass."

Hotu Matua's exiled party searched the ocean for a hundred and twenty days before they found the island. Immediately upon landing, Hotu Matua's queen gave birth to a boy. They named the island *Te-Pito-o-te-Henua,* "The-Navel-of-the-World." The landing place was called Anakena—what we would call August—in honor of the month of its discovery.

The real relationship between the two "brothers" Machaa and Hotu Matua seems hidden in allegory. Both came from the east and from the same country, but at different times. Yet it was the one who came last who named the island and was celebrated as the discoverer and founder of the royal line. Thomson noted this discrepancy, but he and his informants stressed: "The island was discovered by King Hotu Matua, who came from the land in the direction of the rising sun." It was not unlikely, according to Thomson, that the reference to an earlier voyage of a "brother" from the same land represented an "attempt to account for the presence of an earlier people in this way . . . it would account for Hotu Matua finding a tomb or burial-place on the beach at Anakena, when he first landed."

The texts cited by the two old men included a description of the original fatherland:

"Hotu Matua and his followers came from a group of islands lying towards the rising sun, and the name of the land was *Marae-toe-hau,* the literal meaning of which is 'the burial place.' In this land, the climate was so intensely hot that the people sometimes died from the effects of the heat, and at certain seasons plants and growing things were scorched and shrivelled by the sun."

Thomson says: "It is difficult to account for the statement, so frequently repeated throughout the legends, that Hotu Matua came from the eastward and discovered the land by steering towards the setting sun, because the chart shows no islands in that direction which would answer the description of '*Marae-toe-hau.*'"

In the tablet known as *Apai,* where the reading was interrupted because of two unintelligible sections, there was another reference to the original settlement period, given in a still more clearly allegorical manner:

"When the island was first created and became known to our forefathers, the land was crossed with roads beautifully paved with flat stones. The stones were laid close together so artistically that no rough edges were exposed. Coffee-trees [possibly an erroneous translation by Salmon] were growing so close together along the borders of the road that they met overhead, and the branches were laced together like muscles. *Heke* was the builder of these roads, and it was he who sat in the place of honour in the middle where the roads branched away in every direction. These roads were cunningly contrived to represent the plan of the web of the grey and black-pointed spider, and no man could discover the beginning or end thereof." After the second interruption because of unintelligible text in another language, a reference is made to a different "spider," this one living in the aboriginal fatherland "where the black and white-pointed spider would have mounted to heaven, but was prevented by the bitterness of the cold."

According to the old men, fifty-seven generations of kings had ruled on the island since Hotu Matua came from the east, until the last of his descendants was kidnapped and died as a slave in Peru. The recorded memories from this long period were sparse:

"The tradition continues by a sudden jump into the following extraordinary condition of affairs: Many years after the death of Hotu Matua, the island was about equally divided between his descendants and the 'long-eared race,' and between them a deadly feud raged. Long and bloody wars were kept up, and great distress prevailed on account of the destruction and neglect of the crops. This unsatisfactory state of affairs was brought to an end, after many years' fighting, by a desperate battle, in which the 'long-ears' had planned the utter annihilation of their enemies. A long and deep ditch was dug across Hotu-iti and covered with brush wood, and into this the 'long-ears' arranged to drive their enemies, then the brush wood was to be set on fire and every man exterminated. The trap was found out, and the plan circumvented by opening the battle prematurely and in the night. The 'long-ears' were driven into the ditch they had built, and were murdered to a man."

Thomson doubted that the "long-ears" and the "short-ears" could both have come at the same time as Hotu Matua, and wrote:

"The 'long-ears' appear to have been a power in the land at an early period in the history of the island, though they were eventually defeated and exterminated by the others. It is possible that there has been more than one migration of people to the island. . . ."

Thomson was told by the islanders that peace reigned on the island for some time after the defeat of the Long-ears. But a certain King Kaina, chief in Hotu-iti, started new hostilities. He was driven with all his followers to seek refuge on the precipitous islet of Marotiri and into a large cave on Poike peninsula. In the course of the long and cruel wars that followed, which lasted until the missionaries arrived, the cannibalism started. Captives were taken, cooked, and eaten. Vivid memories from this recent period abounded, especially feats of personal bravery, but were considered by Thomson to be of little value to the history of Easter Island.

Since the days when Thomson and Cooke surveyed the prehistoric remains of Easter Island, many important ruins have been lost. At least three of the most remarkable *ahu* have tumbled into the sea, together with a vast village of lenticular stone houses considered by their discoverers to be the oldest and most important on the island. The American investigators also arrived just in time to witness the circular stone houses seen by the early voyagers being turned into sheep fences. Those that were not torn down by the foreign shepherds to provide stones for their extensive walls were converted by the islanders, with little or no repairs being made, into tiny garden plots. Thus the most remarkable house structures of the island's original population were so completely erased or camouflaged that the former existence of such utterly non-Polynesian dwellings was ignored by twentieth-century investigators.

The ceremonial stone-house village of Orongo somehow survived this destruction. These low, corbel-vaulted slab houses up on the narrow rim of the Rano Kao crater served neither the shepherds nor the farmers down on the plains. Even the religious paintings inside the houses have survived, sheltered from wind and rain. Although the reliefs outside these houses, of turtles, fishes, and the hunchbacked creature with claws considered by Thomson to be the oldest of all, are no longer visible, the numerous carvings of long-beaked bird-men that dominate all surrounding rocks still remain. Why was the supreme god Make-Make

Strange figures carved on the rocks in the ceremonial village of Orongo were still visible in the nineteenth century and were discovered by Thomson. He made drawings (*left and center*) of figures he described as half-human, half-feline, with arched back and long, clawlike arms and legs. The islanders told him that this figure represented their ancestors' chief god, Make-Make. The frequent occurrence of catlike figures in Easter Island religious art is remarkable, not only because there were no animals of the cat family in Polynesia, but even more so because the puma and large members of the cat family symbolized the supreme god and his divine descendants in the royal lines of all advanced American cultures from Mexico to Tiahuanaco.

Thomson also drew (*right*) a variant of the figure with the "weeping-eye" motif previously observed by Geiseler, another symbol of the supreme god of Tiahuanaco.

symbolized as a man-beast with hunched back and claws? The gods on the other islands were all in human form. And pigs, dogs, and rats were the only land mammals in Polynesia, yet the features of Make-Make suggest those of a feline.

The feline was the symbol of the supreme god of Tiahuanaco and all related cultures in pre-Inca Peru. These early South American artists also represented the sun god surrounded by servants, symbolized by bird-men—human beings with the heads of birds, just like the servants of Make-Make on Easter Island. Equally as un-Polynesian as the feline and the bird-men is the figure with the weeping-eye motif copied by Thomson from the interior Orongo walls. The weeping-eye motif is typical of Tiahuanaco, where it is another special symbol for the supreme sun god, whose tears bless the farmers in the form of rain. Wherever this motif is encountered in continental South America, it is considered evidence of Tiahuanaco influence.

It is important to know that the three religious figures peculiar to the ceremonial stone-house village of Orongo all reappear in the land nearest to the east, where stone houses also abound. None have Polynesian features. It would therefore seem logical to assume that the Polynesians were the newcomers; they encountered and to some extent accepted the Make-Make worship and its associated symbols and structures from their predecessors from the east.

No doubt Thomson and Cooke's greatest contribution was to verify the claim already recorded by Commander Clark that the first settlers had come out of the east, and to obtain details of these traditions independently from two real old-timers who were already senior citizens before the time of the slave raid. Most of the *ahu* and *moai* would remain and be studied in greater detail by subsequent generations, but the memories of the people were transient.

According to the island traditions, the country that lay to the east was a most unusual place, totally unlike anywhere else in Polynesia. Salmon translated the word for it for Thomson as "island," which is *fenua* in Easter Island speech. But *fenua* is the Easter Island word for *any* land, irrespective of size, and the islanders refer to Chile and all of South America as *fenua* even today.

As we have seen, Hotu Matua, their most venerated king, had fled from a desert country of large size, with an intense and burning climate. This country

The first explorers who came to Easter Island in the eighteenth and nineteenth centuries were astonished to find that the islanders did not fish for a living, but in fact were skilled farmers. They saw a few examples of exquisitely fashioned basalt fishhooks, but the natives refused to part with them. These stone hooks were regarded as precious heirlooms, and the Europeans never saw them being used. According to tradition, the natives' ancestors had such poor catches that they gave up using these traditional stone hooks and made fishhooks of human bone instead. Fishhooks of stone are foreign to Polynesian culture, but have occasionally been found along the American Pacific coast from northern Chile to California. An exhibition at the American Museum of Natural History in New York in 1947 showed a stone fishhook from Easter Island side by side with an archaeological find from Santa Barbara Island in southern California. The two hooks were so much alike that it was hard to tell them apart, except that the American one was smaller. The stylized Easter Island stone hook is still frequently cited in the literature as the acme of stoneworking art among pre-European cultures. This specimen, from the Kon-Tiki Museum collection, is shown life-size.

was known as "The Burial Ground." Man could climb up from the desert heat at sea level and reach such altitudes that only the bitter cold prevented him from reaching the sky. The country was accordingly described as a continent rather than a small island, and was divided between two mutually hostile kings.

Observe: There is no land but South America to the east of Easter Island. And the Pacific slopes of this continent are a vast desert, stretching for thousands of miles along the coast. One of the unique aspects of the climate in the coastline region below Lake Titicaca is that green grass and violets grow on the naked sandhills and plains from August to December, after which it becomes so hot that the sun dries up all vegetation, leaving an expanse of bare sand. It is no easy task to dispose of bodies or to arrange for burials in these dry, sparsely inhabited bays and valleys. The skulls, bones, and sun-dried mummies have accumulated over the millennia in such incredible quantities that the cemeteries have become larger and more crowded than the villages of the living generation. Ilo, for example, a main port on the Pacific where the pre-Inca road descends from Tiahua-naco in the highlands, deserves no more fitting name even today than "The Burial Place." The entire modern town rests on an ancient burial field dating back to pre-Inca times, and all the surrounding hills are covered with tombs that offer evidence of close contact with Tiahuanaco. Ascending inland from this old port to reach that most important landmark of prehistoric American culture, more than thirteen thousand feet above sea level, one is surrounded by still higher hills and peaks that are covered with stone houses and have been terraced for agricultural purposes. These traces of earlier living continue until further human ascent is made impossible by the snow. A better description of the land to the east could not have been preserved by the Easter Islanders. Inland and westward the land rises from a sun-scorched desert to mountains so high that they are uninhabitable because of the cold. There is nothing that links these descriptions to any islands to the west, all of which are renowned for their pleasant climate and luxuriant vegetation.

One allegory or legend collected by Thomson speaks of the spider, Heke, who had spun a network of roads that were found by Hotu Matua when he arrived. In the abandoned fatherland another spider would have mounted to heaven if not prevented by the cold. Presumably the mainland spider also moved along the roads of his own net. Indeed, a network of prehistoric roads radiates from Tiahuanaco toward the north, east, and south, and several lead westward down to ports on the Pacific coast below, including Ilo.

Hotu Matua had fled in search of one island he knew had been settled by his own kin. Yet the early settlers were no longer there when Hotu Matua arrived. Nothing is said about the time span between the voyages of Machaa and Hotu Matua. Perhaps Easter Island was known to both as a secure place of refuge, too far away from their common homeland for the arms of revenge to reach them. The humble description of the first king as a refugee makes the beginning of the island's history sound more like a realistic tribal memory than an invented hero-myth.

The two ships of Hotu Matua were described as ninety feet long and six feet deep, each carrying one hundred and fifty people. No seaworthy canoe or log raft could have been built to such measurements, but a reed ship could. The Easter Islanders use the term vaka-paepae, "boat-rafts," for these vessels. This could very well have been a boat-shaped reed raft structurally related to the little totora floats that survived on the island until the Europeans arrived. A landing from the east in such ships would make sense, as they were made of the totora reeds cultivated in vast quantities for boat- and house-building in every river valley on the continent east of Easter Island. If we accept that the flimsy Easter Island mini-canoes were the modest survivors of proper Polynesian dug-out canoes, then the tiny local reed floats could be correspondingly modest vestiges of former South American reed ships. Neither type could have carried men to Easter Island if they had only been of the size seen by the Europeans. Only large reed bundles could have been combined to make vessels of the impressive size cited for Hotu Matua's "boat-rafts." And the peculiar Easter Island reed huts would match the length, depth, and shape of such watercraft turned upside down. Perhaps the first arrivals lived in their overturned boats after landing? If so, this would explain the curious boat-shaped design of the Easter Island reed-houses.

The Chilean annexation, 1888

Easter Island had never been a rewarding place for foreign invaders. If Inca Tupac went ashore on "Fire Island," he could have found nothing whatsoever of value to add to his already great empire. Roggeveen found the island unworthy of being claimed for the Dutch throne. The viceroy of Peru sent Gonzalez to annex it for the king of Spain, but the Spanish government was not tempted to follow up the Peruvian annexation. Commander Clark's appeal for British protection of the same island was simply ignored. Brander and his shepherds from Polynesia had wanted Easter Island to become part of French Oceania, but in 1888 even the French rights were formally renounced.

It was in that year that Captain Policarpo Toro arrived, and annexed Easter Island to Chile. The captain had been to the island before, as a cadet during the Chilean Gana expedition, and returned intent on establishing a Chilean settlement there. This unexpected turn of events caused the shepherds from Tahiti to lose control of local affairs, and Alexander Salmon left after eleven years spent among the Easter Islanders. He never returned, but his impact on the community remained undisturbed by the change in foreign administration. As we have noted, during his long stay he had done much to improve the miserable living conditions left by his murdered predecessor, Dutroux-Bornier. He had had new homes built, and had encouraged the islanders to resume their ancestors' agricultural efforts. He noted that visiting foreigners were interested in acquiring Easter Island art objects, and started a new kind of local industry. He had discovered that Geiseler, and Thomson after him, had almost completely exhausted the supply of original examples of local art and artifacts in their eagerness to acquire Easter Island antiquities. Tablets, figurines, carved clubs and feather

The Gana expedition, which visited Easter Island in 1870, brought a splendid collection of *moai maea* carvings back to the museums of Chile. Some of the stone heads were carved without necks or bodies. Two were masks representing men with goatees, one with a topknot and the other with a vulva sign carved on the forehead. One had inlaid obsidian eyes, while the other appeared to have lost its original inlays.

The *moai maea* carvings brought home by the Gana expedition also included representations of the crouching quadruped, this time with a human head sticking out at right angles to the animal body (*top*).

Another odd sculpture collected by the Gana expedition was a block of stone with a squatting bird-man and an inverted squatting human figure carved in relief. The head of the human figure is egg-shaped with a bowl-shaped hollow. Behind the figure of the bird-man is another, deeper hollow; both probably had magical functions. Fish and vulva signs are engraved on the surface of the stone.

crowns had all been in great demand. Up until this time, the islanders had created these solely for their own use. Why not make them for sale?

To assist the poverty-stricken islanders—and perhaps at the same time to make a personal profit—Salmon encouraged the redevelopment of those types of carvings that had been most in demand. He thus started a vivid commercial operation, which began after Thomson's visit in 1886. It gained impetus during the Chilean annexation, because at that time a Chilean navy vessel began to visit the island annually. Since the time of Captain Cook's visit, the most highly prized objects created by the islanders were the male and female figurines carved from reddish toromiro wood. These figurines were known as *moai kavakava* and *moai pa'apa'a*. The male was always represented as tall, emaciated, and stooped, with a hooked nose, goatee, clearly delineated ribs, concave abdomen, and circumcised penis. The female was always depicted as wide but flat as a board, sometimes showing hermaphroditic traits and always with one hand placed near the vulva and one under a pendulous breast. Unlike these figures, the *moai maea* had never been put on public display; they were too crude, grotesque, and dissimilar to be in demand. But the smaller stylized woodcarvings had already gained a certain popularity, mostly because of Bishop Jaussen's interest in them. The idea of producing miniatures of the giant *ahu* busts had not occurred to anyone—at least not during Salmon's stay on the island; but the annual navy visitors from Chile soon found that the repertoire of the island artists began to include ceremonial clubs and paddles of the types used in their ritual dances, moon-shaped and egg-shaped pectorals, and the elaborate ancestral feather headdresses.

Any object obtained on Easter Island after Thomson's visit in 1886 should accordingly be viewed with suspicion. During the first years of the Chilean annexation, the very same artists who had carved the artifacts for their own personal use now began to carve them for sale. Consequently there was at first very little difference between the old and the new, at least as far as quality was concerned. Earlier carvings, however, were usually worn smooth; this was especially noticeable in the perforations made to hold the suspension strings. Gradually, less care came to be paid to the work: it was done faster and became cruder. The circumcized male genitalia were now commonly omitted in deference to the chastening missionary influence. And, finally, the supply of native toromiro trees diminished rapidly, forcing the artists to resort to less attractive imported wood.

Two full-length human figures carved in high relief on stones were also among the Gana expedition's finds. One is of a man with goatee and topknot. The other represents a woman with long ears and vulva symbols carved on her head and body. The odd hollow occurs again on the male figure, this time on the abdomen.

No sooner had Easter Island become Chilean territory than the Chilean government leased almost the entire island to the British Williamson and Balfour Company. A restricted area around the village of Hanga-roa was fenced in and left for the Easter Islanders. Policarpo Toro's attempt to colonize the island with three Chilean families failed, and once again the Easter Islanders were left to themselves, with half-forgotten Christian rites and ancestral spirits haunting the caves and *ahu*.

In the first decade of Chilean annexation, Easter Island was twice visited by Father Albert Montilon. He tried to reinforce the Christian faith and to persuade the natives to bury their dead in consecrated soil at the cemetery in Hanga-roa. Although the island population had been formally baptized, Montilon found them to be still strongly influenced by pagan beliefs and customs. A body interred in a coffin at the cemetery would be secretly dug up the following night, and placed in an *ahu* or inside a secret family cave.

After the Chilean annexation, Spanish gradually became the main foreign language on Easter Island, but in the nineteenth century the Chilean influence remained slight. From Eyraud's first landing to Salmon's final departure, Tahitian had served for oral and written communication with Easter Islanders. Well aware of this fact, Father Montilon, on his last visit, chose a Polynesian-speaking islander from the Tuamotu group to be put in charge of religious services when he left.

This new immigrant, Nicolas Pakarati, was well received, but his power over

A comparative study has failed to demonstrate the existence of similar stone sculptures elsewhere in Polynesia, but some striking parallels are to be found in the area round Lake Titicaca. This figure of a bearded man with extremely long ears is likewise carved in high relief from a block of stone and shows the same distorted proportions; the head and legs are the same length. What makes the comparison especially interesting is that this sculpture comes from Rapa, an island in Lake Titicaca. There are only two other islands in the world that bear the name Rapa: Rapa-Nui (Great Rapa), an old name for Easter Island, and Rapa-Iti (Little Rapa), another island of the same size lying farther to the west in Polynesia. According to local tradition, Little Rapa was populated by pregnant women who drifted there from Easter Island.

the Easter Islanders was distinctly limited. Soon he became one of them in every sense. And the little island community, now fenced in at Hanga-roa, entered the twentieth century as if on a planet of their own. And with a very thin veneer of Western acculturation.

Knoche's hearings: A joint community agrees on their past

The fence erected by the Williamson and Balfour Company around Hanga-roa village was mainly symbolic. It may have served as a boundary or border in the daytime, but never at night. We know today that the islanders continued to frequent their family caves all over the island—perhaps even more than they did before, except, of course, for those periods of civil war during which they lived in caves. We also know that the immigrant Pakarati was welcome to conduct Christian services on Sundays—and we know, too, that he, like the rest, crawled into caves at night. He hid sheets of paper covered with ink drawings of *rongo-rongo* inspired by Bishop Jaussen's list as if they were sacred objects, preserved along with his own *moai maea*. It would not be until our visit in 1955–half a century later—that these hidden treasures would be removed from their hiding place by his own descendants.

During the daytime, the carving of the wooden figurines continued openly, their design slavishly following the ancestral examples. The sculpting of an unrestricted variety of *moai maea* also continued as before. These, however, were not for sale, and, as in pre-Christian times, were done in secrecy. A number of new motifs appeared: lava sculptures of rabbit heads, horses, sheep, and even of the Virgin Mary, crowned and carrying the Infant Jesus, were added; they were created to bring the owner good luck, and hidden away. They were for himself and his family alone.

There was no more war or murder on Easter Island. There were angels in the air around the church when psalms were sung, and in the huts where the Sign of the Cross was made at mealtimes. But where there were angels there were also devils. The stone colossi lay within sight everywhere on the island and testified to the power of the demons who—as many Christians believed—had helped their pagan, pre-European ancestors perform superhuman tasks. And when night fell and the angels slept, the bird-men flew about. So, too, ancestral spirits crawled unmolested out of every cave and chicken house.

Throughout the early decades of the present century, the secret lives of the Easter Islanders flourished as never before. The church was on the surface, its doors wide open to everybody; it became the favored meeting place for both worship and choral entertainment. And underneath the churches, their entrances narrow and tightly closed, were the private hideouts where the secret rituals were performed. These caves contained their ancestors' bones and the families' sacred figurines. This was the place where the past became most closely related to the future. Easter Island was now a world working on two levels: below were the roots of the past; above, new branches spread out freely in the sun, giving a bright promise of eternal security. The existence of a supreme god presented no problem: he was the same on both levels. It was his name—his new name—only that the islanders accepted, and the new images of friendly saints made connection with him easy. There was one problem, however: these new saints gave the people no contact with their own pagan parents, those who had gone to the devil. It was this that their *moai maea* did. So the islanders needed both wooden saints and stone images.

By the time the grandchildren of the newly baptized congregations had grown up and begun to loosen their tongues, to speak once more without fear, most of the obscene practices in this confused transitional period had been forgotten. But, judging from what went on sporadically all the way up to our own generation, it is easy for us to visualize the lonely silhouettes that must have appeared in the starlit nights, sneaking among lava outcroppings and overthrown *moai*. Shadows crawling catlike over the dark cliffs, seen only when the light of the sea glittered behind them. No sound but the whisper of the wind and the distant rumbling of the ever-present surf. A sudden whimper somewhere from a stolen sheep. Occasionally the wind bringing a faint odor of burnt wood, betraying a secret food offering being prepared by someone getting ready to enter his ancestral cave. A so-called *umu takapu* for the invisible cave guardian.

Such was the atmosphere among the Easter Islanders when, alone, they literally sailed their own sea into the twentieth century. When Dr. Walter Knoche arrived with a Chilean scientific mission in 1911, he found that very little had changed since Salmon had left in 1888. Officially the island had been Chilean territory for twenty-three years, and many of the younger generation spoke Spanish. Knoche could thus converse directly with the islanders, unlike the previous investigators who had used Salmon, or before him the missionaries, as middlemen.

Knoche went to Easter Island intent on saving what was still left of tribal memories before the last of the premissionary generation passed away. Ten years earlier, a Chilean meteorologist, E. Martinez, had spent a year on the island. When he returned, he told Knoche that the traditions of Hotu Matua were still so vivid among the older people that one of them sat and wept with emotion on the day of the year which marked the king's landing in Anakena.

Although Knoche found that the Tuamotuan catechist, Nicolas Pakarati, faithfully continued his Sunday services on the island, he detected a continuing reverence for and veneration of the old stone images that he interpreted as some sort of ancestor cult. The rich collection of carvings brought back to Chile by Knoche reflected the now-flourishing trade in newly carved wooden figurines. He also obtained a few *moai maea* as well, all genuine though very crude and fragmentary. The exceptions were two unique sculptures, one of them a strange, knobbly image in polished black obsidian, representing a froglike monster with a single pair of limbs flexed in a jumping position. The face, which dominates the front of the figurine, has large eyes, a grinning mouth and a nose split into eyebrows with a continuous curve that outlines a heart-shaped mask. The second sculpture, which was subsequently stolen, was just as unique, to judge from Knoche's description. It was of "outstanding execution, carved as a relief figure in hard light-red tuff, and somewhat recalling Greek art . . ."

By the time of Knoche's visit, about twenty genuine *rongo-rongo* boards had emerged from hiding and reached the outside world. Knoche brought with him reproductions of the three taken to Chile with the Gana expedition. Two of the oldest men began to recite from these copies, but the crowd listening to them interrupted. They declared that the old men did not read, but "merely narrated one of the numerous traditions which were known also to the others without assistance from the script."

Knoche found that several of the elders could still remember the early festivals in Anakena Bay that featured recitals of *rongo-rongo* boards and commemorated Hotu Matua's landing. He therefore interviewed the two old men in the presence of sixty or seventy other islanders, all of whom took an interested part in the procedure. As a result, Knoche was able to obtain unanimous agreement from the crowd on a number of tribal memories that were not necessarily recited from the ceremonial tablets:

"In former times there were two races that mainly differed through the size of their ears.

"We know from the traditions that the island was peopled twice, the first time by the *Long-ears* and the second by another race, the *Short-ears*. According to the myth, the Long-ears had been the builders of the monuments, yet the Short-ears, who came to the island later, had, under the command of the Long-ears, apparently helped. On this point we are informed in detail by the myth of 'The Long-ears and the Short-ears.'

"Many profess that the Long-ears were the master builders of the large stone sculptures which were manufactured in Rano Raraku, and which were found scattered over the entire island. This must probably be so, for according to the tradition they were the ones who produced the *marae (ahu)* which served as foundations for the statues.

". . . The overthrow of these statues was the work of the Short-ears, i.e., the population stratum which, arriving as the second settlers to Easter Island, came under the power of the existing population, i.e., the Long-ears."

It could not have been set out more clearly. Long-ears came first and began making statues. Short-ears came later and helped. But in the end, the newcomers overthrew the statues.

A remarkable piece of information on this period of collaboration had been mentioned to Martinez in 1891 by an old Easter Islander, and was now confirmed to Knoche. The peaceful coexistence between the Long-ears and the Short-ears had lasted for a period of "*karau-karau*—i.e., 200—years," from the arrival of the Short-ears to the war between the two peoples.

Knoche was told that the Long-ears and Short-ears lived in different kinds of houses and had different burial customs. The Short-ears had not invented the *rongo-rongo*. "We were told that the written tablets were not the products of the present population, but by those of the earlier immigration."

The Long-ears were not totally exterminated in the war. Apart from their women and children, at least two of the adult men escaped and were spared from massacre in the pyre. One of them, Ororoine, had direct descendants to whom Knoche spoke personally.

No sooner had the Chilean expedition left when Vives Solar was sent from Chile to serve two years on the island as a Spanish-speaking schoolteacher. He was able to get Knoche's records reconfirmed in all particulars before time ran out. After the last old-timers of Easter Island had been carried to the Christian cemetery, the island traditions degenerated in much the same way the quality of the commercial woodcarvings had done. Traditions told to subsequent visitors were often modified or concocted.

The testimony of the ancestor worshipers

The Easter Islanders are taught by us that the history of their island began on Easter Day, 1722, when a European named Roggeveen discovered their ancestors. But that is not what they learned from their ancestors. *Their version of history began when Hotu Matua came from the east and named the island "The-Navel-of-the-World."* And he came fifty-seven generations before their last king was carried back to the east as a slave.

Now that we have taught them our writing, the descendants of Hotu Matua can read our own version of their history. But, as we have seen, when the first Europeans tested them they could not read their own *rongo-rongo* tablets: they just pretended to read, while actually reciting texts learned by heart. How much can we trust the oral traditions they preserved?

Our ancestors are said to have first encountered them as half-naked barbarians with no real culture. Visitors from the civilized world looked upon them as ignorant pagans, shot them for fun or trapped and enslaved them. But they also marveled at their monuments, their art, their perfect fields. Learned men from the most developed nations came to admire their technical achievements, and remarked that they physically resembled us. As soon as the linguistic barriers fell, our ancestors asked the islanders about their techniques and their origins. What they discovered was recorded. Published. But ignored. The visitors returned home to ask learned European societies for the truth.

Today, now that the Easter Islanders have donned shoes and lipstick, making them rather indistinguishable from ourselves, we understand that they are our equals. Mentally and physically they were our equals in the last century as well, but they were totally isolated from trade or incentive of any kind, and their only available raw materials were restricted to stone, bone, wood, and bark. Their success in handling stones as tall as four-story buildings indicates that they had well-developed brains. To be sure, there were differences between them and us. Not only in dress and in customs, but in philosophy. They were ancestor-worshipers, with a proud belief in their descent from the gods. We look back with horror to our descent from ape men or from a sinful Adam. Their desire was to preserve the good past, ours to improve the dubious future.

As among the Incas to the east and the Polynesians to the west, history was the main religion on Easter Island. The islanders strived to preserve their celebrated links back to the divinity and glory to which their *moai* and tablets testified. Evolution and change was not what these islanders strived for; instead, they desired to maintain the styles and customs their sacred ancestors had created. The European effort to change this attitude caused a rapid loss of historic interest in Easter Island.

The religious teachers sent from Tahiti after the slave raids, and the schoolmasters sent from Chile after the annexation, brought our religion and our version of world history to the islanders. But schools and teachers had also been part of the island's much earlier community life. Memories of the last school of the premissionary era survived well into the present century. The schoolhouse itself was in Anakena, where Hotu Matua had landed. It was remembered as a circular building with low but thick stone walls and a conical roof thatched with reeds. The entrance was through an opening in the roof. In this traditional type of building, the pupils were instructed in the island's history, and punished if they failed to learn their lessons. Royal genealogies were important because, as in Peru and Polynesia, the names of the first sacred kings they remembered were fused with that of the creator god. Though the descendants of Hotu Matua were all named and considered ordinary human beings, they were assumed to have been endowed with some degree of *mana*, or supernatural power. Hotu Matua's ancestors in the fatherland became fused together as the children of Make-Make. Clearly, there was little else to put an excessive demand on Easter Island memories except the lessons at school and the *rongo-rongo* texts that were learned by heart. At least the main facts would not be lost. East would not become west, and long ears would not become long noses.

If we recall that all ancient civilizations have ended in misery after cultural collapse caused by war or other calamities, then history has been unfair to the little group of survivors who lit fires to welcome the first Europeans. They, too, had a history to look back upon. Given this inevitable concession, we should take a fresh look at what they had told us before we imposed our schools and our own version of history upon them. Perhaps the texts recorded by the earliest foreign visitors were not the fables of uninformed barbarians. Perhaps they can give us further clues to the mystery of the island's past. And we owe it to the present Easter Islanders to give them back today what we took from their ancestors last century.

The traditional history of Easter Island

To recapitulate and sort out what we have seen in fragments: The Easter Islanders believed in an immortal soul and in a supreme and omnipotent god who had created the world and the first man and woman. He rewarded the good and punished the wicked in afterlife. He was referred to as the Great God. His personal name was Make-Make. From him descended the line of sacred kings, who were taboo and ruled with unrestricted power. One of them was, as we have seen, Hotu Matua, the Prolific Father, who became the founder of the Easter Island dynasty and the progenitor of the next fifty-six generations of local kings.

Machaa was also a descendant of Make-Make, from the same country; he was traditionally referred to as a "brother" of Hotu Matua. Machaa had learned from Make-Make that, by steering for two months in the direction of the setting sun, he would find a lonely island far out in the middle of the ocean. After having been severely defeated in a war against a neighboring king, he fled from his own country to take refuge on that distant island. And then no more is heard from him: tradition is silent about Machaa's fate.

124

Hotu Matua was the next to get into trouble. He was constantly feuding with King Oroi, the ruler of a nearby country. Following the disrupted reign of his own father, Hotu Matua lost three major battles against the enemy; finally he, too, had to flee to save his life. The desert provided him with no means of escape, so he decided to follow Machaa's example and set sail for the distant island. Considering himself to be its first discoverer, Hotu Matua named the island *Te-Pito-o-te-Henua,* "The-Navel-of-the-World." A burial platform was found at the landing place, and, inland, a network of stone-paved roads that had been built by the earlier settlers.

After exploring the island, Hotu Matua and his followers decided to settle in Hotu-iti Bay, at the foot of the Rano Raraku volcano, where there was a fresh-water crater lake, situated literally above their heads. Coming as they did from a desert country, the refugees from the east were stonemasons, not carpenters. There was plenty of wood available when they arrived, for the trees stood so closely packed along the roads that their branches were laced together overhead "like muscles." Yet Hotu Matua's party preferred to use stone to build their village of circular houses, the ruins of which remained throughout the tribal wars until they were torn down by the foreign shepherds.

Fifty years after Hotu Matua's landing, the first *moai* was erected, presumably on the occasion of the first king's death.

Although these seafaring immigrants had found their way to a lonely island, they were not primarily fishermen. They brought cultivated plants with them from their homeland, and subsisted primarily as agriculturalists. Presumably they were the ones who brought the sweet potato, the bottle-gourd, the manioc, and the totora reeds to the island. These species were among the most important local cultivated plants in the east, from where these people had come. They had no chickens as yet, so the eggs of seabirds were of great importance; the sooty terns, which arrived annually in their migration from the east, became celebrated as the messengers of Make-Make.

Hotu Matua's group had settled an island that had already been discovered but abandoned by people from their own home country: both Machaa and Hotu Matua had sailed on the same course. An untold number of generations later, their intrepid descendants were dragging huge stone blocks across the island and building long-eared statues with the help of another people, secondary immigrants who had arrived from the west. They remembered their progenitor as being named Tuu-ko-ihu. Exactly when they came and how they managed to find the island is not stated in the traditional legends, but they seem to have come humbly and in peace, for they willingly accepted Make-Make as their god and abandoned their own religion. Since they came from the west, they were probably the ones who brought the chickens, the bananas, and the sugar cane. And since they found the island despite the wind and the current, and made a peaceful landing, they were probably both guided and welcomed. For two centuries they toiled willingly to erect the monuments that represented the long-eared chiefs of the original population. The two cohabitating populations were distinguishable mainly through the custom of ear-piercing and lengthening of the ear-lobes practiced by the earlier settlers, the Long-ears, but not by the newcomers, the Short-ears. The Short-ears admitted that not only had the Long-ears started carving the *moai* before the Short-ears arrived, but that they were also the ones who had begun the custom of making the *rongo-rongo* boards.

But before the fifty-seven generations of Hotu Matua's dynasty ended, and after two hundred years of peaceful collaboration, the Short-ears, either tired of working for the Long-ears or on some other pretext, revolted. The Long-ears dug an extensive trench and laid a pyre in it, then withdrew behind these fortifications to the eastern headland of Poike. But they were outwitted by the Short-ears, who faked a head-on nocturnal attack. When the Long-ears, believing the attack was real, lit their pyre, another unit of Short-ears secretly sneaked around the trench, fell upon the Long-ears, and pushed them into what became their own death trap.

Ororoine was remembered as one of the Long-ear men who escaped the conflagration to become the head of the families of those of his line who, through the women and children, survived the raid.

The revolt of the Short-ears put an end to all work in the quarries. Some statues remained unfinished and others were abandoned while "walking" along the roads. The fatal war brought victory to the Short-ears but no lasting peace to the island. New family feuds sprung up among the descendants of the intermarried groups, and a terrible period, traditionally known as the *huri-moai,* or "over-throwing-of-the-statues" era, began. It was during this time that the first Europeans made their short visits to the islands and recorded their impressions. And it is the horror and havoc of these most recent centuries that is best preserved in the traditional stories remembered by those islanders living today. Their predominant memories concur with the impressions of their European observers, from Roggeveen to Eyraud, but for the most part they cover a period in which former well-regarded members of a highly organized community were reduced to the rank of miserable cave dwellers.

The Short-ears won the battle of the trench, but lost their share in a prehistoric civilization.

Spotlight on the Long-ears

The Long-ears played the most important part in Easter Island's traditional history, and although the Short-ears ended up the winners, they themselves recognized that the Long-ears had been the first to come to the island, and that they were the architects, the artists, and the engineers behind the great works, the great statues. The Short-ears were merely laborers. The Long-ears even got the credit for the treasured *rongo-rongo,* and for having converted the later-arriving Short-ears to their own religion.

It was not easy for the scientific community in the outside world to believe in the Easter Island story of the Long- and the Short-ears. It was hard enough to see how primitive barbarians could have reached this island once, let alone twice, before the Europeans came. A single arrival had, of course, to be accepted, since people were found ashore by Roggeveen. Captain Cook had found Polynesian words in their vocabulary. Hence it seemed clear enough that the people on this island were of Polynesian descent and had arrived from the west. The claim that Hotu Matua had come from the east therefore had to be fictitious. Besides, to the east lay only America, and America had seen no seagoing boats before those of Columbus.

The church had brought a new name for the old creator-god to Easter Island. Now science brought a new direction to the ancestral fatherland: it lay to the west. And the Easter Islanders were quick to learn. The Short-ears had, after all, heard that their ancestor Tuu-ko-ihu had come from the west, and they liked the idea that he and Hotu Matua had perhaps come together in the first two ships.

It is, indeed, only because of the records of those early visitors that we know today what the Easter Islanders told us before we converted them to a new faith and a new religious history. To put it plainly: the Easter Islanders had told us that the first people to settle their own island had come from what we call South America. There was no other land to the east. And the Short-ears, coming later from the west, would of necessity have been Polynesians. This is what the old Easter Islanders originally told us—a combination of early tradition and geography.

Today we know that there really were Long-ears to the east, and none to the west. Nobody lengthened their earlobes in Polynesia, while Peru was ruled by Long-ears. The Spanish conquistadores called the Incas *Orejones*, "Big-ears," because they pierced and lengthened their earlobes artificially. Since there really was a land of Long-ears in the direction from whence Hotu Matua was said to have come, the Easter Island tradition makes sense. But if only Polynesians had reached the island, the cohabitation of Long-ears and Short-ears on Easter Island makes no sense at all. Who, then, were the Long-ears? Were they invented, mythical figures, or had the Easter Island term *Hanau-epé* been incorrectly translated as "Long-ears"?

The latter theory has actually been proposed, and it has been considered plausible to those whose migration theories ran contrary to Easter Island tradition. It has been argued that "Long-ears" and "Short-ears" are erroneous translations. The correct terms should have been "stocky race" and "slight race." Given this translation, both groups could have been Polynesian and the problem would have been solved. All it would have taken would have been for some Easter Islanders to have been stouter than others.

The origin of this theory is a modern mispronunciation of the old Easter Island word *Hanau-epé*, now commonly spelled *Hanau-eepe*. *Epé* is the ancient and strictly local term for the lengthened earlobe, whereas *eepe* means "bulky" or "stocky." Hence the recent confusion. Until the visit of Katherine Scoresby Routledge half a century ago, early visitors used the correct spelling: *Hanau-epé*. Knoche's assembly of informants left no room for doubt: "In former times there were two races that differed mainly through the size of their ears." The present descendants of the Long-ears confirm this claim and point to the long ears on the wooden figurines and ancient stone statues depicting their ancestors. Roggeveen and Cook actually saw these people, and wrote that the Long-ears paid more reverence to the statues than the others. They were at that time real flesh-and-blood people, who kindled fires in front of the *moai* and prostrated themselves before the rising sun.

The people encountered on Easter Island did not impress the early Europeans, except by their tall stature and fine features. Nevertheless, they were descended from a line of outstanding navigators, organizers, architects, and engineers. It is presumptuous of us to believe that they confused east with west and invented their own history. Yet that is what we have done. We have turned our backs on South America, and stared only in the other direction. Unless we,

All the typical statues of Easter Island's Middle Period have long ears. According to legends recorded during the nineteenth century, it was the people called Long-ears who erected the statues. Ever since Europeans first learned to communicate with Easter Islanders, the tale has been told of how the Long-ears and Short-ears coexisted peacefully until the Short-ears revolted and defeated the Long-ears in battle on the Poike peninsula. After toiling for two hundred years to raise mighty monuments to the Long-ears' ancestors, the Short-ears rose and took over the rule of the island.

The long ears of the Easter Island statues are their most outstanding feature, and some of them show earlobe plugs. One fallen statue (*right*) shows signs of having had some kind of plug inserted in its stone earlobe.

like the Easter Islanders, begin to look in both directions, the mystery of that lonely island will never be disentangled from its scientific web.

There is no reason whatsoever to turn our backs on South America. South America was the sole gateway to Easter Island in the days of the early sailing vessels. As shown, until the nineteenth century, all vessels bound for Easter Island were advised to depart from the coast of southern Peru or northern Chile. Any earlier vessel, provided it would float, would benefit from the same movements of wind and water.

Inca Tupac Yupanqui was a Long-ear who ventured on a sailing expedition into the open Pacific. Before he embarked, however, he had first traveled by land throughout his continental empire, conquering all tribes from Ecuador to Chile. He was not himself a mariner, and according to the chroniclers, he used local captains and steered for islands already familiar to merchant mariners from his own coast. Yet Tupac reached Fire Island half a millennium too late to have been the Long-ear who introduced ear lengthening to Easter Island. His voyage took place some three generations before the Spaniards conquered his empire, which would be some fifty generations after Hotu Matua's exodus. If tradition is correct in giving the island genealogy fifty-seven generations of Easter Island kings, then Hotu Matua must have lived in pre-Inca times, for the Inca dynasty was founded in the twelfth century A.D.

But there were also Long-ears in Peru long before the time of the Incas. Art and history throughout ancient Peru indicate that the local civilizations were introduced by Long-ears. The Mochica people, who founded the first pre-Inca kingdom on the northern coast of Peru, always depicted themselves as Long-ears. Their traditional history begins with a certain King Naymlap, who came sailing down the coast from the north with a fleet of balsa rafts, with his queen and a large number of followers. Iconographic art from that early period depicts long-eared mariners on board huge raft-ships, and accompanied by mythical bird-men.

The Incas were Quechua Indians from the highlands, but claimed that their royal line had intermarried with an important group of white and bearded Long-ears, who had come down the coast from the north and taught them ear piercing and lengthening before they left to go westward into the Pacific. Being ancestor worshipers, they venerated these progenitors, who had brought culture to their primitive forefathers and were recalled by many names. When the chronicler Zarate came to Peru in 1543, the Inca *amautas*, or historians, told him that originally their people had no king, until from the region of Lake Titicaca "there came a very warlike people which they called ingas. These . . . had the ears perforated, with pieces of gold in the holes which enlarged the apertures. These called themselves *ringrim*, signifying ear. And the principal among them they called Zapalla inga, the only chief, although some say that he was called inga Viracocha, which is 'foam of the sea,' since, not knowing the land whence he came, they believed him to have been formed out of that lagoon."

All the Spanish chroniclers recorded stories about Viracocha and the *Viracocha-runa*, or Viracocha-people, who were claimed to have brought civilization to Peru. They were recalled in all parts of the empire as white and bearded like the Spaniards, and said to be the builders and sculptors of the megalithic platforms and colossal statues of Tiahuanaco. Their leader, who claimed descent from the sun, was known as *Tici* or *Ticci* in the highland and as *Con* on the coast. Viracocha, or "Foam of the Sea," was his Inca name, and the early Spaniards were unclear as to whether this alluded to his white skin or his seafaring skills. The famous chronicler Sarmiento made it clearer. When the white Viracocha-people finally left Peru by sea, "they appeared like foam over the water and the people, therefore, gave them the name of Viracocha, which is the same as to say the foam of the sea."

As is well known, when the first little contingent of Spaniards arrived they were able to conquer the mighty Inca military empire because they were mistaken for the Viracocha-people returning. Among the Indians around Lake Titicaca, *viracocha* is still the name given to any white-skinned foreigner. According to the chroniclers, the last act of the original Viracochas before they left the country was to pass through Cuzco and instruct their Inca successors as to how to continue the custom of ear lengthening that was to set them apart from their common subjects.

It is interesting to compare the manner in which the Long-ears of the two separate areas performed this operation. Father Sebastian Engelbert was told by the descendants of the Easter Island Long-ears that their forefathers pierced their ears and then inserted a piece of totora reed. By gradually adding more reeds, the holes became larger and the weight of the reeds caused the earlobes to lengthen. The Jesuit Oliva, who came to Peru in the late sixteenth century, wrote about the Inca: "They pierced their ears and placed in them large rings of a kind of reed called totora, and subsequently enlarged these rings enormously."

The history of the Incas tells us that Viracocha was the first, and Tupac Inca the last, of the important Long-ears recalled to have sailed into the Pacific. There might have been many others, as neither of these two are positively identifiable with Hotu Matua. Also, both Viracocha and Tupac were popular royal names in Peru, and repeatedly listed as names for rulers in those long genealogies that go

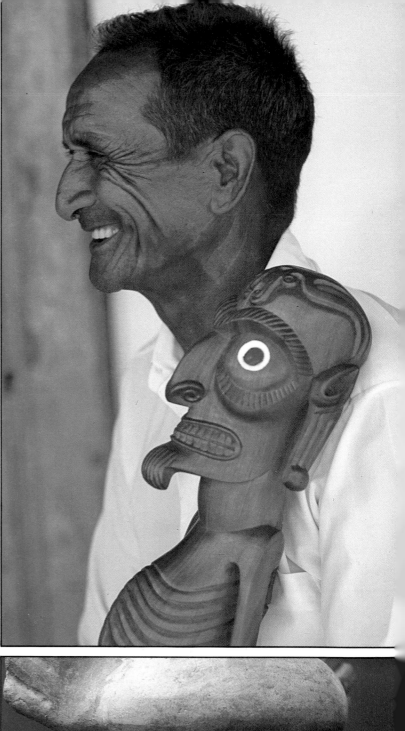

The Long-ears are also depicted in the standardized *moai kavakava* figures which the Short-ears continued to carve in memory of the last refugees of an exterminated population group, which they found hiding and perishing with hunger inside Puna Pau topknot quarries. To this day, skilled woodcarvers still produce astonishingly accurate likenesses of one and the same type of Long-ears. It is both striking and comical to see how closely the full-blooded Easter Island sculptor Pedro Pate *(top right)* resembles his own wood-carving. The likeness proves that the legendary Ororoine cannot have been the only Long-ear to survive; women and children must also have lived to pass on their physical traits to later generations.

The custom of distending the earlobes with large plugs was characteristic of pre-Inca Peru, where the long-eared and bearded god-king Kon-Tiki, surnamed Viracocha ("Foam of the Sea"), was immortalized in ceramic by the Mochica Indians of the coast *(bottom right)*. The practice of ear lengthening is unknown in Polynesia, but Incas of royal birth adopted the habit of their predecessors by piercing their earlobes and putting large plugs in them. This caused the Spaniards to give them the nickname *Orejones* (Big-ears).

back to pre-Inca times. In the old Spanish texts, *Tupac* is occasionally rendered as *Tupa,* sometimes prefixed or affixed to the title *Inga,* such as in Tupa-inga. When the French ethnologist Métraux recorded Easter Island's genealogies, he discovered that the name of Hotu Matua's father in his original homeland was Tuparinga, with the affix *Anga. Anga* is the verb "to create." Since Hotu Matua himself had come from a desert land to the east, that must be the direction to the sacred land where his divine father had ruled. With Tupa-inga being a royal name for long-eared rulers in Peru, and Tuparinga-the-Creator being recalled as the name of the father of Hoto Matua, who ruled in a land to the east, a connection seems a more realistic explanation than coincidence.

An earplug of ceramic from Villahermosa (*left*) is of the typical shape found in early America in an area ranging from prehistoric Mexico to the Tiahuanaco region.

An earplug made from a seashell (*right*) was excavated from an *ahu* by our expedition to Easter Island in 1956.

131

Science comes to Easter Island

Disagreement in the scientific community

The last of the Easter Islanders to accept the Gospel brought by Eyraud had not yet been carried to the Christian cemetery when World War I broke out in Europe. By this time the baptized islanders must have been as confused about Christian morals as about their own origins.

They had been told that their ancestors worshiped the wrong god, and that they were mistaken about the direction of their own fatherland. In postmissionary times, the Galápagos, the Tuamotus, Rapa-iti, the Marquesas, and Mangareva had, in that order, been suggested to them as Hotu Matua's likely home. The Galápagos was accepted as a last resort by those who still clung to the ancestral claim of a homeland in the east. The islanders had never heard of the Galápagos before, but they had gathered from the Europeans that this group was the only one that did not lie to the west. They formed a fairly close idea of Polynesia from the missionaries, the shepherds, and Nicholas Pakarati, all of whom came to visit them from that area to the west. In the end, it seemed reasonable to think that Hotu Matua must also have come from the west. There was, at any rate, a legend that said that, when he died, he looked from Rano Kao toward the bird islets—in other words, to the southwest.

But once it seemed established that both Hotu Matua and Tuu-ko-ihu had come from Polynesia, members of various learned societies in Europe began to cast doubts on their own conclusions. They began to search further west. In the early part of the twentieth century, Dr. Paul Rivet of Cambridge University believed that the Melanesians must have been great navigators long before the Polynesians entered the Pacific. He suggested that they had originally swept right across the entire Pacific from their continental islands off Australia, and peopled South America. T. A. Joyce, an anthropologist at the British Museum in London, measured some skulls from Easter Island in the museum's collection and found them to be "far more Melanesian than Polynesian." And the ethnologist H. Balfour, researching Melanesian art motifs, found many representations of birds, and a wooden float for a fishing net carved to resemble a man wearing a birdlike mask. This was sufficient evidence to allow a new school of thought to develop, one that ignored Cook's early word list. Easter Island was not peopled from Polynesia, but from the Solomon Islands in distant Melanesia.

In the midst of this discussion, another problem began to be even more apparent. If the Easter Islanders actually had been Polynesians, who were the Polynesians? The negroid Melanesians caused no difficulty. They lived on large continental islands so close to the mainland of Australia and New Guinea that they could have walked most of the way from Asia, since each new mountain island was almost in sight of the next. But the light-skinned Polynesians had found their way to all the tiny oceanic isles and atolls on the American side of the ocean. Had they bypassed Melanesia, which had been inhabited by dark-skinned people for several thousand years? A search through the literature by assumed authorities opened fascinating vistas to anyone willing to tackle the riddle of Easter Island looking for unanimous agreement. It will suffice to list them by surname only:

Huxley (1870), like Saint-Hilaire, Flower, Topinard, and Peschele, had classed the Polynesians as Mongoloid.

The same year, Wallace accepted all Huxley's classifications of mankind, except that of the Polynesians, who should "be classed as Negroid instead of Mongoloid."

Thomson (1871), wrote of the Polynesians: "*They are a mixed race*, and may be divided into brown, reddish, and black. . . . Barata, South India, was, therefore, the Whence of the Polynesians."

Shortland (1875) believed that some migrants from India, along with a lost, prehistoric Papuan type on Celebes, pushed on east as Polynesians.

Coleman (1875) strongly opposed any Polynesian kinship with the Malays and indicated a more likely relationship to Madagascar or Central America. His own opinion was that the Polynesians are indigenous to their own islands, but "the origin of the Polynesian race is a problem that has yet to be solved."

Gill (1876) held the view that the Polynesians were a branch of the Caucasian or "white race."

Fernander (1878) saw the Polynesians as a branch of an Aryan people which for ages had been influenced by a Cushite civilization before they left southern Arabia on their long migrations through the Old World and into the east Pacific.

Fenton (1885) likewise linked the Polynesians to a European-like stock.

Tregear (1886) tracked Polynesian speech patterns by way of India all the way back to Iceland.

Volz (1895), on the basis of skull measurements, took the very opposite view, and held that the Polynesians, in spite of their fair skin, were related to the dark-skinned people of Australia and Melanesia.

Ripley (1899) considered the Polynesians to be mongrels, products of straight-haired people from Asia and frizzy-haired Melanesians.

Brigham (1900) was so confused as to propose: "Let the theories await a more complete knowledge. In the meantime all theorists in this domain are helping towards a final solution."

Keane (1903) wrote: "That they are one people is obvious and that they are an Oceanic branch of the Caucasian division is now admitted by all competent observers . . ."

Thompson (1906) considered the Polynesians as one of the purest of all known people, and suggested they were Caucasians of the Alpine branch who had learnt the art of seamanship from the Phoenicians before they reached the Persian Gulf and pushed on to Polynesia by way of Sumatra.

Macdonald (1907) attempted to prove a Semitic origin.

Giddings (1909) agreed with Keane.

Percy Smith (1910) again disagreed and believed the Polynesians had come from North Africa and migrated from Egypt by way of India.

Oetteking (1914) admitted, by the time World War I started, that the racial relations of the Polynesians still remained totally obscure.

Indeed, who had solved the Polynesian problem? Had the Polynesians come from Egypt, India, Arabia, Iceland, Celebes, Australia, or Central America? Were they Caucasian, Phoenician, Mongoloid, Melanesian, Alpine, Negroid, Cushite, or autochthonous to their own islands? Were they mongrels or the purest race in the world? All this had been proposed, but nobody agreed. Because nobody knew.

With this complete uncertainty as to Polynesian origins, the Easter Island problem itself would only be pushed into a whirlpool of contradictory theories, if the island's inhabitants were listed as Polynesians, before we knew who the Polynesians really were. None of the authorities would accept the theories of the others. Only the general public and the Easter Islanders themselves assumed that the authorities knew the answers.

It was amidst this atmosphere of scholarly confusion that a daring British woman sailed into the Pacific, hopeful of throwing new light on the riddle of Easter Island.

Mrs. Routledge's impressive enterprise

Easter Island in 1914 was still the navel of a rather peaceful world, when a beautiful white yacht sailed into Hanga-roa and anchored. It was the Sunday before Easter Day, and the white yacht must have come like a dove of peace to the Christian sons and daughters of cave dwellers in the mood to go to church and sing Polynesian hymns with Nicholas Pakarati. No one on shore or aboard ship suspected that war clouds were about to darken the sky over the rest of the planet.

The streamlined twin-masted vessel had been specially built for this visit, and was the first private yacht to reach the island. It flew the swallow-tailed flag of the Royal Cruising Club, and had been christened *Mana,* the pan-Polynesian word for "supernatural power." Behind the enterprise were the British Admiralty, the Royal Society, the British Association, the Royal Geographical Society, and the leading British scholars of Pacific Island cultures of that time. The learned societies of Europe all felt that it was time to solve the mystery of Easter Island.

The person to attack the riddle was the intrepid Mrs. Katherine Scoresby Routledge. In her book *The Mystery of Easter Island* she humbly refers to herself as "The Stewardess of the *Mana,*" and to her helpful yachtsman husband as "S." Mrs. Routledge was a very remarkable woman. Her book about her adventures remains a classic for laymen and scientists alike.

Mrs. Routledge went to Easter Island at the suggestion of Joyce of the British Museum and Rivet of Cambridge University, the two protagonists of the theory that Melanesians had settled the island against the wind. But she personally, or her husband, wisely chose to sail *with* the wind, from South America. She made a point of having followed Roggeveen's course from Chile, her own arrival coinciding with his discovery on Easter Day. But she seemed unaware of the fact that she had also sailed along Hotu Matua's course, recording that *Mana* bypassed the dangerous rocks of Sala y Gomez, "steering directly into the sunset."

When the members of the British expedition were set ashore in Hanga-roa Bay, the entire island population was there to greet them. Two hundred and fifty in all. As we have seen, since 1897, Chile had leased the greater part of the island to Williamson & Balfour in Valparaiso. The aboriginal population was still, as in the days of Brander, confined to the restricted area around Hanga-roa village, "to secure the safety of the livestock," but the British expedition obtained permission from the leaseholders to move freely beyond the village fence.

The islanders' confinement to the village area, combined with the linguistic barriers, caused considerable inconvenience to the British investigators. Mrs. Routledge and her cook were furthermore forced to spend most of the time alone on shore, while, because of the lack of a harbor, the *Mana* came and went at long intervals.

The first brief period was spent in the house of the murdered Dutroux Bornier in Mataveri, a short distance from the village. This was now the home of the English manager, Mr. Edmunds. He was the only white man on the island except for, as Routledge says, "a French carpenter who lived in Hanga-roa with a native wife being always included in the village community."

The village people at first continued to be very friendly. There was no reason to suspect that trouble was in the making. But church services were in the hands of a native lay reader, and Mrs. Routledge was uncertain as to how much these services conveyed to the worshipers. It soon became clear that an old and feeble woman named Angata, referred to as "the Prophetess," was a leading personality in the village. She represented a link between the ancient and the new religions. Her visions would shortly cause an event that could have put an end to the British expedition soon after its landing.

Once installed at Mataveri, Mrs. Routledge ventured undaunted into the village area to meet the people. She entered their small new houses of planks or stone, in which the inhabitants slept on the floor in company with their hens.

If she had come prepared to find descendants of the dark Melanesians, she must immediately have received a different impression. She stressed that Roggeveen's description of a people of mixed shades of color was still accurate. When she collected genealogies, she wrote, the islanders gave the colors of even remote relations as "white" or as "black." Intrigued by this evidence of a "white" element on Easter Island, she questioned the elders at great length, and concluded: "It is obvious that we are dealing with a mixed race, but this only takes us part of the way, as the mixture may have taken place either before or after they reached the island."

Routledge never lived up to her plan of publishing her extensive field notes, but they were recently discovered in the archives of the Royal Geographical Society in London, and abound in Easter Island family genealogies, specifying those who were fair skinned and even red-haired. In spite of her special interest in this physical type, she formed no theory as to their origins. As a working hypothesis, she merely proposed that "a negroid element" might have arrived from Melanesia, but only to become dominated and largely exterminated by what she terms "a whiter wave."

The islanders' skill both in theft and in hiding the loot had not changed any more than had the color of the skin. And Routledge realized that this was the reason for the absence of any portable objects in the village houses. Indeed, soon after the expedition's arrival, the company's woolshed, which housed Routledge's precisely calculated stock of supplies and traveling equipment, was broken into, and a quantity of items stolen. Worst for the lady was her loss of three-quarters of the expedition's soap. After this, the old prophetess Angata came up

The Mystery of Easter Island was a fascinating account of the first expedition that tried to solve the riddle of the giant statues. Katherine Routledge came to the island in her private yacht *Mana* in 1914. She camped at the foot of the quarry on Rano Raraku to get as close to the great images as possible, wanting to absorb the atmosphere of the lost civilization that surrounded her. They made the visitor feel, she wrote, that he stood "in the antechamber to something yet more vast which is just beyond his ken." Archaeology was still a young science in those days, and no attempts at stratigraphic excavation were made. However, Mrs. Routledge dug around the torso of one of the images buried in the silt from the quarry to investigate the shape of the base. By sheer bad luck she chose a defective statue that was broken off just below the shoulders. Assuming that all the images in the ground below the quarry were the same shape, she came to the erroneous conclusion that they all consisted simply of heads on a wedge-shaped base. Because all the other statues on the island had been toppled so that their faces were buried in the soil, the only ones the outside world saw illustrated were those that stood upright, half buried on the slopes of Rano Raraku. As a result, Easter Island became widely known as the Island of the Giant Stone "Heads."

to the manager's house one day accompanied by two men, and declared that she had had a dream of God. The chairman of the company in Chile was "no more," and now the island again belonged to the people. They were to take the cattle and have a feast the following day. The British party was also to contribute—the "contribution" to take the form of Mrs. Routledge's clothes. A declaration of war, written in Spanish, was formally handed to Mr. Edmunds:

June 30, 1914

Now I declare to you, by-and-by we declare to you, which is the word we speak to-day, but we desire to take all the animals in the camp and all our possessions in your hands, now, for you know that all the animals and farm in the camp belong to us, our Bishop Tepano [Jaussen] gave to us originally. He gave it to us in truth and justice. There is another thing, the few animals which are in front of you, are for you to eat. There is also another thing, to-morrow we are going out into the camp to fetch some animals for a banquet. God for us, His truth and justice. . . .

Your friend Daniel Antonio Hangaroa.

The delivery of the document was immediately followed by action. The islanders went into the field and secured some ten head of cattle. The smoke from many kitchen fires was shortly seen ascending from the village area. One beast was even offered to the British in place of their stolen property.

Edmunds could only muster a half dozen more or less reliable islanders for his defense. And in Mrs. Routledge's party were only four men and a boy from the Juan Fernández Islands. Everybody else was against them. Armed resistance would have been futile. After her husband failed in an attempt at negotiation, the brave woman rode down to the village to speak to the people. She knew neither Spanish nor their language, but was accompanied by the Spanish-English speaking boy from Juan Fernández. A gift was brought for Angata, but the old prophetess refused payment. "Food comes from God," she said. And God had now told her that the Englishmen could have a share of twenty head of cattle if they wished. But none for Mr. Edmunds, as he was a Protestant and had no god.

Mrs. Routledge returned to Mataveri with no positive result. New raids in the field began, and the number of cattle killed on one day rose to fifty-six. Edmunds and the foreign visitors lost all control. They could only hope that the Chilean warship would soon arrive on its annual visit.

Such was the state of affairs when the Routledge party decided it would be wisest for them to load the remainder of their stores on an oxcart and transfer their work and belongings to the opposite side of the island. Thus they came to set up their expedition camp, protected by an armed guard, at the foot of Rano Raraku.

For five weeks the Easter Islanders ruled their island. They left the expedition group in peace. But the Chilean warship arrived just as they were assembling to march on the foreigners in Mataveri the afternoon before the planned action was to take place. The riot died when four of the ringleaders were put in irons.

A Chilean schoolmaster was set ashore along with the materials necessary to build an expensive schoolhouse, courtesy of the warship. The English visitors were entertained in it with celebrations of Chilean Independence Day. School was duly started, but after a few days the children ceased to appear. The master declared he was "not an attendance officer," and from then until the Routledge

Fallen roadside images with others standing partly buried in the silt below the Rano Raraku quarries, which appear in the background. Mrs. Routledge discovered and mapped the prehistoric system of roads along which the images were transported. These roads had been followed by Cook's men in the eighteenth century, when some statues still stood upright along the way. Mrs. Routledge discovered that the images lying by the wayside were full-length figures with bodies, long arms and hands folded on their bellies. There was thus little to distinguish them from the fallen *ahu* images, except that, like the heads standing below the quarry, they were eyeless. She assumed that the eyeless statues along the roads belonged to a third category of monument that differed from all the other images on the island, concluding that they had been placed as decorations along the roads.

party left nearly a year later, no school was held. The blackboard and counting frame were last seen rotting in the field two miles away.

Once peace was in some measure restored, the Routledge expedition could resume fieldwork in the quarry area without having to carry arms. Then, shortly after, on October 12, 1914, a whole fleet of German warships steamed into Hanga-roa Bay. The lonely island, totally isolated from any kind of contact with the outside world, would soon learn that Europe was involved in a global war. The German Admiral von Spee had cleverly picked Easter Island as the most secluded spot for a secret meeting of his fleet. The battleships *Scharnhorst* and *Gneisenau* were brought from Japan to meet the *Nürnberg* and *Leipzig* that turned up from Mexico, and the *Dresden,* which arrived from the Atlantic coast of South America. An escort of smaller vessels anchored alongside these giants.

Chile was neutral, so Edmunds sold the Germans a fortune in meat. "Mr. S." rode over to see the German fleet, and he was able to send letters back with the Germans to Europe. The expedition had barely started to dig in the quarry area, so Mrs. Routledge did not care "to ride for some hours to gaze at the outside of German men-of-war. What did interest us was that presumably . . . the officers would come over to Raraku, and being intelligent Germans, would photograph our excavations. We therefore turned to, and with our own hands covered up our best things."

The Germans, however, did not go ashore. Thus the islanders received from them neither food, clothes, nor soap. According to Mrs. Routledge, the Easter Island sentiment would therefore at that moment certainly have been pro-Allies.

Until the last moment, Admiral von Spee tried to keep it a secret from the people ashore that a war was going on in Europe. The *Scharnhorst* had just come by way of Tahiti, where it had bombarded the town of Papeete because the islanders had risen and killed some Germans. When the news about the war finally leaked ashore on Easter Island, von Spee gave as the reason for his silence

Fallen *ahu* images lying face down over the sloping inland ramp, their lost topknots in the foreground. It was when Mrs. Routledge made a complete inventory of all the monuments on the island that she noticed that the images that had once stood on the *ahu* platforms differed from those at the quarry and along the roads in having deep eye sockets and having been crowned with cylinders of red stone. She therefore concluded that the great images could be divided into three categories: (1) the eyeless and bodiless heads at the quarry, (2) the roadside statues with bodies but no eyes, and (3) the *ahu* statues having bodies, deep eye sockets and red stone cylinders on their heads.

his desire to avoid a native uprising on this island, too. The fleet used the island as a base for a week, then one evening at dusk sailed around the coast and disappeared, the flagship first, never to return.

Following this impressive enemy naval visit, the other members of the British expedition left for the mainland to ensure the *Mana* against war risks. The brave Mrs. R. remained alone with the cook. She took up life once more in her tent by the grave of the murdered manager, awaiting her husband's return with the *Mana*.

Then the German cruiser *Prinz Eitel Friedrich* entered the bay with captured English seamen on board. Mrs. Routledge was desperate with fear the *Mana* would return at the same time. The cruiser left, however—but came back with a captured French barque laden with coal. She towed the barque into the bay and shot off its mast and spars before the Germans sacked the cargo to prevent the hull from capsizing without ballast. Before they left, the Germans set forty-eight French and British prisoners ashore with provisions from the French barque, which they then sank outside the bay.

After this episode Mrs. Routledge remained alone in her tent at Mataveri for months. She had every reason to worry about the fate of her husband, as *Mana* might have been sunk. To her the world must have seemed turned upside down. In Europe, civilized people had entrenched themselves underground; on Easter Island there was peace among the former cave dwellers. In the short time she spent near the settlement, she made a serious effort to learn the local language and thus obtain information directly from the elders. But she encountered unexpected linguistic complications.

"The natives speak, not only their own language, but, side by side with it, that of Tahiti, which is used in their religious books and church services: there are affinities between the two, but they are quite dissimilar, and to understand conversation it was necessary to learn both."

As her main field informant, Mrs. Routledge chose a young islander named Juan Tepano, because he had served in the Chilean army and knew a little pidgin English. She admitted that his previous interest in the ancestral remains had been nil, but he had a vivid imagination, and unfortunately he was to be considered a real authority by later investigators.

Routledge was well aware that her chances of obtaining new information on the island's past was meager unless she dug for it herself in the field. Thirty years of producing commercial carvings had also had a considerable impact on the story-telling. Memories of the distant past became more elaborate than in the days when Salmon and Knoche had been able to obtain short texts memorized by the elders. While new legends flourished like the production of wooden images, the earlier ones were either distorted or forgotten.

Mrs. Routledge was puzzled by the fact that the traditional stories of Hotu Matua coming from the east that had been recorded by earlier travelers were no longer recalled by her informants. With Juan acting as interpreter, she asked an old relative of his, Kilimuti, about this, but he did not know whence Hotu Matua came, and Juan unhesitatingly put his home in the Tuamotu Islands.

No other visitor, however, has caught the atmosphere of Easter Island like Katherine Routledge. Nor has anyone else been so long ashore in a period when petrified giants were the only representatives of mankind outside the Hanga-roa fence. Camping, as she did most of the time, next to the unfinished giants in the quarries, she was astounded by the extraordinary extent of the work. She was able to relive an average day in the life of the ancient stone sculptors, because everything was still there exactly as they had left it. Impelled by motives unknown to the present islanders, professional sculptors had hacked their way into the mountainside and altered the shape of the whole volcano—all just to fill a fanatical desire to secure eternal life for the men found worthy of living on as colossal stone giants. The landscape itself was left barren. Only these silent giants, brought from the volcano wall, lay everywhere, as she saw when she rode around the coast. On Easter Island, she wrote, the past was the present. It was impossible to escape it.

With the missionaries gone, with ancestral images hidden underground, and religious services conducted by themselves, superstition flourished as never before on Easter Island. The numerous *aku-aku*, or inherited ancestral spirits, were now mixed with the introduced *tatane*, the Christian "Satans." The islanders had difficulty explaining to Routledge the difference between them. She was given a list of about ninety supernatural beings, both male and female, with their places of residence on the island.

Much information on the *aku-aku* was recorded by Routledge. The spirits were part of the everyday life of the Easter Islanders. Not all of them were friendly. For several months Routledge lived in a small house built in Hotu-iti, at the foot of the Rano Raraku volcano. "I was later given the cheering information that a certain 'devil' frequented the site of my house . . . who particularly resented the presence of strangers, and was given to strangling them in the night. The spirits, who inhabit the crater, are still so unpleasant, that my Kanaka maid objected to taking clothes there to wash, even in daylight, till assured that our party would be working within call."

Some *aku-aku* helped the various families guard the entrances to their sacred caves. Undaunted by such spirit guardians, Routledge made every effort to locate certain of these hideouts. Her first thought as she saw Easter Island from

Mana's deck had been that it "looked an alarmingly big land in which to find hidden caves." She had been told, before the yacht departed from Chile, that Easter Island was full of caves containing hidden sculptures. A genuine *moai maea* found in a cave in one of the offshore bird islets had been brought to Valparaiso just before she arrived. It was a two-foot tall miniature of an *ahu* statue. The discoverer had given it the name *Titahanga-o-te-henua* and claimed it was a "boundary stone." Yet it turned out to be the very type of doorway image that Pierre Loti (Julian Viaud) had sketched when he visited the island as a midshipman in 1872.

We learn from Routledge that the islanders had now eagerly started to look for hidden entrances to caves belonging to others. Whatever they found would save them the work of making their own images, those they carved to sell. A whole chapter in her book is devoted to cave hunting. On its arrival, the expedition found the area surrounding a cave near Mataveri being dug over and ransacked by treasure hunters from the village. An old Easter Islander, one of the emigrants to Tahiti, had disclosed before his death that something was hidden there. She observed that cave-prowling in search of hidden objects was now the only work the population really enjoyed. Easter Island, she found, proved to be a land of underground caves, and she personally visited a large number of them during her stay. The entrances to some larger ones in the coastal cliffs could be seen from the sea, but were found inaccessible. However, these were not used for treasure deposits; it was the little ones, those with entrances that could easily be concealed, that were most valued. The islanders were so secretive about their hiding places that often when a man died his hoard was lost forever. Sometimes a man on his deathbed would give directions to his son about the whereabouts of the family cave, but the new owner might not always recognize the place. Routledge recorded an authenticated case of a man who had disappeared, along with his secret stores. After bargaining with a visitor, he then went to fetch some carvings he had for sale and was never heard of again. He had either fallen down a cliff or been buried alive.

In the course of her investigations, Mrs. Routledge discovered that the blind upright images below the quarry had the same facial features as all the other statues on the island, but that the backs of the heads and necks were of two different types. Some of the heads had a rough-hewn neck projecting like a keel at the back, where the statue had been cut away from the living rock, while the backs of others were just as finely shaped and smoothly polished as their front and sides. She even found that a few of the upright heads had been abandoned in the midst of the work of chipping away the keel-shaped neck. This convinced her that the backs were sculpted only after the heads had been raised to an upright position. On the other hand, she did not accept the island legend that these statues had only been placed upright temporarily so that their backs could be finished before they "walked" erect to the respective *ahu* platforms.

Orongo, the center of the bird-man cult. Mrs. Routledge also made a thorough examination of the ceremonial village of un-Polynesian stone houses on the rim of the crater of the island's tallest volcano, Rano Kao. It was here, according to the missionaries, that all the inhabitants of the island regardless of family or tribe had gathered to celebrate the vernal equinox, and it was here that our Norwegian expedition excavated the remains of a solar observatory.

The bird-man cult was recorded in detail by Mrs. Routledge. The feline figures that Thomson had been told represented the god Make-Make were now so badly eroded that Mrs. Routledge does not mention them in her book, but the bird-men were clearly recognizable, prominent on every rocky outcrop. Among these, Mrs. Routledge was shown some masks consisting mainly of two large round eyes, which the islanders explained were the face of the god Make-Make. These masks were evidently older than the bird-man reliefs, for the bird-men had often been disrespectfully superimposed on the older Make-Make masks. This corroborates the later discovery by Ferdon during our excavations in 1955–56 that the bird-man cult was typical only of the Middle Period in the island's history. Mrs Routledge confirmed what had been told to two earlier visitors, that the chief activity of the ceremonies held at the village of Orongo up on the rim of the crater was to watch for the return of the first sooty terns from their annual migration to Sala y Gomez Island off the coast of South America. This was the starting signal for the bird-man contest, in which men swimming on reed rafts raced to the three uninhabited bird islands visible from Orongo.

For the benefit of our Norwegian expedition in 1987, the young men of the island revived the bird-man contest of their forefathers. The contestants rushed out of their respective stone houses when the sacred migratory sooty terns—called *manu-tara*, meaning "sun birds"—were reported to have landed out on the rocky islands to nest. In former times the contestants climbed down the cliffs and plunged into the water on their *pora* rafts, which were of the same kind and made of the same reeds as the ones used all along the coastline of prehistoric Peru. The first to return to Orongo with a sooty tern's egg announced his victory with loud exultant shouts, holding the prized egg up high for all to see. Thereupon the winner could triumphantly claim the title of sacred bird-man of the year, with privileges comparable to those enjoyed by the king.

Mrs. Routledge spent two days with Juan looking for a cave belonging to his family, the whereabouts of which had been confided to him by Kilimuti, but they did not find the place, and Juan described his old relative as a liar. In the end, she concluded that the natives possessed, not "castles in Spain," but caves in localities they spoke of as "theirs," but which were as reluctant to materialize as any Mediterranean châteaux. The eagerness to search for these caves would most likely have petered out if the village people had not been aware that many others, like themselves, were owners of objects they had hidden and refused to dispose of. After all, had the storage caves been easy to discover, they would have been useless for hiding treasure. That they were not readily detected was proved by the fact that neither the legitimate former owners nor other potential island thieves were able to locate Mrs. Routledge's stolen supplies. Nevertheless, she did personally stumble upon the entrances to some interesting caves.

One had a small, traditionally narrow doorway, two feet high and eleven inches wide, from which a short passage descended underground at a sharp angle, and through which Routledge had to wriggle. The cave below proved to be a circular vault, less than ten feet in diameter. Four corpses lay side by side on the floor, while a fifth had been shoved in hurriedly, headfirst, through the doorway above. The ceiling and walls were cut into the solid rock and were covered with a white pigment. On the wall were three heads, carved in relief and adorned with touches of red paint. One had a pronounced "imperial,"—a pointed tuft of beard.

In another burial cave of similar type she found more of these unusual stone heads, but again irremovably attached to the wall. She realized that another treasure hunter had located the openings to these two caves before her, and ended by assuming that all movable sculptures hidden in caves had by now been stolen and sold to visiting travelers. She never found her own soap.

Her camp being conveniently located at the foot of the Rano Raraku quarries, Routledge took more time and opportunity to study the work of the prehistoric image makers than any previous visitor had done. Nobody had hitherto paid much attention to the large number of unfinished statues left still attached to the quarry walls. Cook's party had been close, but had not even recognized the quarries for what they were, and yet they cover the entire southern wall of the volcano from rim to base. In Routledge's day, like today, they can be seen from miles away. Probably in Cook's time the steep hillside had been covered by ferns and underbrush, but later the herds of imported animals had grazed and trampled everywhere. At any rate, one of Routledge's surprising discoveries was the high percentage of *moai* left in the quarry area, compared with the numbers carried away to the *ahu* in various parts of the island.

Routledge studied in all some five hundred statues. Of these, two hundred and thirty-one had fallen from about a hundred image *ahu* scattered around the coast. Few were inland. All the other statues were still left lying or standing in the quarry area, or abandoned in the terrain along the barely visible vestiges of prehistoric roads.

Routledge noted that none of the statues in the quarry area had eyes, not even those left standing. Even those abandoned along the road were eyeless, as if blind. Only those that had been standing on the *ahu* had deep, oval concavities to indicate the position of the eyes. And only these *ahu* images had carried the red stone cylinders or topknots on their heads. Now these superimposed ornaments lay on the ground next to the overturned *ahu* images they had once capped. Why were all the other statues blind and bald?

At first Routledge was overwhelmed by the confusion of carved rock, stone faces, shapeless bodies, empty niches, and manmade walls that combined to make the whole mountainside a gigantic monument to human tenacity and ardor. Little could be understood at first glance, but day by day she began to see a system in the chaos. She recognized a hundred and fifty statues abandoned at different stages. The hard but fine-grained volcanic tuff of the mountainside had been quarried by means of crudely pointed, handmade picks of a still harder, dark basalt. Used and worn-out stone picks lay scattered in the quarries by the thousands. In most cases the sculptor had started work by chipping out the frontal contours of the image down into the bedrock, but in some cases work had begun on the image in profile, cutting into a vertical cliff so that the image took shape face up under a kind of canopy. When the front and sides were completed, the undercutting commenced. The rock beneath was chipped away and the image chocked up by stones. A couple of finished images were found abandoned in the very middle of descent.

The statues in the quarries all followed the same norm, varying only in dimension and degree of completion. All were full-length busts with completed torsos, the bodies reaching all the way to the groin and hands held in a strange pose on the belly. An impressive number of statues had been in the making simultaneously when activity throughout the quarries had suddenly ceased. But in some cases the sculptors had abandoned work on an image because a flaw had been found in the rock, or some hard igneous rock had showed up on the nose or chin which the basalt picks were unable to cope with. Nevertheless, hundreds of sculptors must have been busy in the volcano at the moment when work was interrupted.

Routledge fully understood the method of procedure in the quarries. The prerequisites for the birth of this mass of megalithic men were those basalt picks, abrasive stones, patience, time, organization, capable designers, and several teams of highly qualified sculptors, as well as experienced engineers able to move the colossal images unscratched down the mountain wall. But another problem awaited Routledge when she confronted the statues that had been safely lowered to the foot of the hill and set up in the silt just beneath the quarries. Why were they standing there? There was no *ahu* to support them. They had been set up in the ground without any order, some alone, some in clusters and facing in every direction, as if bewildered about their own existence; all were blind and bald-headed. According to tradition, "The statues were set up to be finished."

This claim was not taken seriously by Routledge at the time, although she admitted that it seemed to be based on certain lingering memories. Intent on solving the problem, she proceeded with her own investigations, and observed that many of the forty statues standing in the silt of the quarry had unfinished backs. Some had a rough convex back resembling the keel of a ship, while other backs were beautifully modeled and finished.

She later noted that one image had the right ear carefully modeled, even showing the disk in place in the earlobe, whereas the other ear was left crudely unfinished and the neck was asymmetrical. Digging behind this statue, she found that the carving on its back had been abandoned in the process of transforming it from the boat-shaped to the finished modeled type. When she dug below the neck of some other partly buried images, she found the same thing: the back was only partly finished. She now came to the conclusion that the backs were only finished when the statues were finally set up. In that case, she said, some scaffolding must have been used. But she refused to believe that the statues standing beneath the quarries, once their backs were ready, were awaiting transport to some distant *ahu*. It would have been easier to transport them with the carving on the backs still unfinished, and leave their completion until the image had been set up once and for all on the *ahu*.

While digging in the detritus in her attempt to unravel the mystery of the two kinds of backs, Routledge discovered a beautiful design consisting of two rings surmounting a rainbowlike arch repeated on the backs of several of the images. It was these discoveries that she had kept hidden during the visit of the German fleet. Apart from this, she claimed that digging practically always led to disappointment.

Her first attempt to dig out one of the standing images from the quarry failed completely, as it was found to rest in detritus too hard to shift. Another was found embedded in looser silt, and successful digging revealed that it had no foundation and terminated crudely in a peg-shaped base. Assuming that all the statues set below the quarries were of the same type, she concluded that they had all been destined to remain standing on that particular spot, and were not meant to be transported. She did not realize that the statue whose base she had managed to uncover was a defective specimen, abandoned because its body had been accidentally fractured.

Why the images standing beneath the quarries had been set up in such a disorderly fashion, why they were left blind and without red cylinders on top, and why statues with keel-shaped backs were not to be found outside the quarry area remained a mystery to her.

Much of her time and ingenuity was spent trying to resolve the major problem: how were these colossal monuments transported across miles of rugged landscape? She suspected there must be roads of prehistoric origin and, riding up a hillock one late afternoon, the level rays of the sun helped her to detect the old

Members of the Norwegian expedition to Easter Island in 1986 study the painting of a bird-man on a rock from one of the houses at Orongo. The painting was undergoing conservation treatment by experts in Santiago, Chile, pending transfer to the museum on Easter Island. *Left to right:* Pavel, Figueroa, curator Guillermo Joiko, Skjølsvold, and the author.

Top: Bird-man relief from Easter Island. The bird-man is a very important motif in Easter Island art, often represented as two crouching figures with human bodies and limbs but with the heads of birds, sitting facing each other, hand to hand and foot to foot. This position recurs in both stone reliefs and in frescoes, and is so characteristic that it must have had a special significance (upper right). Men with birds' heads are typical of religious motifs in pre-Inca art from coastal Ecuador to highland Tiahuanaco. In Polynesia, apart from Easter Island, bird-men do not occur in any form of art.

Bottom: Bird-man relief from South America. The pair of crouching bird-men depicted on a ceramic bead from the island of Puna off the northern coast of the Inca empire bear a striking resemblance to their Easter Island counterparts. This cannot be explained away as a coincidence.

tracks which, since Cook's visit, had been partly hidden by the stones scattered by the imported herds of cattle. She discovered three main roads branching out from the Rano Raraku quarries, each about nine or ten feet wide, raised over the lower ground but somewhat depressed through the higher. Abandoned statues lay on them at irregular intervals. One of the roads could be traced all the way across the island from Rano Raraku to Rano Kao. Twenty-nine statues were scattered on it, all of them far apart and placed in a completely haphazard fashion. Some of the statues were twenty and others more than thirty feet tall. Another road ran through a gap in the crater wall toward the western districts; there were fourteen images lying on it. A third road disappeared northward and bore only four giants, but the most distant of these statues was also the largest, measuring thirty-six feet. It was badly broken, but had once been a single piece of rock that would have stood as tall as a four-story building.

Routledge's immediate conclusion was that all these images lying along the roads had been abandoned during transport, but a closer examination posed a curious problem. Some statues lay on their backs, some on their bellies. Some were even broken transversely, into two or three pieces, as if they had fallen from a great height. She dug around and under two of them without finding traces of pavement or platform. Yet her detective work yielded a result: She noted that the lines of weathering on one of them showed that the rain had for a long time run down all sides from the top of the head. Obviously the statue had been standing in a vertical position *before* it fell.

The islanders had a ready explanation: "They walked, and some fell on the way." It was not easy for Routledge to accept this statement, particularly when her young informant, Juan, added extra spice to the old tradition: The *moai* walked on the orders of an old witch, but one day, angry because she had not been invited to take part in a meal of lobster, she caused them to fall. Routledge admitted: "So wedded, however, were we at this time to the theory that they were in the course of transport, that it was seriously considered whether they could have been moved in an upright position."

Concluding that transport of these tall and slender monuments in an upright position would have been impossible, Routledge could only deduct from her observations that they had been set up to stand where they later fell. She devised an imagined description of Rano Raraku as formerly approached by at least three magnificent avenues on which the pilgrim was greeted at intervals by stone giants guarding the way to the sacred mountain. Her conclusion was:

"No statues were, therefore, found of which it could be said that they were in the process of being removed, and the mode of transport remains a mystery."

The weight of some of the colossi amounted to as much as forty or fifty tons, she pointed out, yet all had reached the *ahu* without a scratch, and none were abandoned during actual transport, although the quarries were full of statues in many different stages. She doubted there had been timber enough for rollers under the enormous images, though the red cylinders on their heads could have been rolled from their own quarry at the other side of the island. She heard a tradition about one of these cylinders being placed on top of its image by means of a temporarily constructed embankment, and suggested that the images were probably erected in the same way, "being hauled up on an embankment of earth made higher than the pedestals and then dropped on them."

From her own observations, Routledge concluded that the finished statues on Easter Island could be classed in three distinct categories: Those set up below the quarries with a peg-shaped base; those set up along the roads with completed bodies; and those set up on the *ahu,* also with complete bodies, with concavities for eyes and red stone cylinders on top.

Routledge assumed that these superimposed stones represented a kind of ceremonial headgear. Nobody had told her that the Easter Island term for them was *pukao,* which means "topknot," the coiffure common to men on the island at the arrival of the Europeans. Asking young Juan what they were, she got their name as *hau hiterau moai* which in fact means "hats of red stone for the images." She visited and measured those left inside the red scoria quarry in the Puna Pau crater as well as those left in a cluster outside the crater rim ready for transport. She found others in the field abandoned as they were being rolled toward some distant *ahu.* Unlike the images, they were rolled as crude cylinders, with a boss or knob on top and an oval depression that would fit into the apex of the image.

Some two hundred and sixty masonry *ahu* were studied by the Routledge expedition. Not a single one was found to remain in its original condition; all had been rebuilt. Fragments of older images were seen in the walls, and all those that had formerly been erected on top of the *ahu* lay overturned, their red cylinders rolled some distance away. Juan volunteered that all the sixteen *moai* in Hotu-iti Bay had toppled when an old magician had stamped his feet because he did not get some chicken heads to eat. Routledge put more trust in the old story about havoc at the time of tribal warfare. She discovered how the giants had been overturned: the removal of stones from underneath their bedplates caused them to fall forward.

Juan had more luck in convincing Mrs. Routledge that the old masonry mausoleums opened by Geiseler were *hare moa,* chicken houses. She admitted being greatly surprised—the dwellings for chickens were far more imposing than those for human beings—but she was told that chickens were important to the islanders, and nobody could steal them from inside these structures because the roof slabs could not be removed in the dark without making a noise.

She was also given to believe that the colossal megalithic towers known to the islanders as *tupa* had been built for "turtle-watchers." It was never explained to her why the narrow entrance was so low that no turtle would be seen unless it came in front of the opening! And a turtle-watcher would get the same view if he sat on any nearby promontory far more comfortably than if he sat on the vaulted boulder roof of a turtle-watching tower.

Routledge made a most puzzling discovery that had not been commented on by earlier visitors, and yet it made a considerable impact on her. Some prehistoric tracks known to the Easter Islanders as *Ara Mahiva,* or "Mahiva's Road," were said to encompass the whole seaboard of the island, and were considered to be the work of a supernatural being. The road could be seen as a continuous furrow, and on the northern and western coasts it ran for much of the way along the top of the cliffs. Wherever it had been interrupted, either because of landslides or erosion, it resumed its course on the cliff on the other side. On Rano Kao it showed up best in certain lights, running up both the eastern and western edges. "This silent witness to a forgotten past is one of the most mysterious and impressive things on the island."

Mrs. Routledge remained on Easter Island until the spring of 1915, when, happily, "Mr. S." came safely back with the *Mana.* Three months later the expedition left.

Summing up on her own impressions after sixteen months ashore, Katherine Routledge carefully avoided choosing any single answer to the riddle of Hotu Matua's origin from the chaos of conflicting theories that so confused Pacific Island research. She dismissed, however, the futile speculations of those who had recently begun to ask if this lonely island could be the remains of a sunken continent. And she excluded an arrival from South America. The suggestion that Easter Island had been populated from that direction may be ruled out for practical purposes, she explained, as even the earliest voyagers had noted language resemblances to the other islands. "Having reached this point, however," she said, "we are faced by the larger problem. Who were the race or races who populated the Pacific?" She gave no answer.

But she returned from the Pacific fully convinced that two different peoples had mingled to form the population she had seen on Easter Island. She assumed that the present population descended from the image makers. Her expedition brought back to London a collection of Easter Island skulls for examination by Dr. Keith, which, it was hoped, would clarify the problem. Keith found the Polynesian type to be fairly purely represented in some cases, but his general conclusion was that the Easter Islanders were "absolutely and relatively a long-headed people, and in this feature they approach the Melanesian more than the Polynesian type."

Routledge adds that the same craniological study resulted in another remarkable observation. The skulls showed that the islanders were the largest-brained people yet discovered in the islands or shores of the Pacific, with a cranial capacity even exceeding that of "the inhabitants of Whitechapel."

The skulls she brought back added to the existing problems. Why should the brain capacity of the Easter Islanders exceed that of all other Pacific tribes? In addition, one type of skull confirmed what linguistic evidence had shown: There was a Polynesian element on Easter Island. But the other type was so long-headed that Keith found it necessary to go all the way to Melanesia to find something comparable. But the Melanesians were a dark-skinned, negroid people. If Melanesians and Polynesians mixed, the descendants would be darker than the Polynesians. Routledge and everybody before her had stressed that the Easter Islanders were fairer than any other tribe in the Pacific. Routledge's problem, therefore, was to find the origin of those among the Easter Islanders whose skin was whiter than the Polynesians, even whiter than her own. It made no sense to look for them among the Melanesians.

Eliminating the South American continent for linguistic reasons, nobody took into account the fact that the burial grounds along the Pacific coast of Peru were full of long-headed skulls. The Indians of Peru and the rest of South America today are just as round-headed as is the average Polynesian, but the pre-Inca rulers of Tiahuanaco, and many of their contemporary relatives on the Pacific coast, were extremely long-headed. Deliberate head deformation was practiced among the round-headed Indians to increase the length of their skulls, but the undeformed cranial type of pre-Inca mummies, both in the highlands and on the coast, is remarkably long-headed. These were the people who, according to reliable Inca history, had a skin as white as the Spaniards. And they were the same people who had instructed the Incas to lengthen their earlobes—the people whose stone statues left at Tiahuanaco were found by Markham to resemble the monuments on Easter Island.

Routledge ended her book with the following words:

"And now the story is told. The expedition has, we hope, brought some new pieces to fit into the puzzle which it went out to study, but the help is needed of every reader who has more to bring, from whatever part of the world; so alone can be finally solved the Mystery of Easter Island."

Footprints in the vegetation

Among those who were drawn to Easter Island by Routledge's reports was the Swedish botanist Carl Skottsberg. World attention had again been focused on a lonely spot that contained prehistoric remains which continued to confound the scientists.

Skottsberg wrote a book and several papers on his observations. But a book about wild herbs does not attract a wide reading public. Even anthropologists prefer to read about human bones and potsherds. Admittedly, sweet potatoes and bananas can also tell a story about human voyages, but who cares about weeds? As a result, the testimony of plants is all too often overlooked by anthropological detectives, yet plants can speak a clearer language than legends. The story they tell is as reliable as fingerprints. As the noted plant geographer George F. Carter once expressed it: "Any fool can make an arrowhead, but only God can make a sweet potato."

Skottsberg was able to spend ten days on Easter Island following his botanical survey of the Juan Fernández Islands off Chile. His interest was focused on wild plants collected from the uninhabited areas. Like others before him, he was struck by the fact that the Easter Islanders were for some reason not primarily fishermen. Their subsistence was derived mainly from agriculture, and included the use of a number of wild plants. Among the very few that had managed to reach the island were, to his surprise, two species of freshwater plants. They grew abundantly in the two crater lakes of Rano Raraku and Rano Kao. Both were useful to man, and there were no other freshwater species on the island. Both had come from South America. How had they managed to cross the ocean?

One of these aquatic species was the totora reed, which dominated the banks of South America's Lake Titicaca and was cultivated in vast irrigated fields in all the desert valleys on the coast down below, being used for thatching and boat building. The other was known to the islanders as *tavari*, and was used by them as a medicinal plant. Like the totora, it also grew in Lake Titicaca, where the aborigines, too, used it for medicinal purposes. Both were strictly American plants unknown in the Pacific except in the crater lakes region of Easter Island.

The totora reed had been recognized and mentioned by the earliest voyagers. Skottsberg described it as the most useful wild plant on the island. It had been used for houses and for the making of boats similar to those found on Lake Titicaca and along the coast of Peru. Totora mats were the only form of furniture used on the island, apart from stone pillows. Hats and baskets were plaited

South America: A reed boat among totora reeds in Lake Titicaca, with the snow-capped peaks of the Andes behind. The totora reed is a strictly American species, growing wild in the highland lakes and cultivated in irrigated fields in all the lowland valleys and settlements along the desert coast of the former Inca empire. Since pre-Inca times this particular freshwater reed has been one of the most important plants to the coastal population of Peru and northern Chile, who use it as building material for boats and houses and for braiding mats and baskets. The fibers of the totora reeds served for making string of all dimensions, from thin lines to thick cables, and the tender section near the roots could be eaten uncooked.

Right: Easter Island: A reed boat among totora reeds in the crater lake of the Rano Raraku volcano, with the interior image quarries in the background, where giant stone heads emerge from the silt just as they do below the main quarries outside. When the Swedish botanist Carl Skottsberg came to Easter

from totora, and fishnets, twisted cord and thick braided cables were made from its fibers. It would have been a really lucky strike for the local people if totora alone had been borne on the wind to their crater lakes, let alone in the company of a useful medicinal plant. It would also have helped if directions for its use had been provided, for the Polynesians who arrived from the other direction had no idea as to how to build reed boats. The seabirds that reach Easter Island come from the rock islet of Sala y Gomez, not from South America. Nor do they eat seeds. The normal way to plant totora is by rootstock, not seed. The totora *(Scirpus riparious)* and the tavari *(Polygonum acuminatum)* in themselves are evidence supporting the traditional Easter Island tale of arrival from the east.

With the exception of a peat-forming moss, no other plants grew in the Easter Island crater lakes, but on the edges of the lakes, in the moist soil, Skottsberg found one more strictly American species, a *Cyperus* with edible roots. Its homeland was Peru. The only wild Easter Island shrub, *Lycium carolinianum*, could have come with it from Peru. It was also strictly American, and had edible berries.

The trees growing on Easter Island were, with one exception, widespread in that ocean area and presented no problems from a botanical point of view. The exception happened to be the most useful of the wild trees on the island, the toromiro tree, endemic to Easter Island and used by the population for the carving of all their religious figurines and royal paraphernalia. The islanders had told Salmon and Thomson in the previous century that this tree had been deliberately imported by Hotu Matua. As building material, the toromiro tree was second in importance only to the totora reeds. Skottsberg agreed with Chilean botanists, who found this Easter Island tree so close to its continental Chilean relative that it could be considered one and the same species. No other closely related species

154

Island to study the wild flora there, he was surprised at how few species had found their way to this island. But a remarkably high proportion of the species there consisted of plants used by man in South America, including the only two freshwater plants found in the crater lakes. One was the totora reed, by far the most important wild plant in the Easter Island culture, and the other was a medicinal herb. Both were at home in the Tiahuanaco area. In view of the vast distance from Lake Titicaca to the crater lakes of Easter Island, Skottsberg first assumed that the totora on the island belonged to a different species from that on the mainland. But when the *Kon-Tiki* expedition proved that it was possible to sail from Peru to Polynesia on an Inca type of raft, he re-examined the reeds from Easter Island and found that they were identical with those from Lake Titicaca.

existed in Polynesia. After talking with the local population, Knoche had in fact assumed that the royal toromiro tree was a naturalized Chilean species, and he included it in his list of Easter Island cultivated plants.

Relevant to our story is the fact that Skottsberg originally believed the Easter Island totora reed to be a local variety of the South American plant. But after the *Kon-Tiki* raft experiment had shown that ancient Peruvians possessed vessels capable of sailing thousands of miles, he re-examined the species and found it to be identical with those found at Lake Titicaca. He concluded that it was difficult to conceive that even its seeds could cross the ocean without human assistance.

In his later years, Skottsberg was to have an unpredictable confrontation with the toromiro tree in his own backyard, so to speak. In 1956 our Norwegian archaeological expedition arrived on Easter Island just in time to be shown the last surviving tree of that species. It was a badly mutilated and dying stump, found inside the Rano Kao crater. The toromiro wood was still so popular among the local woodcarvers that they hoarded every piece they could find and hid it in their caves. The species was extinct but for this particular stump which had one live twig with some seed pods attached. I collected the pods, and they were brought with the expedition pollen samples to our Swedish collaborator, Professor Olof H. Selling, director of the palaeobotanical department of the Swedish Museum of Natural History in Stockholm. Selling planted the seeds in Göteborg's Botanical Gardens. Skottsberg knew of this rescue attempt. Three toromiro trees came up; the last specimen on Easter Island died. By an amazing

stroke of luck, combined with Selling's thoughtful action, we were able in the twelfth hour to save a species that otherwise would have become extinct on our planet. During the final days of our excavations on Easter Island in 1988, the botanist Björn Alden, from Göteborg's Botanical Gardens, landed at the new airport on Easter Island with two large cartons in his luggage, each one containing a beautiful little green toromiro tree, which was planted with professional care in the soil of its age-old ancestry.

On the track of the stone giants

Giant statues of human shapes have been left by unknown sculptors all down the chain of the Andes from San Augustin in Colombia to Tiahuanaco in Bolivia, and reappear on the nearest habitable islands in the ocean: Easter Island, the Marquesas, and Raivaevae. The first man to visit them all was the famous travel-book author J. Macmillan Brown. He was also familiar with the rest of the vast pacific region— Micronesia, Melanesia, and western and central Polynesia—where not a single statue of this kind is to be found. He was struck by the remarkably rare marginal occurrence of these stone giants on the few islands lying closest to the comparatively limited area of distribution in northwestern South America. He visited Easter Island in 1923, and camped among the images for four months to investigate the mystery. His conclusion was that the stone giants of the islands were closely related to those of the mainland, and that the differences were simply due to stylistic and artistic variations on a common source of inspiration.

A well-known globetrotter and author, J. Macmillan Brown, had roamed both the Andean highlands and the Pacific islands prior to his decision to tackle the riddle of Easter Island. He had literally followed in the tracks of the prehistoric stone giants. He was personally familiar with the colossal walls and statues of Tiahuanaco, as well as with the related megalithic walls and stone men in adjacent regions of Peru. And in addition he had traveled widely in Micronesia, Melanesia, and Polynesia, and managed to visit the very few sites where stone statues had been erected in those areas. He realized that prehistoric monoliths in human form had a restricted but unbroken distribution in the marginal East Pacific. They had been erected and later abandoned by unknown sculptors from Mexico

and Central America in the north, down the Pacific side of South America, through Colombia, Ecuador, Peru, and Bolivia as far as Tiahuanaco at Lake Titicaca. After that they reappear only on the few nearest islands in eastern Polynesia. In other words, apart from those on Easter Island, stone giants of fair size stand only in the jungles of the Marquesas Islands and on Raivavae. Some statues the size of dwarfs were found on the uninhabited Pitcairn Island by the *Bounty* mutineers in 1789, which the mutineers threw into the sea. Apart from the few islands facing Peru, no other statues existed anywhere in the entire Pacific, which covers half the world.

Macmillan Brown spent five months on Easter Island, a record for local field study exceeded only by Routledge. Like her, he was a devout amateur observer, more incautious in his personal conclusions, but with a wider geographical experience that enabled him to draw more extensive comparisons. His verdict was that, in their rude outlines and conventionalized features, the great stone statues from Central Peru down to Tiahuanaco showed a striking similarity to those of Eastern Polynesia. A unique masonry technique also appeared in this area:

"The tooling and fitting of cyclopean blocks are exactly the same in Cuzco and in Easter Island. Both demand the same skill and the same organization of vast armies of labour. On Easter Island there was plenty of stone, but nothing else to make the megalithic art possible; in the Andes all conditions existed."

More attention might have been paid to Macmillan Brown's observations had he not used his comparisons to bolster his pet theory: that Easter Island was the remains of a sunken land mass. His readers were asked to accept his vision of the images being raised on the last visible peaks of a country that then sank into the sea. Routledge had discarded such a possibility. All evidence was against major geological disturbances having occurred in this part of the Pacific in the last hundred thousand years. But Macmillan Brown found no other explanation,

157

as in his own mind he had eliminated a transoceanic spread in either direction:

"Easter Island was not the teacher of the great-stone art of the Andes," he wrote, and at the same time he argued: " . . . we may accept it as an axiom that it was not Peru that taught the builders and sculptors of Easter Island their art."

The already established axiom that Peru was short of seaworthy vessels, made Macmillan Brown resort to his theory of a sunken land bridge. The Argentine ethnologist J. Imbelloni sided with Markham and Macmillan Brown in arguing a connection between the great-stone fitting of Easter Island and Peru. He refused to believe in the sunken land mass, but he accepted the axiom. Thus, unlike Macmillan Brown, he concluded that it was the Easter Islanders who had inspired Peru.

Few competent scholars could accept this interpretation. Indeed, it seemed most unlikely that a small and probably rather recent island tribe could have influenced the ancient architecture of a whole subcontinent. The American ethnologist E.S.C. Handy came up with yet another explanation. As a staff member of the B. P. Bishop Museum in Hawaii, Handy had personally explored the stone remains in the Marquesas Islands. He proposed that, during the hundreds of years of active voyaging, some Polynesians had visited America and then returned to Polynesia. They could have seen the Mexican or Peruvian stonework, and possibly brought a few masons back with them.

This new theory—that Polynesian canoes might have gone to South America and perhaps even brought back Peruvian stone workers—seemed acceptable to many of Handy's colleagues. But one of them took the idea one step further. The noted archaeologist Kenneth P. Emory, also of the Bishop Museum, was the first to challenge this idea. Emory had studied the stone remains elsewhere in Polynesia, and saw that nothing comparable to Easter Island stone-fitting was found anywhere in Oceania. He pointed out that, since the same technique predominates in the cut-stone facings of ancient Peru, South America seemed a more likely source. He argued:

"It is quite within reason to entertain an American origin for a culture element so specialized as this stone facing. It is a conspicuous element localised in the part of America nearest to Polynesia, a part where currents strike out and flow in the direction of Easter Island and the Tuamotus. This current in 1929 carried a flock of drums of gasoline from some wreck on the South American coast into the Tuamotus, bringing timely aid to the nearly exhausted supply of our party. May not one of the seagoing rafts of the early Incas have been swept into this current carrying survivors as far as Easter Island, 2000 miles to the west?"

No modern scholar had so openly challenged the universal disapproval of the Inca balsa raft theory, which assumed that such craft were incapable of reaching Polynesia. Emory was in fact so scorned for his unorthodox reasoning that he was soon forced to abandon his own proposal. The reason he later gave for giving up his original view was, that "the balsa craft of the west coast of South America quickly became waterlogged." This idea was imposed on him by his colleague, the Americanist R.B. Dixon, who had managed to convince him that balsa rafts become waterlogged within a few days if not taken out of the water to dry.

Dixon himself had never seen a balsa raft. His source was an otherwise well-founded study on aboriginal navigation off the Pacific coast of South America by the leading authority on this subject, S.K. Lothrop of Harvard University.

Lothrop quoted a book written in 1850 by G. Hyam, a British traveler, who had seen a strange sail on the horizon off the coast of North Peru. Asking the captain of his ship what it was, he was told it belonged to a balsa raft, built from a wood so water-absorbent that such rafts had to hug the coast and be pulled ashore at intervals to dry in the sun.

This rumor had been quick to spread, both by word of mouth and in print, right into the heart of Polynesian literature. It became universally accepted when the dean of Pacific island studies, Sir Peter Buck, wrote in his *Introduction to Polynesian Anthropology:* "Since the South American Indians had neither the vessels nor the navigating ability to cross the ocean space between their shores and the nearest Polynesian islands, they may be disregarded as the agents of supply."

They were indeed disregarded, and with them the remarkable observations of Macmillan Brown.

The Franco-Belgian expedition: Petroglyphs and Polynesian roots

In 1934, twenty years since Mrs. Routledge's yacht had arrived on Easter Island, a French man-of-war set ashore the first team of professional scholars to study the past and present culture of the island—an island in which little had changed since 1914. The team was to be picked up by a Belgian training ship six months later.

The only archaeologist with the team was the Belgian Henri Lavachery; his French colleague had died on board. France was also represented by the ethnologist Alfred Métraux, and Chile by a young medical doctor, Israel Drapkin. The Chilean government had sent Drapkin to the island to vaccinate the population against further smallpox epidemics and to attack the growing problem of leprosy. As a special service for the expedition he also collected blood samples in an attempt to make the first classification of the inheritable A, B, and O blood groups found on the island.

Little unified teamwork could be achieved by this trio—their aims and personalities were very different. Lavachery and Drapkin were extroverts, and got very close to the islanders; Métraux had more difficulty making contact, although it was he who was to collect ethnographic data. All three were based in Hangaroa, where Routledge's former interpreter, Juan Tepano, became their main informant.

Lavachery took to the field determined not to duplicate Routledge's intensive study of megalithic works. He searched for less spectacular remains from the past that might have been overlooked by others. And he was successful. It seemed unreasonable to him that skilled carvers in stone had left nothing but stereotypical stone giants. And then he began to discover petroglyphs all over the island.

When a Franco-Belgian scientific expedition disembarked on Easter Island in 1934, the Belgian Professor Henri Lavachery became the first professional archaeologist to set foot on the island. His French colleague, Dr. Alfred Métraux, was the expedition's ethnologist. Both were convinced that the rocky island lacked enough topsoil to conceal ancient ruins, so no excavations were made. Nor, in view of Mrs. Routledge's thorough study of the statues, did they make any fresh attempt to examine the megalithic monuments.

Lavachery did, however, discover an entirely new type of archaeological remains that none of the previous visitors to Easter Island had noticed. He found large numbers of figures and symbols engraved in the living rock all over the island, and undertook the first systematic study of these petroglyphs. They proved to represent a hitherto unknown local art form, with a variation in style and motif that was in sharp contrast to what had previously been found in this island and in the rest of Polynesia. It was later discovered that this bizarre variation of motifs could only be compared to the small forgotten lava sculptures then still lying hidden in the secret family caches. A variety of masks with prominently featured eyes and goatees recur constantly in Lavachery's reproductions.

They displayed a wide range of motifs and testified to a strange imagination. The only thing they had in common with the large *moai* was that they were carved on rocks so large that they could not be carried away and hidden. Bizarre human masks and eye motifs, birds and bird-men, turtles, fish, whales, spiders, lizards, monsters, boats and strange symbols reflected an unrestricted imagination. Lavachery suspected that there might also be a similar variety of motifs carved on smaller, moveable stone figurines, and searched all the caves he could find, but only in one did he come across two stone faces of the *moai maea* type. These were lying on the floor of the cave, and one of them was so eroded that it broke when he turned it over.

Lavachery's main contributions to the success of the expedition were a two-volume report on Easter Island petroglyphs and a popular book on the island's surface archaeology. He recorded and described one hundred and four separate groups of petroglyphs from fourteen different parts of the island, but did not attempt any stratigraphic excavations. He dug a number of test pits, but always found a sparse carpet of earth covering the volcanic rock. He therefore became convinced that deeper excavations were impossible, and that all that remained from the past must lie on or just below the surface.

Métraux, as an ethnologist, naturally attempted no excavations, but accumulated a mass of information on customs and beliefs, tools and art in his volume *The Ethnology of Easter Island.* He refused to believe in the early traditions of the Long-ears and the Short-ears and claimed that the story of the battle in the Poike ditch was inspired by the native desire to explain the presence of a natural depression. His two principal informants contributed a large number of previously unrecorded traditional stories. Some perhaps reflect tribal memories, as most of them dated from the recent period of civil wars.

He concluded dogmatically, "Easter Island culture is homogeneous." As the expedition archaeologist, Lavachery was more cautious: "The Polynesians probably found Easter Island devoid of monuments and uninhabited; but this statement lacks proof."

The two did not agree on the origin of the monuments, although they both considered them to be non-Polynesian and of local origin. Lavachery proposed that many of the unfinished statues Routledge had found attached to the quarry walls were intended to *remain* there as some sort of gigantic reliefs. He suggested that the idea of erecting free-standing statues had evolved from these decorations of the mountain wall.

Métraux did not support this view. He accepted a theory advanced by K. P. Emory of Hawaii, who proposed that the idea of carving images had evolved from the unshaped upright stones of *marae* enclosures in Tahiti or the Tuamotu Islands. Inspired by the abundance of tuff, the immigrants to Easter Island from those islands began carving their plain uprights into human form, and finding how easily these sculptures could be transported across the treeless country, they created larger and larger figures. In support of this theory, Métraux pointed to some unworked stone pillars he had seen set up on an Easter Island *ahu.*

This hypothesis was in turn found untenable by Lavachery, who conducted a special survey of all Easter Island stone uprights. He discovered that they had been erected at the end of the prehistoric period to imitate the earlier standing *moai:* "The substitution was an act of decadence and not of primitivism, and may in no case be considered as evidence of evolution from the form of stone uprights to that of statues."

Once Lavachery had been able to convince Métraux that the Easter Island statues could not have evolved from the unworked uprights of the islands to the west, the Frenchman came to favor the Marquesas as a more likely Easter Island homeland. Lavachery was at first impressed by a photograph of a statue from Mangareva, but the idea of Mangareva as the source of the Easter Island statues was opposed by Métraux; Lavachery finally abandoned the argument after learning that the photograph had been published erroneously. The statue it depicted came from Tahiti, and was made of wood.

Métraux had a simple solution to the old problem of transportation: he underestimated the weight of the statues. He suggested that their weight was only a tenth of what Routledge had estimated, and went on to claim that they had been dragged on their unfinished backs to their destinations, a short distance at a time. He disregarded Routledge's observations that all the images had their backs carved and polished before transportation began. Métraux did, however, accept Routledge's conclusion concerning the one statue she excavated that had a defective base. Like her, he assumed that this one statue represented a common type, and wrote:

"The fundamental difference between the images of Rano Raraku and those on the *ahu* terraces lies in the shape of the base. The Rano Raraku images were originally destined to be planted in the ground, for they taper into a sort of peg, whereas the *ahu* images have expanded bases."

This idea caused a whole new set of hypotheses to find their way into the scientific literature on Polynesia, rather like the story of one feather that gossip turned into five hens. Sir Peter Buck wrote:

"The images with pegged bases were never intended to be placed on the stone platforms of the temples, but were to be erected in the ground as secular objects to ornament the landscape and mark the boundaries of districts and highways. Because the images remaining in the quarry all have pegged bases, it would appear that the orders for the platforms had been filled and that the people had embarked on a scheme of highway decoration when war and contact with white foreigners caused operations to cease forever."

Métraux was the first to note that the Easter Island term for the red stone cylinders was *pukao*, or topknots, and thus did not represent red hats at all, but red hair. He was also clearly told by one islander that his ancestors had moved the *pukao* up onto the head of the *moai* by means of a pile of stones placed against the body of the figure.

The *ahu* in Vinapu was described by Métraux as the masterpiece of Easter Island stonework; the edges of the marvelously smooth slabs meet with mathematical accuracy, and small holes or chinks are filled with perfectly fitted stones. "Such a facing resembles the famous walls of the Inca palaces at Cuzco," he asserted. But he hastened to add that the similarity was coincidental: "There is neither geographical nor chronological link between the two cultures." The abundance of stone and scarcity of wood were the only stimuli the Easter Islanders needed to build such walls, according to his opinion. He wrote: "Several authors have attempted to show parallels between Easter Island culture and the civilization of the South American Indians. These parallels are so fanciful or naive that I do not think it worthwhile to discuss them here."

Indeed, he did not discuss them, and ignored the entire continent east of Easter Island. He does, however, make a head-on attack on the theories of a link between Easter Island and Melanesia, and fails to agree with Routledge and her tutors. His arguments against there being a blood relationship to the Melanesians were based partly on the study of the blood samples which were taken by Dr. Drapkin during the expedition and subsequently analysed by the American anthropologist H. L. Shapiro. Shapiro said that any theory of racial association between Easter Island and Melanesia "does violence to the known facts." Dixon's theory, which claimed the Easter Islanders to be fifty-five percent proto-Negroid mixed with Caspian, proto-Australoid and palaeo-Alpine, was called "a monument of industry." The Easter Islanders were found by Shapiro to have a frequency of blood groups A and B so low as to be almost absent, a deficiency shared by the rest of Polynesia and all of aboriginal America. Genetically, the possession of blood group B is a dominant trait, yet the gene it produces has its world maximum frequency in Melanesia, Indonesia, and Southeast Asia. Thus the islanders of Melanesia can never have formed any part in the racial composition of the Easter Islanders.

This discovery created a new problem for Shapiro and Métraux. With America excluded from consideration, and Melanesia and Southeast Asia eliminated because of the blood factor, the Easter Islanders could have come from nowhere except Polynesia proper. Shapiro admitted that the Easter Islanders deviate significantly from the Polynesians in the shape and dimensions of the cranium, but proposed that this might be due to "selective migration followed by isolation and inbreeding." Métraux accepted this theory, at the same time admitting that it provided the Easter Islanders with only a very short period in which to undergo any substantial and significant evolution. Both he and Lavachery emphasized the great distance between Asia and Easter Island, and assumed that man could not have reached this outpost closest to America prior to the twelfth or thirteenth century A.D. This would indeed have the local settlers very little time to change cranial shape and skin color or to come into contact with a different religion, let alone develop skill in carving and erecting stone statues and imitating the marvelous pre-Inca type of masonry found in Peru.

The continually changing theories about the origin of Easter Island had thus barely culminated with Dixon's complete hodgepodge involving two Negroid and two Europeoid people, when a new proposal was added to the list: that the Easter Islanders were just plain Polynesians of "a somewhat specialized and exaggerated type." To the many who still took the study of comparative craniology seriously, this must have seemed an oversimplification.

Métraux ends his book with the following admission:

"The aim of this book has been to show that Easter Island is a local Polynesian culture which developed from an archaic and undifferentiated Polynesian civilization. . . . On the most solitary inhabited island in the world, Easter Islanders were able to develop and perfect the culture which they received from their Polynesian ancestors to the west."

Métraux's fundamental aim was to solve an old ethnographical problem by making it disappear: There *was* no Easter Island problem. The magnificent statues were not, after all, so very impressive, and the people were just Polynesians whose physical characteristics had changed through inbreeding and isolation.

Nobody could doubt that there were people of Polynesian descent on Easter Island before the arrival of Europeans, but Métraux was the first to claim that the island culture was purely Polynesian. And he was the first to set about proving this point. It is thanks to his research that so many details of the island's aboriginal culture are preserved. No other ethnologist has made such a meticulous survey of all Easter Island cultural traits in a deliberate attempt to trace them back to some area in Polynesia. And no one will be able to improve on his results, as he seems to have left almost no stone unturned in his attempt to find cultural parallels between Easter Island and the islands to the west.

Métraux's conclusions completely ignore the existence of all the land mass on the windward side of Easter Island. As we have seen, the only argument he gives for this one-sided approach is that there is neither a *geographical* nor a *chronological* link between the culture of Easter Island and South American civilization. He made no attempt to elaborate or explain this assertation. It is time to test the logics in his reasoning, as it has all too long remained unchallenged:

● The sailing route to Easter Island that was recommended by Moerenhout and followed by all early European sailing masters, was from the coast of Peru and Chile below Lake Titicaca. This puts the geography straight. There is *indeed* a geographical link, in the form of what we might call a marine escalator. We even know today that in the years of the disastrous Niño Current from the north, which caused famine and catastrophe all along the desert coast of Peru and northern Chile, the Humboldt Current from the south was deflected earlier from the South American coast, and bore down full force upon Easter Island.

● The chronology suggested by Métraux implies that there must have been a settlement of Easter Island sometime in the twelfth century A.D. The fact that this was a century of considerable unrest, a time during which royal lineages changed throughout most of Polynesia, probably influenced him in assigning this date to the settlement. But it was also the century during which the Inca rose to power in Peru, thus bringing about considerable unrest and the expulsion of many earlier settlers of the region. The story of a king who fled to Easter Island from a country to the east fits perfectly into the chronology of the period. There is *indeed* a chronological link.

An appraisal of Métraux's search for outside parallels to Easter Island cultural traits would require that we, unlike him, take both sides of the surrounding sea into consideration.

● The clearest evidence of Easter Island's prehistoric culture are the hundreds of colossal statues erected on megalithic platforms. Both Métraux and Lavachery agreed that these could not be traced to Polynesia, but they disagreed on the theories they proposed to explain the statues' presence on the one island closest to Peru. If Métraux had not excluded all of South America from his comparative study, he would have had to admit that colossal monoliths in human form are not only to be found but are *characteristic* of the pre-Inca period of northwestern South America.

● Métraux admitted that Easter Island's megalithic walls resembled those of ancient Peru, but as no parallels were discovered in Polynesia he suggested that they must have been the result of the development of a native talent inspired by the abundance of available stone. However, there was also an abundance of stone on all the other volcanic islands of Polynesia and elsewhere around the Pacific, but no similar creativity took place. The possibility, even probability, that the inspiration for the Easter Island statues came from the nearest continent, where huge stone men stand on similar megalithic platforms, should therefore not have been ignored.

● None of the other stone structures on Easter Island, whether religious or secular, were found by Métraux to be of Polynesian origin. He accepted Juan Tepano's explanation that the structures opened by Geiseler were "chicken houses," though no such houses were built for chickens in Polynesia. The ruins of the circular houses he likewise accepted as originally having been some kind of garden structures, though nothing similar was found to have been built for plants or for any other purpose in Polynesia. Thanks to the records of the early European visitors, we know that his informant was wrong. And turning again to the nearest shore to the east, we find that low, circular walls—the remains of stone houses—both alone and built together in continuous clusters just as on Easter Island, are the most typical archaeological feature in the desert area between Lake Titicaca and the Pacific coast.

● Corbel-vaulted stone tombs are common in the Lake Titicaca area, and another structure typical of that region is the *chullpa*, a cylindrical stone tower with a vaulted roof made of giant stone blocks and with a tiny creep-in door. The *tupa* of Easter Island resemble the *chullpa* in every detail, and a Polynesian would

Lavachery, too, crawled into the ceremonial stone houses of Orongo and examined their interior walls. He was struck by the "weeping-eye" motif that we find repeated in his watercolor paintings now preserved in the Kon-Tiki Museum (*top*).

When the archaeologist Ferdon, on the Norwegian expedition of 1955–56, undertook the first systematic excavation of the houses at Orongo, he found more variations on the "weeping-eye" theme (*bottom*). He was the first to point out the striking parallel to the religious art of Tiahuanaco, where the weeping eye symbolizes rain from the sun-god. Wherever this motif is found on the pre-Inca coast of the mainland, it is interpreted as indicative of influence from Tiahuanaco. Why not when it is found on Easter Island?

Lavachery also investigated a number of caves on Easter Island. Like Mrs. Routledge and other earlier visitors, the members of the Franco-Belgian expedition were told by their friends among the islanders that caves existed in which lay small sculptures. They had been hidden by their ancestors, back in the days when the missionaries had commanded them to destroy all works of art associated with the old pagan religion. The Franco-Belgian expedition, too, spent a great deal of time searching for such caves, but all they found were remains of skeletons and some sculptures that were so firmly attached to the walls that nobody had managed to hide them before the cave was visited by strangers. A few such masks can still be seen in caves out on the bird islands; they have much in common with both the masks in the petroglyphs and the small portable stone heads that later came to light when some of the islanders revealed their secrets to the Norwegian expedition a generation later.

pronounce *chullpa* as *tupa*. As there are no such structures in Polynesia, Métraux accepted that they were locally developed "turtle-watching" towers. In pre-Inca Peru and Chile, *chullpa* were erected as mausoleums for kings and other important persons.

Métraux found nothing in Polynesia that could have inspired the building of such corbel-vaulted stone houses as those found in the ceremonial village of Orongo. He therefore suggests that the architecture had to have evolved locally, perhaps because of the need to resist the wind on the rim of the volcano. He had not noticed that the same kind of houses had been built in sheltered positions at the bottom of the crater. Nor does he comment on Thomson's lost village of corbel-vaulted houses on the north coast of Easter Island, and again he ignores the fact that such houses are common in South America.

● Ignoring the early records, which show that the circular stone ruins were the remains of former dwellings, Métraux was left with the boat-shaped reed hut as the only house form on Easter Island. He admitted that it was "entirely different" from any Polynesian type in every aspect, including the funnel-like door, which is "unparalleled in Polynesia." And even inside these former huts he had found nothing that suggested Polynesian origin. He listed only mats, stone pillows, bottle gourds for water, reed baskets for sweet potatoes, wooden images and tablets hanging from the thatchings. The mats and baskets were made of Peruvian totora reeds. The bottle gourds and sweet potatoes have been found, together with totora, in tombs dating from the second millennium B.C. on the desert coast below Lake Titicaca. About the stone pillows Métraux states: "Such pillows were not used elsewhere in Polynesia," and of the wooden figurines he says: "Like the stone images, the moai kavakava and paapaa are enigmas." Neither house nor inventory could be linked to Polynesia.

● The wooden tablets were no less enigmatic. The lack of script in Polynesia made him propose that the *rongo-rongo* was not a script, merely a locally invented mnemonic device. He admitted, however, that there was no reason why Easter Islanders needed a mnemonic device unnecessary elsewhere in Polynesia, and concluded: "The main difficulty in solving the problem of the tablets lies in the lack of any convincing parallel in Polynesia." He does admit that the nearest place inscribed tablets had been found prior to prehistoric times was in Panama, but he does not mention prehistoric Peru, where the Spaniards burned the inscribed hoards of the Inca historians.

● Métraux stresses the exceptional importance of the bird cult ritual and the social structure that grew up and was built around the annual bird-man competition. Yet he finds: "The complex of the bird cult . . . has no parallel in the rest of Polynesia." But bird-man motifs based on a prehistoric bird cult are typical of the whole pre-Inca empire to the east.

● Searching for other aspects in the Easter Island religion that might have come from Polynesia, Métraux writes: "The most striking feature of Easter Island religion is the unimportance of the great gods and heroes of other Polynesian religions." He suggests that the importance given in Easter Island mythology to gods whose names are unknown in Polynesia shows that the emigrants substituted the old gods with lesser ones who took over their rank, but he fails to provide any documentation to support this statement. Except for what the Incas told us, and what their art reveals, we know little about the deities of the extinct pre-Inca civilizations on the continent to the west. The Incas worshiped the sun and their royal ancestors, and depicted them symbolically as felines, as bird-headed men, or as faces with tear marks below the eyes. As on Easter Island.

● In lengthening their ears, the Incas were following a socioreligious custom inherited from their divine predecessors. The Long-ears on Easter Island did the same, and Métraux wrote: "Deformation of the earlobe to introduce wooden or bone plugs is restricted in Polynesia to Easter Island."

● The two kinds of wooden emblems—the moon-shaped *rei-miro* and the ball-shaped *tahonga*—worn as pectorals by persons of rank on Easter Island are described at length, with Métraux concluding that "the wooden crescents or *rei-miro* are without any parallel in Polynesia." And: "The wooden balls, *tahonga*, are paraphernalia peculiar to Easter Island."

● Important men also carried a ceremonial double-bladed paddle. Paddles with a blade at either end are unknown in Polynesia. Métraux therefore concluded that they "had nothing to do with navigation and are not derived from any known implement." But if we turn to the coast of South America, we see that the double-bladed paddle was common. Many model balsa rafts, all equipped with minature double-bladed paddles, have been found in the burial grounds of Ilo and Arica, facing Easter Island. On the north coast of Peru, early Mochica artists depicted their chiefs holding double-bladed paddles, and, exactly as with those found on Easter Island, the upper blade is shaped like a stylized human mask with long ears, feather crown, and tear marks. Simple coincidence is out of the question. The Peruvian prototype antedates any settlement on Easter Island.

● Métraux mentions the *pora* or tusk-shaped reed boats that played such an

The peculiar round stone towers that the islanders call *tupa* mystified Lavachery and Métraux as they had previously mystified Mrs. Routledge. However, they accepted the ingenuous explanation given to her by a young Easter Islander who had served as a soldier on the mainland and knew a little Pidgin English. He claimed that they had been "look-out towers for turtle hunters" in the old days, and because there was nothing similar to compare them with in all Polynesia, the explanation was accepted. One need only crawl inside to realize that the explanation is untenable. Nobody could see a turtle from in there unless it crawled through the entrance, and the view was no better from the roof than from any hilltop in the vicinity. The enormous stone blocks of the walls and arched roof suggest a ceremonial function, and the design is the same in all respects as that of the pre-Inca *chullpa*—burial chambers for prominent persons—found in large numbers on desert hillsides from Tiahuanaco down to the Pacific coast.

important part in the ceremonial bird-man swimming competitions. He does not trace their origins, since neither the reeds, the type of craft, nor the custom of competing for the election of a sacred man were native to Polynesia. The craft was of a type characteristic of the Peruvian coast.

The largest *pora*, according to Métraux, could carry two men, and thus had the same capacity as the tiny local canoes. The wooden canoes had an outrigger, and thus were definitely of Polynesian origin, but they were so poorly constructed that Métraux made no attempt to track down their exact prototype in any specific area within Polynesia.

● The stone adzes, which were usually used for woodcarving and with which the clumsily put together canoes were made, show a link to Polynesia. Métraux found two types of polished and hafted adzes on Easter Island that were used for woodworking. He stated that the first kind was clearly Polynesian, but represented a type so widespread in that area that it was insufficient evidence on which to link it with any particular place of origin. The second type he felt must have been developed locally, as he found nothing to match it in Polynesia. He concluded: "It would seem, therefore, that the Easter Islanders broke away from the rest of Polynesia before the specialization of the adze took place."

Since the Easter Islanders worked primarily in stone, it was natural that by far the most common cutting instrument was the mason's pick, or *toki,* an unhafted tool of hard basalt, crudely chipped to fit the hand and pointed at one or both ends. Such *toki* are found by the thousands in the quarries and scattered around all the *ahu* and settlements. Once more, Métraux could point to no similar tool used in Polynesia. They are common on the continent to the east, and the Polynesian term *toki* is also the general term for stone ax among the aboriginal tribes of Chile.

● Métraux indicated that the principal fighting weapon on Easter Island was the *mataa,* a crudely chipped black obsidian blade shaped more or less like an ace of spades, with a well-worked tang protruding from it. This was lashed to a wooden shaft, and served as a spear or kind of lance. Métraux admits that spearheads or similar projectile points were not made in any part of Polynesia. Spearpoints and other projectile points made from chipped stone are found on the southern coast of Peru, however, and a few specimens made of black obsidian, completely indistinguishable from Easter Island *mataa,* have been found in the archipelago of southern Chile.

● Pointed bone needles perforated near the blunt end to hold thread are the most common artifacts to be found on Easter Island after *toki* and *mataa.* Outside of New Zealand, sewing was not a Polynesian practice, and Métraux failed to find bone needles among any of the groups from which the Easter Islanders could have come. The reason he gives for this is that the way in which cloth was manufactured on Easter Island differed from the way it was made in Polynesia: "Easter Island is the only place in Polynesia where strips were fastened together by sewing. Elsewhere in eastern Polynesia the strips were felted together, in western Polynesia they were pasted." Again, no links to Polynesia. Yet bone needles, indistinguishable from those found on Easter Island, are frequently found in the prehistoric middens of Ilo on the south coast below Lake Titicaca. Again Easter Island sides with Peru.

● Apart from the fishhooks, no other elements in the Easter Island culture found by Métraux can be considered sufficiently noteworthy to warrant a search for their origin. The fishhooks were indeed remarkable in type and of masterly

Stone fitting. Métraux rejected any possibility of contact between South America and Easter Island, while admitting that there was a striking similarity between the special type of megalithic masonry which was typical of ancient Peru *(opposite page)* and that found at Vinapu, on Easter Island *(this page)*, and which has no counterpart elsewhere in the Pacific. He attempted to explain the singular presence of such walls by arguing that there was no timber on Easter Island, so the Polynesians who settled there started to work with stone until they were as good at it as the stonemasons of Peru. Métraux admitted in his book on the ethnology of Easter Island that he had intentionally disregarded cultural parallels with South America while studying every feature of the Easter Islanders' culture to determine what part of Polynesia the Easter Islanders had come from. In each case he had been forced to conclude that he found no parallels in Polynesia. Every form of local architecture, art, artifacts, customs and religious beliefs was peculiar to this one island closest to Peru. The sole exception was a form of stone axe and a puny canoe made of sewn-together boards, both common.

design, although less useful than might have been expected in an island community. Several scholars have described Easter Island's one-piece fishhooks of polished black basalt, exquisitely designed and perfectly balanced, as the acme of aboriginal stone-shaping art. Yet nobody has actually seen these fishhooks in use, and they are not of Polynesian origin. One old islander refused to dispose of his specimen to Palmer, as it was said to be a treasured heirloom. According to a tradition recorded by Métraux, the ancestors possessed only this one type of stone fishhook, but the fish would never take bait from them, so they began making different kinds, using human bone. Métraux doubted this claim, for had the stone hooks been totally useless, the early fishermen would not have put so much work into their manufacture. An alternative explanation would seem to be that the kind of fish the stone hooks were originally designed for were not present on Easter Island. Perhaps the fish caught in the former fatherland differed

from those of Oceania. Stone fishhooks have been reported as having been used in the coastal region below Lake Titicaca, and a tradition from the Tiahuanaco area claims that the ancient Aymara fished with hooks made of pumice stone. On the northern extremity of the reed-boat area, stone fishhooks have been found in prehistoric middens on islands off California. These are so similar to those of Easter Island that in 1947 specimens were exhibited side by side in the American Museum of Natural History in New York. The exhibitors argued that Easter Islanders must have reached the American coast, and that the point of arrival would presumably have been the nearest region below Titicaca, since the same exhibit also demonstrated the close relationship between the two other Easter Island types of fishhooks to those excavated at Arica in northern Chile.

The simplest of these forms, the U- or V-shaped bone fishhooks, could have reached Easter Island from Polynesia, according to Métraux. But not necessarily, since it was also an aboriginal American form. No kind of fishhook at all was known to people in Indonesia and southeast Asia prior to European arrival. The third type of fishhook—the composite hook with a curved bone point lashed to a straight shank—is more complicated in shape and with a more restricted distribution. This type of hook occurs in early Moa-hunter sites in New Zealand, but is otherwise unknown throughout Polynesia. It is a well-known American type, however, found in archaeological middens on Vancouver Island and in desert burial mounds in Ilo and Arica, east of Easter Island. In the latter area the single and the composite forms are found together, as on Easter Island. And as shown in the 1947 exhibit, the composite hooks manufactured by the prehistoric fishermen of Arica are so amazingly like those of Easter Island that they can hardly have been independently invented. In both areas, hackles made of feathers were inserted into the grooves where the curved point was tied to the straight shank. Any theory that the same concept and design could spread from Easter Island to Arica on the continent is ruled out by chronology. The catalog of the exhibit makes this clear:

"The oldest known occurrence of the two forms is in northern Chile, where they were used by the first inhabitants of the coast, probably before 1000 B.C."

If, in conclusion, we sum up Métraux's total harvest of the elements of Easter Island's culture that could be solely of Polynesian origin, we are left with an unimpressive list: a rudimentary relic of a Polynesian outrigger canoe and one of the two local types of stone adzes. Neither the canoe nor the adze have characteristics that could help him tie their provenance to any particular area of Polynesia. All the other items cited by Métraux, although *not present* in Polynesia, are *characteristic* of aboriginal South America, most of them being clustered in one geographical area ranging from Lake Titicaca to the coast below. Indeed, although Metraux insisted that Easter Island belongs to the marginal subarea of central Polynesian culture, he admitted:

"But in attempting to link Easter Island culture with a specific group of islands within this area we are faced with a considerable difficulty. No specific region of central or marginal Polynesia shows a marked and distinctive resemblance to Easter Island."

We may reverse the statement, and ask: What, in fact, *are* the cultural elements usually considered indicative of Polynesian culture? The usual answer is: the grooved wooden *tapa* mallet for bark cloth, the bell-shaped pounder for making *poi,* and the wooden bowl for the kava-drinking ceremonies. These are the three items commonly listed when citing the material elements of Polynesian culture.

None of them had found their way to aboriginal Easter Island. Nor, as we have seen, did the pan-Polynesian gods.

The first wooden mallets reached Easter Island with the Polynesian companions of the missionaries. Before European exploration began, the Easter Islanders had used smooth beach stones for beating bark, as did the South Americans.

The *poi*-pounder was not an implement native to Easter Island. *Poi* was not produced by the local women. The breadfruit from which it was made did not reach Easter Island until the Europeans brought it, but taro did grow there, and was equally popular for *poi* production among other Polynesians: it kept well, and they used this fermented mash to provision their long voyages. But the Easter Islanders were clearly not accustomed to *poi*.

Kava drinking played no part in Easter Island socioreligious customs. *Piper methysticum*—the Polynesian plant which was first masticated and then fermented in hot water—was not brought to Easter Island.

No matter how we approach the problem of the Polynesian contingent on Easter Island, we find its *physical* and *linguistic* presence quite evident, *while from the cultural point of view it is almost invisible.* This supports the traditional view that the emigrants adopted the customs of their new country. These customs happen to align with those of the people of pre-Inca Peru. The Polynesians do not surrender their own customs and beliefs simply because they relocate to a new area. It is therefore significant to find that they came humbly and empty-handed to Easter Island, bringing only those three things—the chicken, the banana, and the sugar cane—something the people, who either received or brought them, needed.

Ethnographic evidence thus indicates that the Polynesians were indeed brought to Easter Island, either with their consent or against their will, by navigators from a more culturally developed area of ancient Peru, using either force or cunning. Maybe the nineteenth-century Europeans were not the first to sail from Peru into the Pacific as slave raiders. History repeats itself. In any epoch people carried away as slaves would readily change their faith and culture, but not so easily their physical appearance and mother tongue.

1955: The first Norwegian expedition. What the soil had hidden

It then became my turn to challenge the riddle of Easter Island. Twenty years had passed since the efforts of Lavachery and Métraux by the time we arrived from Norway in a converted Greenland trawler. We had read what others had written, of how Hotu Matua picked Anakena for his landing and his first base. So we headed for the same bay, and dropped anchor as close as we could get inshore. We camped in tents by the wide white beach, while our ship rode at anchor off the black lava promontory for six months, the longest period any vessel had visited Easter Island.

There were no trees in Anakena in 1955. Nothing but shining white sand and prehistoric walls built of huge stones. The half-hidden backs of giant statues fallen in rows barely emerged from the sun-baked dunes. There were no shadows but our own, and nobody on this side of the island but our own group of twenty-three foreigners. From what we could tell after we had climbed the hills, sheep and horses appeared to rule the rest of the island. In order to lessen the risk of sheep-stealing, the human community remained confined to the village of Hanga-roa on the other side. The population had increased to around nine hundred, including a Chilean governor, a schoolmaster, and a Catholic priest. We felt as if that other side belonged to Chile and modern times, although there were neither shops nor wheeled vehicles anywhere on the island, except for the jeep we had brought ashore with us. "Our" side still belonged to Hotu Matua and the days of the stone-age engineers.

The former royal habitat did not seem altogether vacant. We pitched our camp between the largest of the stone colossi and the huge red topknot intended for its head. We felt like the humble guests of a race of mental giants, who, for the moment, were out, but had left behind their own images, which were of a size to match their minds. They had come, like us and all the other visitors, by sea; their wake stopped here. We had come, as had so many before us, to look for their tracks. Giants had to leave footprints. And they were there. The invisible giants themselves seemed to be there too, forever, together with their tracks. We felt their presence everywhere—on the hillside, on the beach, wherever they had left their great stone men to serve as sepulchers for their own intrepid souls. They had fulfilled their own desire to become immortal on earth.

As we assembled around the long table in the mess-tent that first evening, I looked at my men. They were all there, except for a watchman who remained on the ship to blow the siren in case the anchors tore loose. The captain and crew of the ship were visibly excited about the adventure, and ready to put their muscles to work. The scientists forming the core of the expedition had already exchanged cautious opinions on the prospect of finding subsurface deposits on such a treeless island. I had known only two of the archaeologists before. Arne Skjølsvold from Oslo University, who had accompanied me on the Galápagos dig and Edwin Ferdon from the Museum of New Mexico, who had been a valuable consultant in my studies on the prehistoric cultures in Middle and South America. There were two more American archaeologists: Dr. William Mulloy from the University of Wyoming, and Dr. Carlyle (Carl) Smith from Kansas University. Then there were two South American archaeology students, Gonzalo Figueroa and Edwardo Sanchez, sent along as official representatives of Chile. Dr. Emil Gjessing, a Norwegian medical doctor, was to provide fresh blood samples of the living population and deliver them at 4°C. to the British Serum Laboratory in Melbourne.

The other scientists had no preconceived idea as to who the carvers of the stone giants might be. They were not concerned about theories. They had come to dig where nobody had dug before, to look for stratification where no one had found it—not to prove that Easter Island had been peopled from Polynesia or from South America, but to look for any traces from any direction. East *or* west. Or East *and* west. As for myself, I believed that the people now living in Hanga-roa village were descended from ancestors who had come from Polynesia. But I

In 1955 the first Norwegian archaeological expedition set sail from Oslo for Easter Island in a converted Greenland trawler, with the author as leader and an international team of archaeologists aboard. At that time Easter Island had no contact with the outside world except for a brief annual visit by a Chilean naval vessel. The island possessed neither harbor nor airfield, so, after having inspected the cliff of Rano Kao (*top*) and the steep coast below the extinct volcano Rano Raraku (*center*) with statues standing up on the slopes, the members of the Norwegian expedition landed on an exposed point of solidified lava, where a large portion of the island's population had gathered to meet us (*bottom*).

also believed what these ancestors had told them: that they were of mixed blood because they were also descended from an earlier people on the island, those who erected stone statues and who had come from the east.

I did not impose my theory on any of the men around the table. On the contrary, I left it to each archaeologist to choose his own area of excavation, and to write up his own discoveries and conclusions exactly as he pleased. I could not help considering us a team of detectives. Time and again I caught myself thinking of the words of a distinguished old archaeologist of the orthodox school: Dr. Herbert J. Spinden, president of the Explorers Club in New York and director of the Brooklyn Museum. He was the one who had really triggered my desire to know the truth about Polynesia. "You cannot solve anthropological problems as if they were detective stories," he had said. "How else?" I wondered. "How else if not exactly like a detective story?"

To me the problem of the original settling of Polynesia was one of the greatest whodunits of all times. At a time when the so-called western world was ignorant of the existence of both America and the Pacific, some men and women had managed to sail unnoticed and unrecorded into the world's largest ocean and take possession of every little lonely island that had soil and water enough to sustain human life. Their route covered thousands of miles of roaring ocean, so no footprints remained. Their fingerprints were gone, too, vanished when skin and bone had withered away, while Europe still believed the world ended in an abyss beyond the horizon. But those-who-did-it brought with them skills and customs that were to survive generation after generation. And their genes lived on in the blood of their descendants, as did the genes of the useful food plants their descendants continued to cultivate until the Europeans arrived. And the winds and currents have continued to flow in exactly the same directions. Nothing should be overlooked. All the clues needed to be combined and added to the evidence of language if we were to understand what had happened in the open east Pacific off the American shores prior to European exploration. It was, to me, a genuine detective job.

Old Dr. Spinden, as grayhaired and friendly as Santa Claus, had told me that no people from South America could have reached Polynesia before the Spaniards arrived, for they had no boats. They had balsa rafts, I said. You try to go from South America to Polynesia on a balsa raft, he answered. I did. And now I had come to Easter Island to dig, because I knew from my experiment with the balsa raft *Kon-Tiki* that even we, novices in this sort of travel, had been able to sail from Peru twice as far as the distance to Easter Island.

Métraux had prompted me to turn to archaeologists in search of the long-lost tracks of the prehistoric seafarers. We had an argument about a stone head recently reported as discovered in the Galápagos Islands six hundred miles off the South American coast. Métraux was sure it was Polynesian, I was sure that it was South American. We were both wrong. I went there to dig with two anthropologists, and we found that the stone head had been carved by a German settler, who showed us his work. But while in the area we began the first archaeological survey ever of that oceanic group, and found thousands of pre-Inca potsherds, which we brought back to the United States National Museum in Washington for identification. The Galápagos Islands, uninhabitable in prehistoric times because of the lack of a permanent water supply, had clearly been a popular fishing ground for raft voyagers from Ecuador and northern Peru throughout the Mochica and Chimu periods of pre-Inca Peru. The oldest ceramic shards we found were polychromed fragments identified as "Coast Tiahuanaco." Voyagers from pre-Inca times had come to Galápagos from coastal valleys as far down the Peruvian coast as Casma, two hundred miles south of Trujillo.

Three years had passed since we took our findings from the arid Galápagos to Washington. This time, when we set up our camp in Anakena Bay on Easter Island and sat around the long table in the mess-tent, we at least knew that on this island there was no lack of prehistoric sites from which to choose. The question was whether we would find anything by digging. Lavachery doubted it. Métraux insisted that everything lay on the naked surface. Certainly the land-

We camped on the shore of Anakena Bay, partly on the advice of the resident Catholic priest, Father Sebastian, and partly because all previous visitors had been told that this was the place where the legendary first king of Easter Island, Hotu Matua, had landed with his followers after a long sea voyage from a great land to the east. Father Sebastian Englert soon became a member in good standing of our party and a popular liaison between ourselves and the islanders, who virtually regarded him as the uncrowned king of Easter Island.

scape looked bleak and barren. Beyond the bright dunes of the beach, the ground was hard packed with gravel and stones of dark crushed lava that barely allowed any grass to take root. The perpetual trade winds brought dust into our tents, however, so we knew that erosion must have caused the soil to drift.

We decided to start work the next day, right in our own camp area, since Anakena played the principal part in all the traditional versions of the Hotu Matua legend. In the sand near our tents lay some long and beautifully carved foundation stones with deep holes drilled in them. These were said to be the remains of what was considered "Hotu Matua's house." Beside it lay a pentagonal stone oven: the king's kitchen. We dug, and down below the first king's oven we found an older oven of the same type. We continued to dig, and thought we had gone a long way back in time when we found a blue Venetian pearl—the very type Roggeveen recorded as having brought with him to the island in 1722. There was nothing deeper. Below, to our surprise and disappointment, lay only sand and silt. But at least it was clear that not everything lay on the surface.

Among the ruins at Anakena, centrally located just above the beach, lay the most impressive ruin of all: Ahu Naunau, with its row of fallen statues. What was visible of the long seaward wall, which disappeared into the sand dunes, had clearly been rebuilt with stones taken from an earlier structure. Although it was crudely put together, it had, mixed in with the rough boulders, several colossal blocks of marvelously cut basalt. Some of these reused blocks were decorated with human figures in relief, but they were inserted wrong side up. The giant head of a statue, broken off at the neck, had been set into the wall sideways, as if it were an ordinary building block. This head was of a different type from those of the usual *moai* statues that had stood in a row on top of the *ahu*. The people who had decapitated this older giant and placed their own ancestral images on top of the *ahu* could not have been of the same lineage as their local predecessors. They were indeed ancestor worshipers, yet they showed no regard for the original function and dignity of this older image. And they had dismantled the incredibly fine wall of the temple to which the old image belonged, only to use the squared-off facing blocks as wall fill. This first *ahu* we saw upon landing thus seemed to me to enclose in its seaward wall the key to the question of whether or not Hotu Matua's party had been the first and only settlers on the island.

Naturally we began test pits by this important *ahu*. But as the archaeologists encountered nothing but sand, they lost interest. It had been agreed that they were to select their own sites for excavation, and as nothing promising turned up in Anakena, they all wanted to try elsewhere. I admitted my disappointment when nobody wished to go on digging in the royal bay where we had pitched our camp, but the other sites selected were so obviously important that we all realized they could not be ignored.

Attention was first turned to some of the circular structures, which by now had become generally known as walled garden plots. Test excavations of a few of them immediately disclosed that they were indeed remains of circular stone houses with thick, low, core-filled masonry walls, and built-in storage cists. One entered through what presumably would have been a conical thatched roof, a structure common in the Lake Titicaca region and on the barren slopes between Tiahuanaco and the Pacific coast. The remains of these houses were sometimes clustered in contiguously walled units, forming regular village patterns, and Ed Ferdon, in his survey of them, later concluded that this form of dwelling was "one of several features that made the Easter Island material culture complex

Like most of our predecessors, the first thing we did after disembarking was to visit the mighty stone heads rising out of the sandy soil below the quarry on Rano Raraku. At the time of our arrival, there were no other images standing upright on Easter Island. All those that had once stood on top of the stone platforms round about the island when the first Europeans arrived had been toppled during the intertribal wars that raged until the missionaries landed in the latter half of the last century. And like everyone else, we were greatly puzzled as to why the monuments below the quarry consisted of heads only, while all those lying prone had bodies and arms.

stand out as markedly different from those of other Polynesian islands. . . ."

Arne Skjølsvold excavated a fireplace inside one of these circular houses, and found the remains of charred sweet potato in the ashes, dating the last local meal to the sixteenth century.

Arne next decided to investigate the Rano Raraku image quarries, with its multitude of stone heads. A pleasant contrast to the stone head that had lured us to the Galápagos!

Ed wanted to work in the ceremonial stone-house village of Orongo, with all its associated features. What was the background of the bird-man ceremonies?

William Mulloy decided to examine the megalithic *ahu* of Vinapu, famous since Captain Cook's visit for its spectacular stonework. Even Métraux had admitted its resemblance to the stone walls of the Andes, but to him it represented the last stage of independent local development. Now Bill hoped to excavate material for a radio-carbon dating, and thus learn if this superb structure was from an early or late period.

Carlyle Smith preferred to work close to camp. But when Carl found the sand around the great central *ahu* in Anakena to be completely lacking in interest, he decided to excavate some open coastal caves in nearby La Pérouse Bay. They showed evidence of former human occupation, and by excavating the floor he hoped to obtain an early radio-carbon date. But to my mind the people who built the great image *ahu* were not cave dwellers. They must have come as an organized group, and lived in village societies accessible to the king. I attempted to convince Carl to dig deeper than he had done along the impressive Ahu Naunau wall in Anakena, but professional competence outranked island tradition, and

It was both fascinating and impressive to see how the whole side of the volcano Rano Raraku had been hollowed out and pitted like a worm-eaten cheese by the prehistoric quarrymen. Everywhere lay more-or-less unfinished stone giants as yet unseparated from the rock. In a few places the sculptors had started on the vertical cliff face and cut out a profile, while in others they had started from above and outlined the full-face figure with equal skill.

excavations at Hotu Matua's royal site had to wait until many years later. Carl also assumed responsibility for the examination of a number of *ahu* and for excavations in the Poike trench, in order to try to verify the story about the pyre in the war between the Long-ears and the Short-ears.

Father Sebastian Englert was the village Capuchin priest, who virtually became part of our team. He was such a central figure among the islanders that we considered him their present-day priest-king. His arrival in 1935, shortly after the departure of the Franco-Belgian expedition, marked the first permanent estab-

Enormous quantities of stone often had been cut away and removed from the quarry to give the prehistoric artists an even surface to outline a stone giant and start the work of sculpting it.

The greatest of all the giants still unseparated from the rock of the quarry is over seventy-two feet long. If cut loose and raised erect, it would have been a single block of stone as tall as a seven-story building. On top of this colossal monolith would come the customary red stone "topknot." It is hard to credit the theory that lack of timber was the only reason why the people who settled on this lonely little island became such outstanding organizers and engineers.

lishment of a Christian mission since the dramatic sojourn of Lay Brother Eyraud and his associates about seventy years earlier. Father Sebastian had encountered a generation of Easter Islanders still torn between two faiths. They believed in the teaching he tried to reinforce, but they also retained a profound respect for the seemingly superhuman achievements their ancestors had accomplished with the aid of Make-Make and pagan *aku-aku*. The entire community was still under the influence of a generation brought up by pagan parents. In fact Father Sebastian spoke of a woman in his congregation who had been born some twenty

We had no trouble in confirming that Mrs. Routledge had solved the problem of how the statues were made in the quarry. The front of the stone giant was carved first, complete down to the last detail except for the eye sockets, which were not even marked (*top*).

When the front and both sides had been exposed and finished, the sculptors began to undercut the back, which was still attached to the bedrock (*bottom*).

years before Eyraud arrived. Successful theft was not only tolerated, it was admired. The islanders needed a special permit from the governor each time they had to go on a legitimate errand outside the restricted village area. On advice from Father Sebastian, we put a rope around our camp the first night to keep the thieves away. Next morning the rope was stolen.

Father Sebastian was full of stories about secret caves, and he was personally convinced that many still held art treasures from pre-Christian times. He had witnessed cases where islanders who had removed such hidden objects, thus vio-

The only tools used by the sculptors were rough coup-de-poing axes of hard basalt. They were without handles, pointed like pickaxes at one or both ends, and fashioned to lie comfortably in the hand. Thousands of such *toki* axes lay scattered all over the quarry, as if the wielders had thrown them down on the day when the work stopped, never to be resumed. In the final stages before the monument was freed from the rock, it lay supine on a back shaped like the keel of a boat about to be launched.

lating surviving tabus, had gone mad from fear. The priest, impressive in his white gown, had climbed all around the island cliffs searching for caves, and had made a valuable inventory of important archaeological remains. He did not accept the conclusions of the Franco-Belgian expedition that only a single people had reached the island before Roggeveen. He strongly defended the view of the islanders, claiming that two people had arrived, one of them definitely "white." Unlike Métraux, he was sure some link with ancient Peru existed, but was vague in his opinion of migration routes or method of transportation. He seemed to

When the statue was finally free, it was propped up with stones pending the difficult maneuver of lowering it down the hillside to the plain below. Some of the giants lying there ready for "launching" looked as if they might go sliding away down the mountainside at the slightest push. Getting them down from the top terraces of the quarry undamaged must have been the hardest task that those incredibly clever Stone Age engineers faced. The job could not possibly have been done without stout ropes of bast or totora reed fibers. Oral tradition on the island points to the huge cylindrical pits on the crater rim, where the poles once stood to support such ropes.

Not all attempts to lower the stone giants from the top of the volcano had been successful. One of the statues broke its neck while being transported over an empty niche from which another statue had previously been removed (*top*). The journey down the hillside was made with the back unfinished, but on reaching the foot of the mountain the stone images were raised upright so that the sculptors could get at the backs to finish them. The great puzzle remained: How could the giants be transported to their destinations many miles away when they were already finished and polished smooth on the front, back, and both sides?

One of the first projects that our expedition decided upon after our arrival in 1955 was a re-examination of the buried parts of the eyeless heads that stood at the foot of Rano Raraku. The Norwegian archaeologist Arne Skjølsvold was put in charge of this project and led a digging team made up of hand-picked islanders and most of the ship's crew. All felt like pygmies from Lilliput in a world of petrified Goliaths. The sculptors and engineers responsible for these hundreds of stone colossi appeared to have performed a superhuman task.

assume, as did Macmillan Brown, that there had been a sunken land mass somewhere in the East Pacific. He wrote a popular book based on the information obtained from his own congregation, and concluded that neither of the two peoples who reached Easter Island had come prior to about A.D. 1575.

We needed labor to help us dig. As work progressed, the dozen or so of the ship's crew was augmented by Easter Islanders picked by Father Sebastian and given permission to come to our sites on horseback and sleep in local caves. Soon we numbered around a hundred men, all of whom were engaged in four separate excavations.

As I climbed about with Arne and our cameraman in the crater walls of Rano Raraku, we shared Katherine Routledge's excitement at her discoveries. Abandoned quarries with unfinished statues were everywhere, and one could clearly witness every stage in the carving of the *moai* except the opening of the eyes. All were blind. But I could not help noticing that every image, whether merely outlined on the rock or already detached for removal, were full-length busts, and all were similar to the type seen along the prehistoric roads and on the *ahu*. Not a single one of them was designed to become a mere head, yet according to the existing literature all the blind images set in the soil at the foot of the hill were supposedly nothing but heads tapering into a buried peg-shaped base.

Arne decided to excavate one of these heads completely, and selected one of the largest on the outer slopes of the volcano. The more the men dug, the clearer it became that the head rested on the shoulders of a body with arms. The body seemed to continue endlessly the deeper down we dug. To reduce the fear of being buried in a veritable landslide, we had to widen the excavations and pass the soil up from man to man, standing on superimposed terraces. Soon we knew that as much statue was hidden below ground as was visible above. The gigantic monolith was a tall, full-length bust, carved with a flat base so as to stand free without support from sides. Just like those on the *ahu*. Like them, they had long arms running down the sides, the slender hands with long nails clasping the abdomen. Nipples and navel were represented, but instead of the penis, so prominent on the wooden figurines, this giant's genitals were hidden by a small rectangular relief resembling a kind of penis cover or shield.

We dug another head, another, and still another, outside and inside the volcano. About a dozen were excavated. All proved to have complete bodies resting on a flat base. These discoveries made Arne recheck Routledge's photograph of the one she had uncovered that reportedly had a "peg-shaped base." He now detected that it was a defective specimen. A large part of the image had broken away along an oblique fracture line, and this gave the remainder of the body its unique wedge shape.

A single broken *moai*, abandoned by its unfortunate sculptors, had thus been cited again and again in the scientific literature, until all the blind images standing at Rano Raraku had peg-shaped bases!

The islanders who helped us dig were not surprised. Their ancestors had always told them there was only one kind of *moai*. Those standing at the foot of the quarries, they said, were only set up so their backs could be finished before they began their march to the *ahu*.

Clearly they were right. The backs of the statues we excavated, and the rear of the heads and necks of all the others, showed us how right they were. In fact, Routledge had noted the variations in the execution of the neck of all these standing Rano Raraku images. They were abandoned while work was in progress on their backs. Each image had come down from the quarries on its rough keel, face up. They were not to leave for their ultimate destination until every detail but the eyes were finished.

In the area between the clusters of standing statues at the foot of the quarries were some conspicuous hillocks. They had always been thought of as natural formations. Arne decided to check. To everybody's surprise, the hillocks proved to be artificial when Arne sank a deep exploratory trench through one of them. He found that it consisted of debris and broken stone picks that had evidently been carried down from the quarries in plaited trays or baskets. Carbon samples

When we reached the place where the eyeless heads stood at the foot of the volcano, we noticed some round, grass-covered hummocks. Until then, everybody had believed them to be natural formations. When we decided to drive a trial shaft through one of them, we discovered that the whole hummock was manmade. It was composed of debris from the quarry, mixed with broken and worn-out stone pickaxes. The debris had been carried down the hill in baskets or woven mats, which had left impressions that could still be seen here and there. Among the debris we also found ashes and pieces of charcoal that would enable us to date the period when the quarry was worked.

We selected a tall statue whose base we decided to examine. The ship's captain, Arne Hartmark, accomplished the difficult feat of climbing up on top of the giant's head so that we could measure its height above the ground before we started digging.

As the excavations proceeded *(opposite page)*, we were obliged to keep widening the shaft to prevent the soil from caving in, as it was composed entirely of silt and debris from the quarry uphill. As the shaft steadily deepened, Skjølsvold could see that this was definitely not just a head with a plug-shaped base like the one Mrs. Routledge had excavated. It was a full-length statue, just like those that had been transported across the island and erected on *ahu* platforms all around the coast. The body had quite simply been buried in debris washed from the quarry above as soon as the sculptors had downed tools, and there was nobody left to haul away the debris that lay scattered everywhere around the unfinished monuments.

found at different levels in the mound indicated that the debris had accumulated from work that had gone on from somewhere around A.D. 1206 to around 1476, with ample margin for error in either direction. There was no way of telling when the first work had begun. Certainly the mass production of standardized *moai* was still proceeding at full speed just a few centuries before the Europeans came to America and Oceania. Once work stopped, prior to the European landing, the masses of debris not yet carried down by man had descended by reason of its own weight. After a few seasons of rain the statues below were buried up to their necks.

While working to expose the complete statues standing below the quarries, Arne found one figure that had a large ship, complete with three masts and superimposed sails, incised on its front. This petroglyph made the statue resemble a giant monument of a mariner, a picture of his sailing vessel tattooed on his chest. But the hull of the vessel was completely curved and pointed upward at each end, just like those of the reed ships depicted in the art of pre-Inca Peru. The deck of the ship was filled with people, indicated by short notches, and a long fishing line ran down to a large turtle carved way below on the statue's stomach. Clearly the carving was old, for the lower part of the statue would have been covered by silt as soon as the quarries were abandoned.

All the "heads" excavated by our expedition proved, below ground, to continue into bodies with arms. Not a single one consisted solely of a head with a plug-shaped support intended to be embedded in the ground. The only exception happened to be the very one that Mrs. Routledge had been unlucky enough to pick; on closer examination this proved to be a defective statue abandoned by the sculptors because it had been accidentally broken off diagonally during the course of the work. All the statues represented busts of naked men, all modeled after the same prototype—presumably the revered basalt figure from the ceremonial village of Orongo, which wound up in the British Museum. Métraux and other earlier visitors had been told a legend of how the first statue acquired its shape. The sculptor who made the first attempt had not succeeded in getting it right until he was advised by a witch to look down at himself when he urinated. In our excavations we noticed a marked difference among the genitals of male images on Easter Island. The small figurines of emaciated Long-ears carved in wood had prominent, circumcised penises, whereas the stone giants generally had no penis at all, usually just a small square patch in relief that could have represented pubic hair or a minimum modesty patch. In answer to our question as to why the stone giants had no *ure*, one old islander replied calmly: "A *moai* [stone image] cannot have two *ure*, a *moai* is a *ure* himself." This strengthens the theory proposed by several observers, that the Middle Period statues on Easter Island had intentionally been given a phallic shape.

On the largest of all the *ahu* images Carl discovered another petroglyph of the same kind of vessel. A colossus that had toppled from the fine *ahu* of *Te-Pito-te-Kura.* "The-Navel-of-Light" had stood thirty-two feet tall, weighed eighty-two tons, and had carried a topknot weighing eleven and a half tons. Before it was overturned and fell nose down, this monolithic bust, Carl managed to clear a passageway underneath the giant, and found an incised carving of a two-masted ship, the foremast running through the huge round navel of the *moai* as if to depict the circular sail of a solar vessel.

When Bill was excavating the famous *ahu* complex at Vinapu, he found two

Some of the excavated Rano Raraku statues that had been finished on the back had a dorsal pattern of the same kind as that seen on several of the statues that had been toppled from their *ahu* platforms. This pattern had been wrongly interpreted as a "belt," whereas in fact it consists of an arched rainbow motif that is confined to the back and does not even continue round to the sides and front. The descendants of the Long-ears claimed, in fact, that the motif represented the rainbow with the sun and moon above it and rain symbolized by the M-shaped sign underneath. Once again it was obvious to us that images so artistically carved on all sides including the back could not have been subjected to the friction of being dragged along the ground.

eroded petroglyphs pecked into the facing wall of *Ahu* No. 2. One represented a boat with three superimposed sails. A study of the talus deposits that covered this design showed that it dated from the image-carving period prior to the civil wars on the island. Carbon dating from material taken from below the plaza wall of the same *ahu* gave the approximate date: A.D. 857.

These early ship designs began to assume religious importance when Ed found them inside the houses at Orongo, among the double-bladed paddle and tear mark motifs. Reed ships with from one to three masts were painted on the slabs of the ceiling; the ships were in red, with white lines running vertically across the hull to represent the rope lashings around the bundles. One ship with three masts and a double set of yardarms had no sails, but a red disk was painted on the central mast. *Ra* and *raa* are the words for "sun" and "sail" throughout Polynesia. The red disk may represent a play on words, but this would not exclude the representation of a sun boat, a motif widespread among reed-ship voyagers in various parts of the world. Ed actually excavated the remains of a solar observatory next to the same stone houses on the rim of the crater.

This came as no great surprise, however, since the missionaries had recorded that the Orongo festivals were determined by the position of the sun, and the Dutch discoverers had witnessed the early islanders prostrating themselves to the rising sun. Ed also found a system of four holes drilled in the rock, surrounding a strange image unlike any *moai* prevously discovered. A pole placed in the largest hole threw its shadow directly across each of the three other holes at the time of the two equinoxes and the local summer solstice respectively. A fire-pit was also associated with this solar observatory. The strange image consisted of a rounded rectangular head without either body or limbs, identified by the islanders as Make-Make. Ed concluded that the great god Make-Make, the sun, and symbolic fire must have been intimately linked together in Easter Island's earliest period. He found no parallels in Polynesia, but as with the whole Orongo complex of buildings and religious art, he could point to direct parallels in Peru.

We had barely digested our own discovery that all so far known *moai* on Easter Island were either finished or unfinished monuments of one single type, when we began to encounter images of different style, so far unknown to science. Some were mere rectangular stones with a flat face carved in relief, like the one found in the solar observatory. They did not surprise the islanders, though they had nothing in common with the *moai,* their ears being short or absent and their eyes huge and bulging. To our workmen they represented Make-Make, the heavenly god of their ancestors. He was known to them from numerous petroglyphs, where he was sometimes shown merely as two big eyes with frowning brows. Clearly he needed no human body, only watchful eyes that kept track of all human behavior. Human beings needed bodies and limbs. But not the god represented by the sun.

It came as a shock to the islanders, however, when a monster with legs was found. Arne had asked his workmen to clear the talus that almost totally covered a seemingly natural boulder below the southeastern cliffs of Rano Raraku, which were supposed to represent the oldest part of the quarries. At first a huge head with a round face appeared, and bulging eyes stared up at them. The face had short ears and a goatee, a feature found on several Make-Make petroglyphs. But as we continued to excavate, the head became the complete image of a giant, face upturned and kneeling as if in prayer. His hands were placed on his thighs, and the soles of his feet were turned up behind so that his rounded buttocks rested on the heels. A stone statue with legs had never been seen or heard of on Easter Island. But here it was, and in a kneeling position with hands on the thighs instead of on the stomach. It was the first truly realistically shaped monument to be found on Easter Island. Using our jeep and many men, we tilted the colossus up on its feet, or rather its knees. This time workmen and scientists were equally amazed. The image did not seem to belong among the *moai* of Easter Island.

The circumstances of discovery gave us reason to think that this might have been an earlier type of sculpture, antedating the final standardization of the stiff and legless local *moai.* It could be a sort of missing link to the art of the outside world.

192

We had brought along three tons of dental plaster to make an exact cast of an Easter Island statue, because we knew that the Chilean authorities would not allow us to take one away. We chose a statue lying rockbound in the quarry (*left*), and the casting of the thirty-one–foot giant was so lifelike when erected in the Kon-Tiki Museum that the Chilean embassy sent a representative to make sure that we had not smuggled out a real statue.

Geographically, Easter Island could be considered the Navel of the World of stone men. The few crude stone *Tiki* of Polynesia were all standing figures with hands on their bellies. But *kneeling* stone giants were typical of the pre-Inca cult site at Tiahuanaco. Two crude prehistoric specimens now flank the entrance to the modern village church there. Two more, beautifully carved and well preserved, were found on top of a megalithic platform in Tiahuanaco and brought to a sunken plaza in La Paz. They have the same upturned face, with goggle-shaped, bulging eyes and goatee, and kneel in the same pose, their hands on their thighs. When he described this resemblance in his report, Arne concluded:

"As we have pointed out, the similarity between this Tiahuanaco statue from South America and our specimen is so great that it can scarcely be put down to chance, but must be ascribed to a close relationship, which implies that there is a connection between these two examples of ancient stone sculptures in the Andes and on Easter Island."

Another surprise awaited us and the island population when Bill started to dig behind the Inca-like wall in Vinapu. On the inland side he discovered a large sunken temple plaza surrounded by earthen embankments. Inside this enclosure he found what at first seemed to be the corner of a rectangular block of red scoria. It proved instead to be a tall and slim pillar-shaped image with rectangular cross section, representing a body with arms resting on the stomach and stunted legs. A deep hole had been cut into the region of the heart and the head was broken and missing, but when set up the red image fragment still stood eleven and half feet tall.

193

Dr. Carlyle Smith, a member of our expedition, examined a number of the *ahu* walls and the statues that had been thrown down from them during the intertribal feuds. He made a drawing of the great statue at Ahu Te-Pito-te-Kura, shown before it was overthrown, with a human figure to scale. He also showed the dimensions of the biggest statue still lying in the quarry as it would look if erected, minus the topknot. Remember that these colossi were intended to stand on the top platform of an *ahu*.

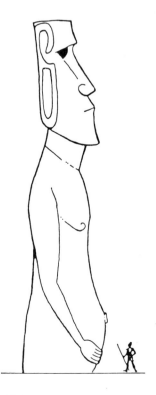

Again, there was nothing to match this kind of monument in Oceania. Again, the statues of Tiahuanaco were brought to mind. The authority on the archaeology of Tiahuanaco, W. C. Bennett, had grouped the local stone monuments into three kinds: The ornate and conventionalized classical monument, the realistic kneeling statue, and what he called the "Squared-Pillar-Type Statue." The latter was the most common local form, and typical for the Tiahuanaco-inspired territory. The bearded image—known as Kon-Tiki in Tiahuanaco itself—is of this type, and it is also carved from selected red scoria and placed, as on Easter Island, in a sunken temple court next to an elevated, sun-oriented, megalithic platform. Typical for most of the squared-pillar-type statues in the Andes is that they have their arms flexed and their hands placed in a peculiar pose on the abdomen, as did that on Easter Island.

According to Bennett, the kneeling statue and the squared-pillar type are the two oldest forms in Tiahuanaco; the ornate and conventional classical monuments are a later local innovation. Markham and Macmillan Brown had compared them to the common *moai* on Easter Island, but, taking our new discoveries into consideration, it now occurred to me that the famous classical monuments within the two areas did not descend one from the other, but were of common ancestry. The link should be searched for in the earlier period, the one to which the kneeling- and the pillar-type statues belong. In his group of squared-pillar–type monuments, Bennett also includes a number of squared heads without bodies. As on the square heads of Easter Island, the artists had emphasized the large eyes, and the nose had been carved in high relief and split into curving eyebrows ending as pouches on the cheeks. Ears were absent or unimportant. Thus the hitherto unknown types of Easter Island stone monuments that were now turning up with the aid of spade and trowel coincided even in diversity and quite specific detail with the stone-shaping art of the pre-Classical period in Tiahuanaco.

Bill then made another discovery at Vinapu, in front of the sun-oriented seaward wall that faced away from the plaza with the pillar statue. Abutting the fine masonry of this wall he excavated a contiguous group of stone cists containing cremation burials. We later discovered cremation burials in front of several other *ahu*. Cremation was not a Polynesian custom, but it was frequently practiced in South America. The islanders' memories of their old traditions were once again correct: there had been two different kinds of burials on their island.

The most important discovery Bill made at Vinapu, probably the most important piece of detective work of the entire expedition, was to identify two distinctly separate cultural periods on Easter Island prior to the final period of civil war and destruction. Many visitors had noted that the *ahu* had been rebuilt, but found no system in the apparent chaos. In the course of his excavations, Bill discovered a dramatic change in religious architecture following an intermission between what he termed the Early and Middle Periods. The Late Period was the time of civil war and destruction. The Inca-like wall facing the sea was built in the Early Period, when the shrine seemed to have been simply a large, elevated platform filled with rubble and faced with the huge, beautifully fitted slabs. It was not designed for, nor able to support, gigantic *moai*. In this Early Period, the statues may have stood in the sunken court, or were of more modest dimensions. But the Early Period came to an end long before the Middle Period began. There was an interval when the shrine was left unattended. In his report Bill explains in detail how silt and weathering during that interval changed the original building. He concluded:

"After Early Period times the structure appears to have been abandoned for

Another of the expedition's archaeologists, Dr. William Mulloy, excavated a buried monument of a kind that no one had ever seen before on any Pacific island. It was the trunk of a shattered statue with navel, arms and greatly shrunken legs, but with the head missing (*above*). The cross section of the pillarlike figure had the rounded, rectangular form so characteristic of the pre-Inca stone giants of the whole Tiahuanaco area around Lake Titicaca.

The third of the expedition's American archaeologists, Edwin N. Ferdon *(top right)*, led the dig at the cult site of Orongo. There he discovered the overgrown remains of an ancient solar observatory, which contained a small statue of the chief god, Make-Make, as well as traces of a pyre that proved he had been worshiped with fire. All these hitherto unknown forms of Easter Island statuary that were now excavated appeared to date from the island's Early Period.

Evidently also from the Early Period were some statues of hard dark basalt that had often been smashed or dragged away from the *ahu* where they had originally stood (*center*). These stone images from the Early Period were generally shorter and more broadly built, and the tops of their heads were rounded because they had never worn the red topknot typical of the Middle Period. In several cases the heads of such early statues had been struck off and contemptuously used as building blocks in *ahu* walls of the Middle Period (*bottom*).

During the excavations at the southeast corner of the volcano Rano Raraku, where tradition holds that the first quarry was located, Skjølsvold found the most astonishing of all the monuments discovered by the expedition. This statue, which must be a product of the Early Period, proved to be a full-length figure of a man with trunk, arms and legs. It had nothing in common with the familiar *ahu* images of Easter Island. Here Skjølsvold views the goatee and staring eyes of the giant, which lay with bent knees and its arms along its thighs instead òf the standard stance with hands on belly. When the colossus was raised (*opposite page*), it was seen to be a fat, rounded male figure, kneeling with buttocks on heels and the soles of the feet to the rear. Nothing like it had ever been seen in Polynesia.

a considerable period, while forces of erosion created changes.''

This remark brought to mind the truth of the islanders' own traditional account: that Hotu Matua had found the island abandoned by Machaa or others, who had left behind their system of paved roads. Bill then stated:

"The Middle Period reconstruction began with the structure in this advanced state of ruin. The people who carried out the repairs were clever stonemasons who did an enormous amount of work, but their techniques were different from that of the Early Period people. Their masonry shows neither the technical perfection nor the artistry of the earlier masons. Their masonry was done principally with small, easily moved and rarely cut stone, though their work with statue bases, statues, and topknots shows skill and willingness to handle large stones at least equal to that of the Early Period. They were not reluctant to reuse a stone without modifying it to obscure its former function. They were apparently not perturbed by juxtaposed incongruities in masonry type. They were apparently not interested in recreating the *ahu* as a work of art or in harmonious details of excellent masonry, but rather in creating a solid base for statues in the quickest and most practical way possible. It would seem that the attention at this period was focused on the statues rather than the *ahu*.''

What Bill discovered about the distinct periods was independently confirmed through the excavations of the other archaeologists. Ed found evidence of an Early and Middle Period when excavating the Orongo ceremonial site, again with signs of abandonment in between. The bird-men were a feature of the Middle Period, when the importance of the sun and the Make-Make masks became less noticeable. Bird-man reliefs on the Orongo cliffs done in that period were even found to be carved right across earlier Make-Make masks and feline motifs.

Carl trenched and studied seven important ahu, and also confirmed Bill's observations. The prehistory of Easter Island could be divided into Early, Middle, and Late Periods. He was not tempted to excavate Ahu Naunau next to our camp in Anakcna, but observed:

"The accumulation of sand hampered efforts to interpret fully the architectural sequence of Ahu Naunau. The occurrence of facing stones typical of the

Early Period, and the inclusion of the stone head resembling that of the statue with legs at Rano Raraku, in a Middle Period wall, argues for the presence of an Early Period structure on the site."

The Late Period activity at the various *ahu* had consisted of simply overthrowing the statues and depositing the bones of the deceased underneath the fallen giants or beneath a carpet of rough stones thrown up on the sloping Middle Period ramp. As Carl discovered, the use of caves as dwelling places was also a feature of the Late Period. His excavations of a number of these caves showed that they were not used as dwellings until shortly before the arrival of the European explorers. The people of the Early and Middle Periods led well-organized lives, lived in houses, and were not cave dwellers. What Carl termed "the *mataa* horizon" after the presence of *mataa*, obsidian spearpoints, was typical of the cave-dwelling era, and purely a Late Period phenomenon. Obsidian was chipped for tools in earlier times, but not used for weapons. There was no evidence of warfare during or between the Early and Middle Periods. Yet Carl, too, found evidence of an abandonment of the Early Period *ahu* before they were utilized for a different purpose at the beginning of the Middle Period.

If we combine facts with the traditional stories of the islanders, we may say that the "brothers" Machaa and Hotu Matua, who sailed at intervals from the same coast without encountering each other, represented the Early and Middle Periods, while the Late Period began with the battle in the Poike trench. Had people from the Early Period left the island before another population group, one with a basically similar culture, replaced them in the Middle Period? Had the mythical Machaa established a temporary settlement, with walls and images like those in Tiahuanaco, before his successor, the substantially historical Hotu Matua, followed in his wake, perhaps having embarked from somewhere further up the coast? Perhaps the second wave of settlers arrived generations after the first, guided by legends that survived in the homeland about the whereabouts of the island. Certainly the Middle Period bird-man cult was as typical for the reed-ship navigators of the north Peruvian desert coast as were the Early Period masonry and the kneeling and pillarlike stone men typical of Tiahuanaco.

Where did the Polynesians come into this sequence of periods? Métraux had found scarcely a trace of them in his survey of the local culture. Archaeology supported the evidence of tradition and ethnology. They had come without deeply affecting religious or secular architecture. They forsook what they had and accepted what they found without interrupting or changing local affairs. They must have come at some time during the Middle Period, however, for they were there when the Late Period of civil wars began, and nobody was there when the Middle Period began.

No one was more fascinated by island traditions than Father Sebastian Englert. He firmly believed that the battle at Poike, which put a sudden end to the image making and started the Late Period of civil wars, had actually taken place. He had collected from descendants of the Long-ears a genealogy of twelve names dating back to the generation of Ororoine who had escaped from the pyre. At Father Sebastian's suggestion, we decided to dig some test pits into *Ko-te-Umu-o-te-Hanau-Eepe,* "The Earth-Oven-of-the-Long ears." Carl first inspected the vestiges of the legendary trench, which separated the cliff-girded Poike peninsula from the rest of the island. Though earlier visitors had considered it a natural feature, Carl wrote: "To the archaeologically oriented observer, the site stands out in sharp contrast with natural features, and is readily identifiable as the work of man."

Our curiosity was fired. The islanders were visibly excited when Carl organized

The case of the kneeling statue. The rectanguloid pillar statue had its only counterpart in South America and not on any other island in the Pacific. Kneeling statues were among the most typical monuments of pre-Inca time. Two were removed long ago from temple ruins and placed on either side of the church door in the village of Tiahuanaco *(top left)*, and two others were found by archaeologists on top of an *ahu*-like stone platform in the cult center itself and moved to a square in La Paz *(top right)*. It was not only the kneeling attitude with hands on knees that matched the new find on Easter Island, but also the facial expression, the characteristic shape of the eyes, mouth, and the goatee. Skeptics pointed out that ribs were a peculiar and essential feature of the kneeling giants from Tiahuanaco. The Easter Island archaeologist Sergio Rapu found fragments of a kneeling image buried deep in the sand by the great *ahu* at Anakena. One from the Early Period on Easter Island had clearly marked ribs.

digging parties to excavate six deep test pits at intervals along the legendary defense line. This line showed up as a long series of elongated depressions, each roughly a hundred yards long and ten to fifteen yards wide. These trenches followed one another at narrow, five-yard intervals right across the peninsula. And on the upper side of each depression lay a mound formed by dirt removed from the trench. Erosion had flattened almost everything, reducing some depressions to barely perceptible hollows, while others remained up to ten feet deep. Everyone on the island agreed that these moats and ramparts were the remains of the Long-ears' defense position.

We watched the islanders working impatiently at top speed with picks and shovels until they disappeared from sight into ever-deepening holes, where nothing was found but more brown sandy soil. All of a sudden, one after another excited face appeared above the rims of the holes, and voices shouted for us to come and look. Here was evidence of the pyre! Picks and shovels were exchanged for small digging trowels, and up came bits of charcoal and ashes, remains of burnt branches and brushwood. Father Sebastian in his white gown ran alongside the trench as triumphant and excited as the islanders themselves, watching as a larger section of the prehistoric structure was re-excavated. The sides of the four walls in each pit were found to be banded with black and red deposits composed of charcoal and burned earth.

The layer of burnt wood was hit upon long before the floor of the manmade trench was reached. We had to dig another five-and-a-half feet before we hit rock bottom. The trench had thus been more than half filled with windblown sand and silt by the time the pyre was prepared. The generation that prepared it could thus not have been the original constructors of the artificial moat. Here again was evidence of a long period of abandonment between the original building of a structure and its use in a later period. Through a stroke of luck, Carl was able to ascertain the date for both periods. Under one of the earthen ramparts he found the remains of a small campfire. The charred bits of wood must have been quickly covered up by dirt thrown up from the trench when it was orignally dug, otherwise they would have been washed down the slope by the first rain. A radio-carbon test on these trapped pieces of charcoal gave a reading of A.D. 386, plus or minus a hundred years. This antedated the assumed settlement of Easter Island by a millennium. There was no evidence of any fire in the trench itself above the thick layer of ashes and charred wood lying five-and-a-half feet below the bottom, and thus dated from a time when the deep trench was half filled with silt. A carbon date for this pyre came out as A.D. 1676, allowing the same margin for error. This was, almost to the decade, the date Father Sebastian had predicted on the basis of twelve generations since Ororoine.

Human bones could not have been preserved in this kind of soil. Three sling stones were found, however, one imbedded in the burnt layer. No *mataa*. This confirmed the idea that the obsidian javelin was a Late Period innovation. The sling, unknown in the west Pacific, was known in Polynesia and was the principal fighting weapon of ancient Peru. Carl suggested it might have been a Middle Period weapon on Easter Island.

Tradition had triumphed over theory. Father Sebastian rejoiced, together with the islanders. The Poike trench was manmade not by the Middle Period Long-ears, who later used it, but by their Early Period predecessors, who built it and left it unused.

The Easter Islanders had known about the disastrous Poike pyre all the time, but we got the credit for finally proving thcm right. And I, as leader of the expe-

The mayor of Easter Island, Pedro Atan, was a goldmine of information to the first Norwegian expedition. Father Sebastian Englert, a specialist in Easter Island genealogy, identified Pedro Atan as the last of twelve generations of direct patrilineal descendants of Ororoine, the survivor of the massacre of the Long-ears at the Poike trench. The mayor confided to the author that his father and grandfather had told him how the Long-ears had organized their statue-raising operations. He had hitherto kept this secret to himself because nobody had asked *him* about it!

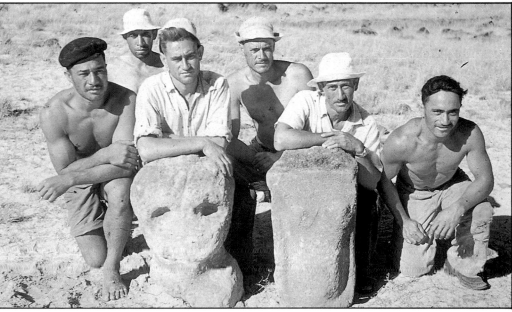

The main collaborators of Pedro Atan. Red hair was common among the Long-ears according to the first Europeans, and several of the mayor's children had red hair, including his son Juan, seen below leaning on an Early Period stone head. Pedro himself is seen leaning on a headless female trunk that was to be reunited with its head thirty years later (p. 246).

dition, who even knew some terms in Polynesian from my year in the Marquesas, was given credit for what the archaeologists had discovered below ground. Father Sebastian told us that the islanders came to him and insisted that I was a reincarnation of Hotu Matua. How else could I have gone straight to Anakena and put up our camp right at Hotu Matua's site? How else could I have come ashore and greeted them with *kaoha,* the salute their ancestors used in former times, before the missionaries came and taught them the Tahitian greeting *ia-ora-na.* They did not know that I learned the word *kaoha* in the Marquesas, which was probably the home of their Polynesian ancestors before they came to work with the Long-ears. But superstition could no longer be suppressed when we began to dig up the kneeling statue and other buried remains from an earlier period, relics that were unknown to everybody on the island. I had indeed "come back" with my followers to dig up what we knew was there!

One of those who seemed most impressed was the native island mayor, Pedro Atan. He looked more like a Palestinian than someone from Polynesia. Father Sebastian pointed him out as one of the few direct descendants of the Long-ears. He was the grandson of Tuputahi, who took the family name Adan, after Adam, when Christianity was introduced in the last century. The names of each of his forefathers were preserved, right up to Ororoine, the Long-ear spared from the pyre twelve generations ago.

The mayor was sitting on the floor, chipping away at a bird-man figure, when I entered his modest village home. He was known as by far the best sculptor on the island. He beamed with pride and his thin lips trembled when I told him I came because I knew he was the elder of the Long-ears. He was an amazing character. His brain was as sharp as his face, and he was always prepared to find a solution to any problem.

Did he know how his ancestors carved and raised the big *moai?* Of course. If he knew, was he willing to show me? Yes, how big did I wish the *moai* to be? If it was to be big, he would need help from some of the men who were Long-ears only on their mothers' side, for he had only three brothers who were pure Long-ears like himself. When I asked him why, if he knew, he had not revealed his secret to all those who had asked the same question before me, he answered calmly, "Nobody asked *me.*"

In my subsequent dealings with the Easter Islanders I was to understand that this reply was symptomatic of the local character. They don't give away anything precious unless you ask for it directly. And anything hidden and not known to others is a treasure. Mental hoards were as real to them as money in the bank is to foreigners. I was also to learn that ancestral spirits were as much part of local society as in the days of Métraux and Routledge. To Pedro Atan and his associates, the *aku-aku* were as real as the flora and fauna of the island itself.

Consequently Pedro Atan did not go directly to the quarries with his men to show us how to carve a *moai.* Their work required ritual preparations that were more serious than we had at first thought. One night Pedro came to our camp with all his relatives, old and young, of both sexes. We were all half asleep, and crawled out of our tents into the darkness to witness a strange spectacle. Never had we heard singing like this. It was out of the past. Beautiful, rhythmic, magically hypnotic. The islanders were sitting in the dark near our tents, singing in harmony in a high-pitched treble while beating rhythmically on the ground with stone picks and double-headed clubs. The singing group was flanked by two children wearing paper bird masks with long, projecting beaks, imitating bird-men as they nodded and swayed to the music while a beautiful young girl danced in slow motion in front of the others. They performed the ritual song of the stone-

One night all the members of the expedition were wakened in their tents by the strangest choral singing any of us had ever heard—beautifully harmonized, but almost eerie and totally unlike any music we knew. It was the mayor and his family, who had come to perform an ancient ceremony essential to the success of their enterprise the following day, when they proposed to demonstrate how the work in the quarry was done. A child danced in a paper bird-man mask.

Early next morning the mayor and his closest relatives had collected a large number of the stone pickaxes that had lain strewn about the quarry ever since the day work suddenly stopped. They held the picks in their hands, and when the points wore down they sharpened them again simply by shipping off pieces with another stone axe of the same kind. The name for these tools on Easter Island was *toki*, and *toki* is also the ancient word for stone axe among the aboriginal population of North Chile.

After three days' work, the outline of a statue had begun to take shape in the cliffs of Rano Raraku. No tools were used except the hard basalt *toki* and water bottles made of gourds. The workers constantly sprayed the surface with water to soften up the rock, the interior of which was very hard.

203

When Pedro Atan claimed that he also knew how the statues had been erected without modern technical aids, the author challenged him to prove it by doing it. A stone giant lying face down close to the camp was selected for the experiment. It lay in a particularly awkward position, with its head pointing downhill toward the former temple court, and was to be erected on a platform that was higher than its base. Using no tools except poles and rocks of all shapes and sizes, the descendants of the Long-ears began to lift the head of the statue by such tiny increments that we could hardly see any movement at all. Small stones were wedged underneath and were gradually replaced by larger ones in ever-increasing numbers. Soon the giant lay horizontally.

Supported by stones that, from now on, were constantly piled under its head and shoulders, the giant slowly reared up until its huge empty eye sockets began to gaze out over the camp.

The pile of stones had reached the giant's chin when its base began to butt against the great rock on which it had once stood. Carefully controlled with draglines, the statue was now tilted to a vertical position.

When all the piled stones had been removed, no clue remained as to how the statue had been raised.

It had taken eighteen days for twelve men using only poles and rocks to re-erect a medium-sized Easter Island statue. The stocky giant now standing atop its ancient *ahu* at the east end of Anakena Bay, where King Hotu Matua had first come ashore, was the first to be seen by the eyes of modern men in its original position. Many other statues were later re-erected on the island. Accustomed as we all were to seeing the eyeless heads of the unfinished statues standing half buried at the foot of Rano Raraku, seeing the deep eye sockets gazing out over our camp gave us a weird feeling. Why did the stone giants have hollow eye sockets like those of a skull when they had noses, lips, and ears like living men? This was a mystery that was to remain unsolved for many years. When the work was finished it was Lazaro Hotu, the mayor's second-in-command, who posed with the author, because the Chilean warship had arrived for its annual visit, and the mayor and half the village had taken to their beds with influenza.

cutters for the first time outside the family circle. We were later to hear it many times. The song was not to any *aku-aku,* but, the performers assured us, to the supreme god.

Early next morning we found the mayor and his men in the quarries, collecting some of the old stone picks that lay discarded everywhere. They sharpened the points by striking off chips, and after a private ceremony among themselves behind a rock, six men set to work as if they had never done anything else but carve *moai.* The mayor outlined the profile of a statue about sixteen feet long on the vertical wall of an empty niche, and then the cutting began. Each man, a pointed basalt pick clenched in his hand, hit the hard volcano wall with his even harder stone pick, so that the dust whirled around and tiny bits fell to the ground. They first pecked vertical parallel lines, to enable them to knock off the ridges in between with greater ease. Water from gourd bottles was splashed on the rock at intervals to soften it. The volcanic tuff was easy to work on the surface, where rain had caused erosion. But it seemed as hard as flint inside—as the Spaniards had found when the *moai* sent out sparks when hit with an iron pick.

By the third day, we began to see the complete contour of the *moai.* We did not have enough time to see them finish the carving, but calculated that it would take about a year for a medium-sized *moai.* There had to be elbowroom between the sculptors, who stood side by side, which meant that the number of men who could work on each statue at one time was very limited.

When next the Long-ears were asked to show us how their ancestors erected the giant statues, they again agreed to do so. The mayor offered to re-erect the lonely colossus that lay face down at the foot of an *ahu* right beside our tent. It lay in an awkward position, head pointing downhill on the ramp. Again the Long-ears came at night, and performed an equally gripping but quite different ceremony. This time a deep hole was dug in the ground, and the mayor's brother stood inside it stamping rhythmically with his bare feet, producing an eerie hollow drumming, which helped to create a truly underground atmosphere. Again, an old crone led the choir in her high, shrill voice, while the young beauty danced like a nymph. We understood the refrain: A *moai* was to be erected on the *ahu* at Anakena at Kon-Tiki's command. *Kon-Tiki* was the name I had received from the moment we had landed on the island.

And the *moai* was erected. Twelve men toiled for eighteen days to get the twenty-ton giant back up on top of the *ahu* where it had formerly stood. They used nothing but their muscles, poles, and a quantity of stones. By prying up first one side and then the other in jerks that resulted in almost invisible movements of the giant, they put progressively larger stones underneath it, until the colossus lay on top of a huge stone pile taller than they were. Then they transferred their activity to the image's head, building up more piles of stones under the face and shoulders until the *moai* tilted on end of its own weight and stood gazing out over our camp with deep empty eye sockets.

When I asked the successful mayor how the statues had been moved the long distance from the quarries, he answered, with natural conviction, "The *moai* walked."

These people had been giving that same answer to the same question ever since the first missionaries had asked it. I did not, of course, take the answer seriously, and asked if that ancestors had a more worldly manner of moving heavy stones. Yes, indeed: for smaller stones they used a *miro manga erua.* And

When the mayor was asked how the Long-ears had transported the statues for miles in all directions across the island, he made the same reply that Europeans had been hearing for hundreds of years: the statues had "walked" to their appointed places. The author at first interpreted this as a sign that the technique had been lost, and that the islanders had invented a myth to cover their ignorance. On his own initiative, the author made an experimental attempt to drag a medium-sized statue on a forked pole sled which, according to the mayor, had been used to transport smaller stones. It took the united efforts of a hundred and eighty islanders to drag the statue a short way across the sand, and everybody was happy—except the mayor and elders of the island, who stubbornly insisted that according to their ancestors the statues had not been dragged but had walked erect.

Pedro Atan made a sort of y-shaped sledge out of a forked tree. But now he said he needed the whole village to come and help pull. With the governor's permission, and following Pedro's advice as how to best recruit labor, we invited all those who could ride a horse to come and eat two oxen and a cartload of sweet potatoes, which the Long-ears baked in an earth-oven near our camp. We found it took a hundred and eighty islanders to pull a less-than-medium-size *moai* over the sand.

"This was not the way it was done," said the islanders.

Leonardo was the name of one of those who argued that the stones had walked in an upright position. It sounded so meaningless that I would long since have forgotten the episode had I not written it down in my own book on the expedition at the time.

"But, Leonardo," I said, "how could they walk when they had only heads and bodies and no legs?"

"They wriggled along like this," said Leonardo, and gave a demonstration by edging himself along the rock with feet together and stiff knees.

The Long-ears had every reason to be triumphant when they had shown us and the entire island population that they knew how their ancestors had erected the stone colossi. Only two logs were used to erect a twenty-ton statue. But this revived an old question: Did the ancient Easter Islanders have access to wood? Métraux's view had been that the giant statues and masonry walls were created of stone because of the local lack of wood. But had the island always been as barren as it was today? The islanders insisted that their ancestors spoke of great forests. Their grandparents had told as much to the first missionaries. Were these claims based on fact or fiction?

This was one of the most important questions we hoped to answer by bringing the first modern pollen-boring equipment to the island. Professor Dr. Olof H. Selling, Director of the palaeobotanical department of the Swedish Museum of Natural History of Stockholm, had taught me how to drill for pollen samples to a depth of twenty-five feet in the swamps around the crater lakes. Selling later examined the stratified deposits from Rano Raraku and Rano Kao under a microscope, and was able to determine that the vegetation found by the first humans who reached Easter Island was different from what it is today. Easter Island had formerly been covered by a forest flora, including trees that later became extinct. Among the surprising discoveries was pollen from several species not known to have grown on any Pacific island. One was an unidentifiable type of palm, another a coniferous *Ephedra*, native to South America. The palm had been so common that its pollen filled every cubic millimeter of the bottom strata in the Rano Raraku crater swamp.

Dr. Selling could demonstrate that the original forest disappeared after the arrival of man. Soot particles from vegetation fires began to appear in the swamp deposits at the time the forest vegetation gradually disappeared. The fires were probably caused by man, who needed to make space for agricultural settlements, and to gain access to the naked rock of the quarries. The destruction was later so effective that palms and other forest trees were lost, and only pollen from grass and spores from ferns blew into the crater lakes. Science had thus been able to confirm what most foreigners had so far doubted—although the islanders had always held it to be true: There had been forests on Easter Island in the days of their ancestors.

While we drilled in the crater swamps to collect soil samples with pollen from Easter Island's former vegetation, our expedition doctor, Emil Gjessing, sampled blood from all those islanders who, according to Father Sebastian, were of pure local lineage. With the ship's refrigeration system, we were able to deliver fresh blood at 4°C to the Commonwealth Serum Laboratory in Melbourne. This would permit the identification of blood genes never previously studied from the East Pacific. Hitherto the lack of refrigerated samples had prevented identification of anything but A-B-O groups, but now we could secure refrigerated blood samples from several islands in the eastern fringe of Polynesia. When R.T. Simmons and his Melbourne colleagues received our material, they could study the A-B-O groups (including A_1 and A_2) as well as the M-N-S, Rh, P, Le^a, Fy^a and K groups, and compare them to blood groups from people across the Pacific. The results they published in 1955 buried many wild theories about Pacific Ocean relationships. They concluded that "there is a close genetic relationship between American Indians and Polynesians," and "no similar relationship is evident when Polynesians are compared with Melanesians, Micronesians, and Indonesians except mainly in adjacent areas of direct contact."

The discovery that Polynesia was genetically similar to America, while the rest of Oceania was similar to Asia, was so unexpected that an independent analysis of new blood samples from Easter Island was conducted by an international work group consisting of E. and A. Thorsby, J. Colombani, J. Dausset, and J. Figueroa. They reached the same conclusion: the blood genes pointed clearly to aboriginal America.

While we were still drilling for pollen in the totora-covered edges of the crater lakes, some islanders arrived who had the governor's permission to harvest reeds for their floor mats. One of them was Leonardo Pakarati, whose four older brothers were fishermen. Father Sebastian said I ought to talk to them if I wanted to know anything about ancient boats and fishing. I asked the Pakarati

The mayor's younger brother, Adan Atan, like Pedro a full-blooded Long-ear, was the first islander bold enough to admit members of the expedition to a secret family grotto. Like Mrs. Routledge, Skottsberg, Lavachery and Métraux, the author had begun to doubt that such grottoes existed when the floodgates began to open— first Adan Atan came forward, and later other families started to bring out their treasures. The mayor himself, however, who claimed to own Ororoine's cave where the very finest sculptures were hidden, was so superstitious that he never showed us his own cave; instead he began to make new replicas of the ancient sculptures, which, he claimed, his grotto contained. The sculptures in some of the caves were covered with dust and cobwebs, or lay wrapped in reed mats so brittle that they crumbled at a touch, while others were well cared for and evidently in use, with ancient sculptures placed on new reed mats.

As more and more of the Easter Islanders revealed the secrets of their family caves to the author, an almost incredible wealth of curious lava sculptures began to come to light. Their owners were often remarkably ignorant of what the figures represented or what the purpose of this art form had been. An outstanding exception was the stone skull with one or more depressions in the crown *(top right)*, which recurred frequently and was always referred to as the "key" to the cave. It was a kind of magical guardian, and was usually the sculpture one was given before being allowed to crawl into the grotto. According to Adan and the mayor, the depressions used to be filled with the powdered bones of a deceased relative, but we were never able to confirm this. At the right of the bottom row of pictures is a kind of sphinx, a long-tailed quadruped with a human head. To the left of it is a whale or other sea-monster shaped like a boat, bearing on its back a typical Easter Island house *(hare paenga),* and on its tail an equally typical pentagonal cooking oven *(umu).* Under its belly, on either side, project three round balls. The owner could not explain what any of all this signified. In the top row is the bust of a woman carrying a fish in a rope across her shoulders. This fine sculpture was later stolen from the exhibits in the Kon-Tiki Museum.

brothers to make me a *pora,* a specimen of the one-man reed floats used to visit the bird islets. They were very pleased to do it. They cut totora reeds in the crater lake, and made excellent rope out of *hau-hau,* the strong fibers of hibiscus bark. A few days later, when the reeds were dry, each man made a tusk-shaped water-craft just like those of Peru, and, clinging to the thicker end while kicking water, they began swimming about. First in the lake, then in the waves of the open ocean.

Father Sebastian had learned from some of the old people that in former times they made large, flat-bottomed barges of reeds. The principle was that of the *pora,* but some of them were huge, like Hotu Matua's craft, the one that could carry a couple of hundred people. These were the *vaca poepoe,* or raft-ships, and vastly superior to the *vaka ama,* or canoes. Father Rousel in the last century was told of great *vaca poepoe* that could carry four hundred passengers. They were curved, with a lofty bow raised like a swan's neck, while the stern, equally high, was split in two parts. This was precisely the way the huge reed-ships looked that, with the bird-men, were shown on jars from pre-Inca Peru. And: the reed was the same.

The Pakarati brothers were sure that the ships shown on the *moai* and on the ceilings in Orongo were *vaca poepoe.* And to everybody's excitement they built us a small one with raised bow and stern, resembling those seen on Lake Titicaca today. The four brothers climbed on board and paddled out of Anakena Bay. The little *vaca poepoe* took the ocean swells with ease and rode each wave like a swan.

"Our grandparents have told us of boats like these," said the mayor, with tears in his eyes. "I feel it here," he added, thumping his chest with emotion.

There were many reasons for what happened next. Eyraud, Routledge, Lavachery, and Father Sebastian had all heard about secret caves filled with old images, but none had ever seen one. We had better luck. Father Sebastian represented the church that had told the islanders to destroy all pagan heirlooms. Thus they could never show him their forbidden heritage. The Franco-Belgian expedition, as Lavachery later put it, brought with them nothing to encourage barter, nor were they "attributed supernatural prestige." They discovered too late that the islanders concealed secrets from them of which even their own guides had been ignorant. Earlier, Mrs. Routledge had been handicapped by linguistic barriers and by being isolated in her hut near the quarries. By the time we arrived, we had members of all the island families working for us in our camp and we were able to converse fairly fluently, since we all shared the same simplified Spanish vocabulary.

It was the Long-ears who revealed the secret. But not Pedro Atan, who was so superstitious that even after telling me he would bring me to his family cave, which he said was the most important on the island, he would always back out at the last moment. But he did encourage his younger brother, Adan Atan, and his right-hand helper, Lazara Hotu, who had Long-ear blood himself, to reveal their secrets. And others followed. It would be hard to forget all the nights I stole away in the dark, alone or accompanied by one of my expedition members, on horseback or at the heels of some barefoot Easter Islander who was supposed to guide us to his cave. There were caves *everywhere*. Some were right under our feet in the midst of a stony field—it sufficed to brush away sand or remove a few rocks and the slab that concealed the entrance to an underground chamber would be visible. There were horrible moments during which I had to be lowered down the black coastal cliffs and use toes and fingers to follow some agile islander along tiny ledges, the surf crashing far below us. Nothing can equal the sensation of crawling by flashlight through tunnels so narrow I had to turn my head sideways, feeling as though thousands of tons of rock were pressing on my back and chest as I forced my way through the narrow passages. And then to sit up inside a vaulted room surrounded by barbaric, bizarre and grotesque sculptures of demons, beasts, skulls, monsters, hands, feet, and boat models carved in lava. They were all lying on the floor, or placed neatly on stone shelves covered with totora-reed mats. Some pieces were badly eroded and showed signs of great age; others had been wrapped in reed mats now so brittle that they crumbled to powder at a touch. Some were covered with a fine layer of airborne dust. In some caves lay the skulls or the entire skeleton of buried relatives. A few of these pagan hideouts were tidy and showed every sign of still being held in veneration.

When the village population realized that the secrets of what lay hidden in the family caves were being revealed, a few quietly found their way to our camp at night and presented me with *moai maea* from their own private hiding places. Some truly amazing stone sculptures turned up, often with motifs that surpassed the imaginations of both donor and receiver. But some young men soon found out what was going on, and realized that, as with the wooden figurines, the *rongo-rongo* boards, and the legends about of Hotu Matua, the market could be replenished when the old stuff ran out. They had begun to carve again, but the newness of the carved surfaces and, even more, the poverty of motif and design, were immediately apparent, and trading was halted. This was later regretted, as a sub-

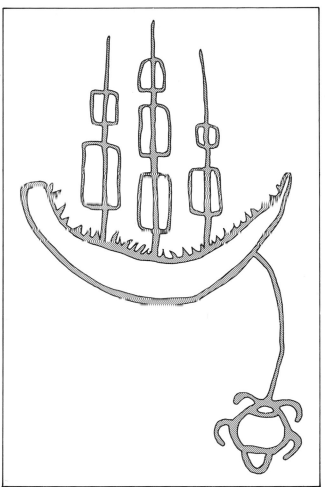

Skjølsvold made one of the most surprising discoveries during his excavations of some of the stone heads at the foot of Rano Raraku. One of the statues looked like a sailor with his ship tattooed on his chest. Only the tops of the masts projected above ground, and a carved rope ran from the ship down over the abdomen to a great turtle beside the navel. The ship had three masts, each with several courses of sail, and the deck was full of small marks which undoubtedly represented men.

Another three-masted vessel was discovered by Ferdon painted on a rock in the ceiling of one of the ceremonial stone houses at Orongo. An odd detail was a round disc painted as a sail on the mainmast, a common symbol of a solar ship in many ancient civilizations. Mulloy found a two-masted sailing ship of the Early Period

in his excavations of the classic walls of Vinapu. And Smith, when he tunneled under the belly of a fallen giant statue at Ahu Te-Pito-tc-Kura, found an engraving of a ship done in such a way that the mast passed straight through the statue's round navel, which thus also assumed the form of a round sail.

The fact that this petroglyph was not of a later date was proved by the rope leading down to the turtle, which must have been quickly covered up by silt from the quarry above after the sculptors had downed tools and the first squalls of rain had washed the debris downhill because there was nobody left to carry it to the dumps at the foot of the volcano.

The old men of Easter Island were positive that the ships discovered on statues and walls represented the great vessels that their ancestors had built of totora reeds. A family of fishermen now offered to construct a miniature of such a vessel. They harvested reeds, dried the stalks in the sun, and built a small boat (top left). The tiny craft rode the waves like a swan, and bore a remarkable resemblance to those still used on Lake Titicaca.

sequent survey showed that a few of what we had assumed to be fakes were actually copies or variations of *moai maea* that were, in fact, definitely old.

Our adventures in the caves are described elsewhere. It took only weeks to put down on paper a book about what we ourselves had experienced on Easter Island. But two decades would pass before I could publish a book illustrating all the peculiar sculptures others had brought from the same lonely island in the period from Captain Cook's visit in 1774 until Salmon stimulated the first production of commercial art in 1886. The vast majority of genuine and properly documented *moai kavakava* and *moai maea* I located in sixty-three museums and

Reed boats of all sizes, from one-man rafts to regular ships, were in use along the coast of Peru from the very earliest times. The largest are usually found depicted in outline drawings on pots from the early Mochica period, while smaller two-man fishing boats made of reeds are also often shown molded as ceramic vessels from the same culture (bottom left), as well as from the later Chimu period.

Double-bladed paddles were quite unknown in Polynesia, but figured prominently in the culture of Easter Island, where ceremonial ao paddles were a status symbol carried by all the important men at ceremonies and meetings (top right, and page 94). A stylized human face was always painted or carved on the top blade, the most characteristic features being the stripes representing the feather bonnet on the head and the hanging plugged earlobes. Double-bladed paddles were used along the coastline of Peru and Chile in pre-Inca times. Miniature paddles, together with miniature models of balsa rafts, were often placed in tombs and are frequently found on the coast below Lake Titicaca.

On the northern coast double-bladed paddles are depicted in Mochica art, which shows chieftains holding them in their hands as a badge of rank just as they did on Easter Island. Here, too, we find a human face represented on the top blade, once again with feather bonnet and big earlobes (bottom right). The connection seems to be obvious, and the Mochica potters have shown us that double-bladed ao paddles were carried by chiefs on the coast of Peru long before Easter Islanders could have brought the idea to South America.

private collections throughout the world and depicted in *The Art of Easter Island* (1975) had been overlooked by science and never published, as they did not conform to the standard motifs known from familiar Easter Island art.

Lavachery came personally to Oslo to study the collection of *moai maea* we brought back from the caves. He was not surprised. He himself had run into unexpected excitement on Easter Island when he had suddenly discovered hundreds of petroglyphs totally different from the early and more stereotyped art forms. The rest of the scientific community was more bewildered, some even loudly skeptical. How could there be such an unrestricted flow of imagination on this one island, when the art of the rest of Polynesia was know to be bound by very restricted conventions? Lavachery revised his earlier view, and in his Introduction to *The Art of Easter Island* he concluded:

"Undoubtedly, as with so many of the problems of this island, we ought to direct our attention toward South America, as Thor Heyerdahl has now taught us to do. Have we nothing to learn as to imagination, variety in motifs, realism and conventionalism, from the unique versatility embodied in the painted or modelled pottery of the early Mochica art in Peru?"

Return to Easter Island: The puzzle falls into place

Thirty years would pass before I returned to Easter Island for further investigation. What tempted me to return was a remarkable discovery made by one of the many young archaeologists who, following us, had tried to wrench more information out of the old ruins.

I had never lost interest in the island, though my contact had mainly been through the archaeologists who had accompanied me on the first expedition. Nearly all had gone back—Arne to do more carbon dating, and Carl repeatedly as a cruise-ship lecturer. Bill and Gonzalo had virtually settled on the island to resume their excavations, as well as reconstruction of *ahu* and *moai*.

My own interest in the Pacific island problems had in the meantime taken a more global approach. The reed ships we had learned about from old Easter Island art and from the living islanders had set me adrift on such craft in other oceans. It was not a vessel unique to the East Pacific, but was the type of watercraft common to three great Old World civilizations: those of Egypt, Mesopotamia, and the Indus Valley. These three, and those of ancient America and Easter Island, were separated from one another by the world's three largest oceans. At least that was what we all felt by looking at a map. But I no longer felt that way: to me, the ocean had *linked* these civilizations together ever since reed ships had been in use. They remained *separated* as before by the Arabian desert, the Peruvian mountains, the Indian jungle, and the icy wastes around the

Bering Straits. Yet early man had fought his way on foot across all these geographical obstacles, carrying his burdens himself. Why should we believe that he lost his courage and his drive for conquest and exploration the moment he became civilized and was able to travel in buoyant craft? For a man who knew his watercraft, traveling took on a new shape when he could sit down with his cargo and let wind and steering-oar do the work.

By the time I decided to go back to Easter Island, I had learned from experience that it is more difficult to build a reed ship correctly than to sail it across any ocean. Reed bundles can be lashed together in many ways for use on a river or lake—but only one specific and highly specialized method gives it the durable curves required to ride and resist ocean waves. This ingenious technique was shared by the widely separated founders of civilization, and survived until historic time in the Middle East and throughout the Inca coastal region. It would have been lost throughout the world, along with the people who knew its secret, had it not been still practiced with undiminished industry by the Indians of Lake Titicaca. On this mountain lake on the borders of Bolivia and Peru, twelve thousand five hundred feet above sea level, the Aymara, Uru, and Quechua Indians have continued their ancient boat-building traditions. Local beliefs held that Kon-Tiki Viracocha first appeared with a flotilla of such totora-reed boats when he and his immigrant party set forth from the Island of the Sun to found Tiahuanaco.

To people who could build reed ships in the correct way, distances between continents shrank to weeks rather than the years or centuries needed by travelers on foot or horseback. I returned to Easter Island with the feeling that the place was not as isolated as it had seemed before. It was part of the planet that had housed the other reed-ship builders. My inexperienced but cosmopolitan companions and I had in recent decades sailed a reed ship from Mesopotamia to the Indus Valley and then on from Asia to Africa. We had sailed another from Africa to America; and an Inca-type balsa raft from there and twice the distance to Easter Island. As a result, I was no longer quite as categorical in rejecting the theories of those who had proposed a relationship between the Old World civilizations and the first settlers of Easter Island. I had sided with Métraux, Lavachery, Buck, and all the others who had ridiculed the theory of the Belgian investigator G. de Hevesy, who believed the Easter Island *rongo-rongo* originated in the Indus Valley, on the very opposite side of the earth. He had pointed to similarities in certain signs appearing in the undeciphered script of these two widely separated areas. Several diffusionists had been so impressed that they proposed prehistoric voyages exactly halfway around the world to bring culture to Easter Island from the Indus Valley, eastward against all prevailing elements. None of us had thought of a voyage in the opposite direction, the way I had now sailed by following prevailing winds and currents. A voyage from east to west, following the sun and all the elements, would bring a reed ship from the Indian Ocean, past the southern tip of Africa into the South Atlantic trade winds and currents, which join the North Atlantic drifts in the Mexican Gulf. The Isthmus of Panama would be the only barrier to the Pacific. This isthmus could have been the gateway from the Old World to Peru and Easter Island.

The parallels between the Indus Valley and Easter Island hieroglyphics to which de Hevesy had pointed had never impressed me, yet his theory of possible common roots seemed less absurd to me than before. In fact, by now I had not only personally crossed the ocean gaps from the Indus Valley to Polynesia on westward voyages in pre-European types of watercraft—I had also revisited the Indian Ocean several times and found unsuspected stepping-stones bringing India closer to America for deep-sea navigators. These stepping-stones were the 1,200 coral atolls of the Maldive archipelago, a lonely oceanic republic scattered like pearls on a string across the equator, far away from any continent. So far away that no archaeologist had been there to search for traces of prehistoric voyagers. Yet they had been there, and in no modest quantities, to judge from what we discovered when we went there to start the first archaeological excavations.

When the president of the Maldives had seen from our voyage with the reed-ship *Tigris* that a Sumerian type vessel could sail anywhere in the Indian Ocean, he invited me to probe the mystery of a long-eared stone statue that had recently been dug up from the sand on one of the Maldive atolls. It was a mystery, since all depictions of the human form were strictly forbidden by the prophet Mohammed, and every single person in the Maldives had been Moslem since Islam was introduced in A.D. 1153, prior to the arrival of the first Europeans. Hence the statue pertained to a still earlier period.

The statue proved to be a large image of Buddha. And when our team of archaeologists started excavation of some strange hills referred to as *hawitta*, they proved to the the ruins of large *stupa*, Buddhist shrines. But not even the Buddhists were the first discoverers of these remote islands: The *stupas* were found to be converted Hindu temples, and images were found both in stone and bronze of Hindu gods and and demons as well as numerous *lingams*—phallus stones. The first seafarers of all to reach these islands, however, were a legendary people recalled throughout the Maldive archipelago as the *Redin*.

To them were ascribed the original building of all the *hawittas*, and excavations revealed that they had first been built as square and terraced pyramidal structures filled with coral rubble and dressed with beautiful stone masonry. The *Redins* had been sun-worshipers, for the walls were exactly oriented to the sun's coordinates and decorated with sun-symbols as well as sculptures of lions and bulls. These earliest architects had also been master masons, who fitted megalithic slabs with the same incredible technique and precision as found in the best walls of ancient Peru and Easter Island. The seafaring *Redin* had even left their self-portraits in the form of stone heads of elegant men with long, slender mustaches and huge blocks in their expanded earlobes. They were Long-ears.

The oldest known practice of ear extension was among the mariners in the prehistoric Indus Valley harbor-city of Lothal, where large numbers of big ear-plugs of the type used by the Long-ears in ancient Mexico, Peru and Easter Island have been found. In the subsequent epoch of India the Hindu rulers adopted the custom, but it was restricted to members of the royal families and images of the Hindu gods. Buddha had long ears because he was born and reared as a Hindu prince, and as Buddhism spread, the images of the long-eared Buddha spread wide and far over modern Asia.

Stone heads and stone statues were common to all the earliest civilizations that spread out of the Middle East and Western Asia, but only those of India and the Maldives had long ears. And it was the stone statues of seafaring Long-ears in western Asia and the Middle East that made me decide to return to Easter Island. The reason for the deep, empty eye sockets on the Easter Island *ahu* images was still a mystery. The small wooden figurines nearly always had inlaid eyes, but the big statues never.

In 1986, when the author returned to Easter Island with a new archaeological expedition, he found many changes. A frightful tsunami, or tidal wave, had thundered into Hotu-iti Bay at the foot of the Rano Raraku volcano and made a complete shambles of everything. The whole row of fallen statues photographed by our first expedition at Ahu Tongariki in 1955 (top) was gone. The huge wall of megalithic blocks and all the statues had vanished without trace, and there were only sea pebbles and waterworn boulders left where the *ahu* had stood. Hitherto unknown small statues from the Early Period, used as fill inside the *ahu* wall, had been exposed. And the giant statues of the Middle Period had been hurled far inland; some were broken and some were lying supine (below).

Inlaid eyes, however, were a common feature shared by many of the oldest images of the Middle East, all the way from Egypt to the Indus Valley. Most of the sculpture produced by the seafaring Hittites of the Mediterranean had inlaid eyes. The Hittites had adopted this practice from the Sumerians of the Persian Gulf, their predecessors and teachers. It was while I was looking at the Hittite stone colossi of Aleppo that I suddenly felt as if a *moai* from Easter Island was gazing down at me, hollow-eyed. Nowhere else but on Easter Island had skilled sculptors cut two deep pits—like those found in a skull—to represent eyes, while on the same image nose, lips, and ears were depicted realistically, as on a living person. Then I noticed another Hittite stone head which had one inlaid eye and one empty eye socket. One eye had obviously been lost.

From that moment I was no longer in doubt. The Easter Island *moai* all had had inlaid eyes from the moment they were erected until they were toppled over. They had lost their eyes when they had fallen face down. I next checked the prehistoric American stone statues in Mexican museums. Several had inlaid eyes precisely like those in the Middle East and the wooden figurines on Easter Island.

But other changes of a more positive nature had also taken place on Easter Island during all the years we had been gone. Close by our old campsite at Anakena, a young archaeologist from Easter Island, Sergio Rapu, had started large-scale excavations round the central *ahu*. He had also raised a whole line of fallen *moai*, so that our own statue no longer stood alone on the neighboring *ahu*. A fine paving of water-polished cobblestones (*top*) had been exposed on the formerly sand-covered temple court in front of the statues.

Two of the members of our first 1955 expedition, William Mulloy and Gonzalo Figueroa, had also returned several times to the island and undertaken extensive reconstruction work in collaboration with the Chilean authorities. They had excavated the inland site of Ahu Akivi and re-erected the seven stone giants that had been toppled there (*bottom*).

I was now so convinced that, in *The Art of Easter Island,* I argued that the finished *moai* of Easter Island must also have had inlaid eyes. I illustrated examples of images from Mexico and Peru with inlaid eyes to show that the custom could have been brought to Easter Island by voyagers from the east. This proposal was vigorously opposed by those who pointed to the fact that inlaying eyes on stone sculptures was not a Polynesian custom.

Two years later the world press announced a new discovery made on Easter Island. An archaeologist named Sergio Rapu declared to an astonished scientific world that the giant *moai* had once had inlaid eyes. He had found a large, complete eye that perfectly fitted the space designed for it. I realized that anybody with the name Rapu had to be of Easter Island origin.

I was soon to learn that Sergio was the bright young boy who was around when some of his relatives dug on our team many years before. He had been brought to Wyoming by Bill Mulloy and, after attending the university there, became an archaeologist. He had returned to his own island and been appointed by the Chilean government as the first native governor of Easter Island.

The irresistible desire to see a staring *moai* brought me back again to the island of the stone giants.

Much had happened on Easter Island in the intervening years. Chile had opened an airstrip linking "The-Navel-of-the-World" to its South American mother country with an airline. A rare miracle had happened; for once a tiny island community had managed to take the long step into the jet age without defeat or loss of dignity. Given modern attire and adequate education, the Easter Islanders had survived and come out on top in a completely new world. They had learned to benefit from the sudden influx of tourism by taking interest and pride in their ancestral art and customs. A couple of small hotels had been built in Hanga-roa and almost every family ran a modest pension or a little shop. Scattered among the homes were a new school, hospital, post office, gas station, a big sports complex, and even two rustic *discothèques* that competed for the islanders' attention. Yet it was still the little village church that drew the biggest crowd and was the focal point of the island's social life. The houses were single-story, and the entire village was almost hidden in a tropical garden of palms and evergreens.

Outside the village the island remained almost unchanged. The open grassland was here and there interrupted by small clusters of newly planted eucalyptus trees and coconut palms, and tourist buses ran along the same dirt roads we had inaugurated with our lonely jeep. There were now some six hundred registered vehicles on the island. The tourists could admire the twenty-seven *moai* re-erected by Mulloy and Figueroa in various parts of the island. The two archaeologists had also reconstructed several *ahu,* restored the Orongo village, and paved the road for the National Park Service set up by Chile to protect the most important sites against tourists. A century of sheep-ranging had ended, so tall grass and underbrush grew everywhere and bush fires frequently ravaged the landscape.

Many young archaeologists had been attracted to Easter Island since our visit, to measure and map monuments and sites, even to excavate some *ahu* and to uncover more varieties of petroglyphs. Further evidence of solar observation and astronomical alignments had been reported. And statistics testified to our suspicion that as time had passed the giant *moai* of the Middle Period were built increasingly higher. The tallest were those that were the last to have left the quarries. A most ambitious project mapping the thousands of prehistoric remains was under way, led by the two Chilean archaeologists Claudio Christino and Patricia Vargas. Through their initiative the University of Chile had built a modest anthropological institute in one part of the village and the island administration had erected a small archaeological museum on the outskirts of Hanga-roa. This was directed by the governor, Sergio Rapu. In spite of the village's modest size, these two scientific units were far apart in every sense of the word. I am personally indebted to both for presenting me with the challenge to return and resume work on the island.

Claudio Christino invited me back as a guest of the Institute, and the University of Chile sponsored the First International Science Congress, which assembled in Hanga-roa in 1984. During this meeting Sergio Rapu showed me the huge eye that fitted so perfectly into its former socket. And he took me to Anakena to show me where it had been discovered. He had dug in the sand around Ahu Naunau, next to our former camp, and, after finding the eye, his team had dug another thirteen feet down without reaching the bottom of the *ahu* wall.

They had stopped digging for fear that the colossal structure would collapse. Its immense blocks now towered high above our heads, with seven re-erected Middle Period statues balancing on top.

After all these years, it was like a dream come true to be back in such a familiar spot and to face the immense wall that had previously been hidden from view. Some thousands of cubic feet of sand had been removed by Sergio's team, leaving a huge depression along the seaward façade, and deep down in the sand where Sergio had stopped working, still half buried, lay the broken heads and torsos of Early Period statues. They were smaller, with rounder heads that were never designed to wear topknots. None of them had long ears, but all had deep eye cavities as if they had once contained inlays.

Sergio's work could not stop there. He seemed to have reached a sort of floor or crust of hard-packed sand, possibly the ground level marking the transition between the Early and the Middle Period. There was more below.

As governor of the island, he had never had time to publish his findings, but those of us who took part in the congress received a briefing illustrated by the objects in his museum. There was the eye. A big disk of dark stone representing the pupil ingeniously slipped into a pocket in a still larger, almond-shaped eyeball carved from white coral. Next to it was a torso fragment of a large statue with ribs, and the lower part of a kneeling statue just like ours, with fat round

221

Even after the end of the first Easter Island expedition, the author had thought a great deal about the purpose of the deep eye sockets on those of the island's stone giants which had been finished and erected on their *ahu* platforms.

He was greatly astonished when, during a trip to the Middle East, he saw a stone head with the same deep eye sockets—a relic of the ancient Hittites. It was the Hittites who taught the Phoenicians to build seagoing ships, first of reeds and later of cedarwood.

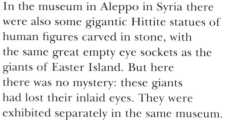

In the museum in Aleppo in Syria there were also some gigantic Hittite statues of human figures carved in stone, with the same great empty eye sockets as the giants of Easter Island. But here there was no mystery: these giants had lost their inlaid eyes. They were exhibited separately in the same museum.

buttocks resting on the heels of its feet, the soles facing the rear. Claudio could tell us that still another complete but badly eroded kneeling statue had been located inside the Rano Raraku crater. It lay in the oldest part of the quarries, just across the crater rim from the one we had found before. Sergio's mutilated image fragments were unquestionably remains from the island's Early Period. His Anakena excavations had shown beyond doubt that the concept of carving kneeling stone giants, otherwise thought to be unique to Tiahuanaco, were present on Easter Island from the time of the first settlers. And the fact that our kneeling specimen had no ribs whereas some, but not all, kneeling statues in Tiahuanaco had them, no longer mattered. Sergio had discovered that even this unexpected feature had been an early element in the monumental sculptures of Easter Island.

There was one more lecturer at the Easter Island congress who was able to report on a significant discovery with direct bearing on sea routes to the island. A British palaeobotanist, John Flenley, had conducted a new series of pollen borings in the crater swamps and confirmed our earlier discovery that the island had formerly been wooded. Like Selling, he had found pollen of a locally unknown palm abundantly represented in his soil samples. According to Flenley, the formerly common Easter Island palm could now be identified as *Jubaea Chilensis,* the gigantic Chilean palm until then never found outside Chile. It was an extremely useful tree, with edible nuts and a colossal trunk of tough, fibrous wood ideal for engineering operations. Endemic to Chile, this palm had not even spread with the coastal current up to Peru. How could it have spread to Easter Island?

Those who had categorically denied that any ocean current existed that would bring drift-voyagers from South America to Easter Island were now faced with

The Hittites could not possibly have influenced Easter Island, but the idea could have spread via an intermediate culture. Was there any such intermediate culture in pre-European America? The author found that several of the advanced cultures in ancient Mexico had been in the habit of putting inlaid eyes in stone images—just like the Hittites. Pupils of black obsidian were placed in eyeballs carved of shell or white stone, which were then inserted in the stone images.

In museums in Peru the author found similar eyes that had fallen out of wooden sculptures, a common phenomenon on Easter Island. In a book on Easter Island art published in 1976 the author put forward the controversial theory that the giants of Easter Island had also had inlaid eyes.

Two years later Sergio Rapu announced the sensational news that he had dug up the first complete eye at Anakena, and that it exactly fitted the eye socket of one of the Middle Period statues lying there.

a dilemma. If this South American palm could not have floated to Easter Island alone, man must have brought the nuts by boat. And if Chilean palm *could* have come by sheer drift long before human voyagers, why could not a boat with people have come the same way?

Two years after the congress, I was back on Easter island for the third time as leader of a joint Norwegian-Chilean archaeological expedition, this time financed by the Kon-Tiki Museum. No sooner had the news about our expedition plans spread to the press than I got a letter from a Czechoslovakian engineer. Pavel Pavel had read my book about our first Easter Island expedition, when the Long-ears showed me how to carve and erect a stone statue. I had believed everything else they had said about the statue, Pavel wrote—why had I not believed them when they said their ancestors made the statues walk?

Pavel had believed it, and made a twenty-ton replica of an Easter Island statue in cement. He had made it walk with the aid of ropes and fifteen friends.

I immediately wrote back. Had he made a *moai* of cement walk, then he could join our expedition if he felt he could do the same with a real Easter Island statue. An urgent reply confirmed his willingness to come, provided I could get him out of Czechoslovakia and into Easter Island, which was a province of Chile. In spite of the political barriers, both countries proved most cooperative and a happy Pavel Pavel was part of our team when Arne Skjølsvold, Gonzalo Figueroa and I landed at Hanga-roa airport in 1986.

El Consejo de Monumentos Nacionales in Santiago, Chile, had granted the necessary permission to let us try to make a statue "walk." We therefore left the continent amply supplied with rope. But before we dared take the risk of seeing a real statue topple and break, we went into the field and examined the bases of the statues that lay abandoned in the quarries and along the prehistoric roads.

The great eye that Sergio Rapu had discovered and identified when it was unearthed by Sonia Haoa, a student of archaeology and like him a native Easter Islander, proved to be a masterpiece of art and craftsmanship. A central disk of dark lava rock was inlaid in a cavity on the inside of the almond-shaped eye of white coral so that the pupil could not fall out, and the whole piece fitted perfectly into the eye socket of the statue. Skeptics who had rejected the theory that the Easter Island giants had had inlaid eyes had argued that it was impossible because the practice of putting inlaid eyes in stone images was unknown in Polynesia. Now they had trouble explaining their origin.

The inlaid eyes of a Hittite statue (*left*) and the similar eyes of an Easter Island *moai* (*right*) are separated by two mighty oceans, with the Isthmus of Panama between them. The distance looks impressive on the map. But we crossed the Atlantic in fifty-seven days in the reed ship *Ra II* and sailed twice the distance from Peru to Easter Island on the balsa raft *Kon-Tiki*. It took the Spaniards a week to cross the Isthmus of Panama on foot, and they built themselves new ships on reaching the far shore. Europe in the Middle Ages never reached the heights attained by the civilizations of antiquity on both sides of the Atlantic.

The bases of those still in the quarries were perfectly flat. As we examined those along the roads, it became abundantly clear that those closest to their point of departure had their bases best preserved, whereas the further the *moai* had been removed from the quarry area the more convex the base had become. There were no signs of wear on any other part of the statue. What we saw supported Pavel's conviction that they must have been moved in an upright position. Some of the statues transported several miles from the quarries had their bases worn so round that they had to be wedged up with stones for balance when set up on an *ahu*. In one case, the base had been so worn away that, on arrival at its *ahu*,

a new pair of hands had to be carved on the belly, as the original pair had ended up too close to the base. This image had four hands.

In certain lights, traces of Routledge's roads could still be detected, and, like her, we were tempted to dig in front and behind some of the fallen roadside images to see what we would find. To our surprise we found that the densely packed surface of broken and crushed lava extended everywhere, but never deeper than a few inches. Below was rich soil—deep black humus that in some cases contained root-holes from former trees, so large that an arm could be put into them. This fertile humus had been produced by the forests of earlier times. The cover of crushed stones and lava boulders that had fooled us and others before us was not the result of volcanic eruption, but the remains of all sorts of walls and cairns torn apart by man and later set throughout the area, then stepped on and kicked around by tens of thousands of sheep, horses and cattle.

During one test excavation we found a large number of stone picks lying in a circle just where one of these lonely roadside giants had stood before it was toppled. Clearly it had been wedged up temporarily with these picks by the transport workers, for fear that the walking image might fall over while they left for a break. This fitted the traditional claim that the *moai* walked for a distance each day and then paused. By digging trenches crosswise behind and in front of these isolated statues we found evidence of hard-packed but unpaved roads. The black humus that formed a belt slightly wider than the image base was as firm and even as if a steamroller had prepared the ground. Obviously, the transport workers had needed no artificial pavement, cuts, or fill over certain stretches. The images had in effect prepared their own way, and wherever possible each giant had followed in the tracks of its predecessors.

It was a great day with an air of suspense and nervous anticipation among the islanders when all was ready for Pavel Pavel to show us how a *moai* could walk. None of the elders doubted that their ancestors had formerly made the statues perform. But their ancestors had *mana* and worked with the help of Make-Make. To us he was the devil, not on our side. Old Leonardo was as sure now as he had been thirty years before: the legless stone busts had walked by wriggling forward from side to side. And again he showed us the motion, with the soles of his feet put together, before we had told him or anybody else about the experiment we were to conduct.

We had selected for our experiment a medium-size statue already re-erected in the field between Rano Raraku and Hotu-iti Bay. Here the terrible tidal wave of 1960 had lifted off the row of fifteen colossal statues on Ahu Tongariki, which no longer existed. The immense building blocks and broken images lay tossed inland in a field covered by ocean boulders. Before we were allowed to start our experiment, our island workmen insisted on pacifying all the invisible *aku-aku* in this haunted area. As soon as the appetizing fumes of pork and sweet potatoes baked in banana leaves in an earth oven tickled our nostrils and satisfied the invisible guests of honor, our work could begin. Leonardo was sitting with his older sister Elodia, the late Father Sebastian's faithful housekeeper, and they were to invoke supernatural support with a monotonous rhythmic song they both knew by heart. Leonardo accompanied their singing by beating time in the air with a string figure held between his hands, resembling some kind of cat's cradle.

Pavel Pavel had two ropes lashed to the top of the statue's head and two others to its base. The upper pair were stretched out to each side and the lower pair

Excavations at Anakena were resumed in 1986 as a joint project of the Kon-Tiki Museum in Oslo and the new archaeological museum on Easter Island named after Father Sebastian Englert. The author's old friend and colleague on previous expeditions, Dr. Skjølsvold, was once again to lead the archaeological investigations. Sergio Rapu had discontinued his excavations when he had uncovered the paving, which had belonged to an *ahu* earlier than the one now visible above ground. We continued to dig deeper and found traces of human habitation at intervals all the way down to bedrock, more than thirteen feet below present-day ground level. The landscape around this bay evidently looked very different in the days of the first settlers on the island. Had there been tsunamis here too?

forward. Fifteen men were divided into two groups, and it took some time before we and they fully grasped that the interplay between them had to be timed to the second in order to work. Pavel spoke no language known to any of us, but he was a genius in making his orders understood by gesture, by waving his arms and feet. The very moment the team with the head ropes made the statue tilt to the right and stand on edge, the team with the base ropes had to quickly pull the opposite side forward, before the giant tipped back onto its full base. In order for the statue to take the next step, both teams had to change sides. Now the statue was tilted to the left so the right side of the base could be twisted forward. Once the men got into the rhythm the system was exceedingly simple, even familiar—we use it ourselves when we move a heavy refrigerator. At first we were scared stiff that the men with the top ropes would pull so hard that the giant would capsize, but Pavel reassured us that the design of the *moai* was so ingenious that the colossus would have to tilt almost sixty degrees before it would fall over. The thickness from front to back of the upper part was so insignificant compared to the bulky lower body that the center of gravity was almost at the navel.

We all felt a chill down our backs when we saw the sight that must have been so familiar to the early ancestors of the people around us. A stone colossus of an estimated ten tons "walking" like a dog on a leash behind a group of Lilliputians, with a little man in front beating his left and right fists in the air each time the Goliath had to take a step. After the successful performance, we all embraced a beaming Pavel Pavel. And Leonardo and Elodia willingly accepted

All the refuse from Ahu Naunau was found outside the wall on the seaward side. The temple court itself had been on the landward side and had been kept clean after the pavement was laid. Most of the refuse was from food-offerings, but included charred human bones from cannibalistic rites. It was on the seaward side that Sergio Rapu's assistant Sonia Haoa had dug up the first eye of a Middle Period statue, and it was also she who found the first fragments of Early period eyes for us. One of them fitted perfectly into the eye socket of the great Early Period head that the architects of the Middle Period had used as structural stone in Ahu Naunau (*left*). But Sonia also found part of a coral eye that had belonged to the grotesque basalt head that we had dug out from beneath the foundations of the same ancient ahu (*right*; see also p. 248).

part of the honor. We could all read from Leonardo's face that he had known the truth the whole time: it was the song he and Elodia had sung that had made the *moai* move.

The statue had indeed walked. I could find no better word for it in any European language. I suddenly had an idea. The Easter Island verb for "walk" is *haere*. But when the *moai* started to move, the old islanders used the verb *neke-neke*. I looked this up in J. Fuentes's dictionary of the Easter Island language, and read: "*neke-neke*: to inch forward by moving the body, due to disabled legs or the absence thereof."

What other language in the world would have a special word for walking without legs?

We were back on Easter Island the next year. Much of what we saw now made more sense to us, even the big cylindrical holes on top of Rano Raraku. As before, the islanders insisted that they had served as postholes for the funiculars used when the *moai* were lowered from the upper terraces of the quarries to the plain down below. But if they needed holes this big, the poles must have consisted of tree trunks so thick that it would take two men to embrace them. Nonetheless, we were willing to believe even this seemingly legendary tradition, for we knew that without some kind of brake the giants would have gone out of control and rushed down the steep mountainside. We had now seen *Jubaea Chilensis*, which grew in Gonzalo's garden outside Santiago. The Chilean palm was enormous, dwarfing any coconut palm. Even two men, their hands linked together, failed to embrace the largest.

In our imagination, we saw the blind colossi being guided on their rough keels down across the empty niches in the crater wall, to be set up and have their dorsal keels chopped away before the long march began. And we could visualize the terrifying sight of several of the carved giants wriggling along the roads in different directions, like robots from another planet, through a green landscape of palms and cultivated fields.

The island could have sustained a much larger population than the three to five thousand inhabitants everybody had formerly estimated it could support. As

Our radiocarbon datings showed that Ahu Naunau at Anakena was totally rebuilt in the thirteenth century, when it was converted into a typical Middle Period *ahu*. The Swedish archaeologist Paul Wallin is brushing a miniature stone head that he has just unearthed. Above him is a block with two frigate birds carved in relief. This block was taken from a once beautifully decorated building and reused as an ordinary building block in the Middle Period.

Paul's wife, Helene, also a professional archaeologist, made the important discovery that chicken bones were present only in the uppermost layers of refuse. The expedition's stratigraphic excavations revealed quite clearly that poultry, a Melanesian-Polynesian type of livestock, was unknown to the original inhabitants of Easter Island and was introduced very late, presumably at the end of the Middle Period. This discovery confirmed the Easter Islanders' own account that seabird's eggs had been an important part of their forefathers' diet until they acquired poultry.

Opposite: Seabirds still nest on the rocky islets off Rano Kao, though the sooty tern that used to play such a vital part in the bird-man rights is now seldom seen. It was eggs of seabirds like this *manu kena* and *makoe poki* which, according to tradition, were so important to the islanders before the introduction of poultry from Polynesia.

we rode across the barren plains, our horses continued to kick and crush the fragile lava stones, but we knew there were large fields of fertile soil underneath.

This time we wanted to concentrate all our efforts on the central Ahu Nauna in Anakena. During the previous year's digging season, the research and work we had done on the transportation of the statues had left us short of time: we had dug only a few test trenches on the plaza side of this great *ahu*. Here, seven feet below the surface, Sergio had exposed a neatly fitted pavement made of boulders when—for security reasons—he had to stop and refill the trench. We had dug three feet further below this pavement and then, while working our way through alternate layers of red silt and yellow beach sand, we hit a dark-brown layer of soil full of human refuse. Arne obtained a radiocarbon date of A.D. 850.

Now we were back to expand these excavations. Our team was augmented by an archaeological friend from the Maldive excavations, Õystein Johansen, director of the Norwegian Academy of Sciences, and a few young archaeologists from Sweden and Chile. Major trenches were opened on either side of King Hotu Matua's *ahu*, this time also on the seaward side, where Sergio had stopped on reaching the crusty sand floor.

Our trained Easter Island workmen were silently scraping down at the bottom of the deep trenches, and up came bits of carbon, human bone, teeth, stone picks, obsidian chips, and refuse from meals of turtle, whale, fish, birds and crabs, all to be neatly brushed free of debris and packed by the archaeologists in their numbered plastic bags. Then Sonia crawled out of her trench with something white in her hand. She was a young Easter Island beauty of few words who had studied archaeology both in Chile and the United States. In a sense we had inherited her from Sergio's former team. Her family name was Haoa, almost the same as that of Make-Make's legendary companion deity, Haua.

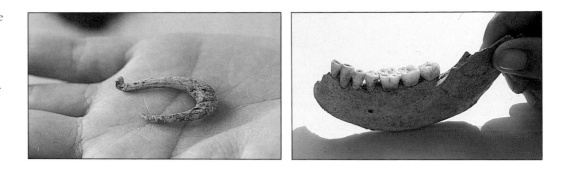

Surprisingly few fishbones were found among the refuse, and fishhooks were also conspicuous by their rarity. This fine specimen (*left*) is made of human bone. Study of the refuse strata has clearly confirmed what the first Europeans reported: the people of Easter Island were first and foremost farmers; in fact, they were peasants who lived isolated in the midst of the ocean and made very little use of the ocean's resources. Our investigations gave no support to the theory that the statues were erected by castaway fishermen from Polynesia.

There were plenty of skeletal finds as well as several megalithic burial chambers in the *ahu* at Anakena. Our new finds were additional to the crania and thighbones of more than one hundred individuals excavated by Sergio Rapu and studied by the American anthropologist George Gill. Gill found traits that deviated from the Polynesian norm; many of the crania, for example, had curved "rocking-chair" jawbones (*right*), an un-Polynesian feature known from the aboriginal population of America.

The piece in her hand was a partly worked fragment of white mushroom coral. Whatever it might once have been, most if it was now missing. Sonia claimed it was part of an eye. Seeing our skeptical looks, one of the workmen hastened to explain that Sonia *knew,* for she had been the one who dug up the eye for Sergio. At that time she did not know what she had found until Sergio slipped it into one of the eye sockets of the statue, and everyone could see it was the eye of a *moai*. Now she showed us that the piece in her hand had a curved part shaped like the corner of an eye, and a round depression for the pupil. I looked up at the megalithic wall above our heads, into which the huge head of an Early Period image had been inserted sideways, used without respect as a mere building block. It had deep eye sockets. We had seen it there in the wall ever since we had landed at Anakena thirty years earlier. The piece Sonia held appeared unlike the eye of Sergio's *moai*: it was thicker, and its proportions were different. An impulse made me suspect that Sonia's eye fragment belonged to that old building-block giant, and we climbed up onto a ledge in the wall from which we could reach the head. Sonia slipped her piece into one eye socket. It did not fit. She tried the other. Yes. It fit the depth and sides of one corner so perfectly that it did not even fall out.

But this was an Early Period head. We now had the first proof that inlaid eyes were not a local invention of the Middle Period, but a tradition, an art form already practiced by the earliest settlers in Anakena.

More Early Period eye fragments appeared among the refuse thrown outside the seaward wall of Ahu Naunau. To Middle Period worshipers, the inland side was the plaza of the temple, which they kept clean.

I was surprised that island traditions had been silent about the remarkable fact that the statues had eyes, until I learned what had happened when Sergio first showed his find to old Leonardo and asked his opinion.

"It is an eye," was Leonardo's calm comment. "for the *moai* had eyes when they stood on the *ahu.*"

Thirty years ago Leonardo had told me that the statues had walked. Why had he not told me then that they had eyes? Of course—because I had only asked how they were moved, not whether or not they had eyes. One must almost know the answer first to be able to ask the right questions on Easter Island.

The new trenches we sank along the plaza side of the same *ahu* revealed a previously unrecorded and truly beautiful wall of immense slabs, perfectly shaped and fitted. This was an unexpected discovery. All had been invisible until Sergio had removed a thick deposit of beach sand. Before we started to dig, only the upper edge of a few stones emerged above ground, but gradually they proved to be huge worked blocks of the same type as those in the famous wall in Vinapu. They were deep below the Middle Period plaza ramp. This was the type of wall everybody had compared to the megalithic works of ancient Peru. Métraux assumed this type of masonry to be the latest stage in a purely local evolution on Easter Island by Polynesians who took to working in stone because there was no wood.

But this was certainly not from the latest stage of Easter Island stone fitting. It was unmistakably an Early Period product that had been totally buried in silt before the Middle Period *ahu* was erected. A closer inspection proved that these fine slabs had been part of an even older structure originally existing elsewhere, one that had been dismantled by man or destroyed by nature. The slabs had been dragged to this place from another site, and although perfectly polished and joined in the original wall, they had then been reworked to fit them together according to another plan. Stone picks as well as chips and powdered debris from ongoing work were found buried in the silt—evidence that the fully developed technique of building stone walls in Peruvian fashion was known to the earliest architects who settled in Anakena Bay.

While we were still at work in Anakena, we had an unexpected visit from a special connoisseur of Tiahuanaco- and Inca-type masonry: Professor Camila Laureani from the Institute of Esthetics of the Pontificia Universidad Catolica de Chile. She arrived from Santiago to re-examine the masonry of the *ahu* walls. To her mind, the mere desire to build an elevated platform for heavy statues was insufficient stimulus to create a wall as esthetic and specialized as the one in Vinapu. In an article devoted to Easter Island *ahu,* she had pointed out that the artisan in charge of Vinapu had confronted the problem of construction with the mentality, the taste and the experience of an architect, not a constructor. If we had found the wall in Vinapu in Inca territory, she wrote, nothing would have seemed strange in either its appearance or the skill with which it had been built. No one would have thought it could have been the work of another culture. Her verdict was clear:

"Ahu Vinapu is an architectonic construction which combines the essential characteristics of the structures in the Altiplano of Peru-Bolivia in a manner so evident that one cannot doubt the arrival on the island of a contingent of these people."

Now, confronted by the discoveries of the Tiahuanaco-type statues—the red pillar type, the kneeling giants and the torso fragment with ribs—she sat down with us on Sergio's terrace and showed us the last paragraph in her new manuscript on Easter Island *moai*. Referring to the stunning similarities between these Early Period monuments and their counterparts in South America, she wrote: "To speak of coincidences or accidents, when they repeat themselves in too many fundamental aspects, is at least as bold as to try to solve the problems through extraterrestrial visitors."

Soon after this we discovered a basalt statue so totally alien to anything found in the Pacific that it could well have fallen from outer space. But in the meantime we had reached rock bottom in our Anakena digs, and another mystery had appeared.

We had dug deeper than last year's culture layer, which had been dated to A.D. 850, and continued to find human refuse, which accordingly had to be still older, until the solid bedrock was reached. A mixture of silt and human refuse thus lay directly on the bare rock, as if the first settlers had lived on cliffs bare of soil or vegetation. Had one of the terrific *tsunamis* or Pacific tidal waves hit this open bay and washed away all the original humus? The deep deposits we had dug through—thick layers of sterile beach sand alternated with layers of equally sterile silt from the surrounding hills—spoke in favor of a succession of local tidal waves. The catastrophe of 1960 that had totally changed Hotu-iti Bay with its colossal *ahu* was certainly not the first to have hit Easter Island.

One thing was sure. We had dug deep test pits looking for human refuse in almost every part of Anakena, and we knew the place to have been settled for more than a thousand years. If we estimated, for the sake of argument, that a thousand people had lived around the royal settlement for a thousand years, that would amount to one million man-years. What had all these people left behind, other than the megalithic stone works? Apart from the sheer refuse of meals we had only found one beautiful little fishhook made of human bone and the shank fragment of another tiny one in stone. Where had all the other evidence of former human industry gone?

Certainly, on the seaward side of the huge wall, excavations had uncovered badly smashed Early Period statue fragments and a couple of stone heads the size of oranges, along with several pieces of broken Early Period eyes of different dimensions. But all this was simply evidence of the deliberate destruction brought about by the Middle Period settlers either in contempt or in fear of the evil eyes of the former residents. They had mutilated the earlier images and fractured their eyes before they dumped them into the seaward dunes to keep their own inland temple plaza clean for their own ceremonies.

Literally fitted into this picture of religious contempt and architectonic reconstruction was a piece set into the wall of the royal *ahu* in Anakena. Ever since I had walked around with Sergio to see the newly exposed walls that year of the congress, I had been almost magnetically drawn to one part of the western wall, where a rather shapeless chunk of dark-gray basalt was visible below the confusion of unworked stones that formed the now exposed flank of the *ahu*. The visible part of this stone in the very bottom layer showed no obvious sign of being worked. But the type of rock was unusual. It brought to mind the stone in a

Left: In 1987, we discovered a megalithic wall of finely hewn and perfectly fitted blocks during our excavations on the landward side of Ahu Naunau. This discovery demolished the popular theory that such walls had appeared at a late stage on Easter Island and represented the high peak of local evolution due to the lack of timber. This buried wall was clearly older than the common vertical walls visible above ground. Nothing like it has been found on a single island in the whole of Polynesia, but it is typical of the megalithic walls of South America. No Polynesian fisherman would have been capable of conceiving, much less building, such a wall, and as it was built in a early period of the settlement of the island, the probability is overwhelming that the inspiration came from the nearest continent to the east.

The splendid wall at Vinapu, which everybody had compared to the walls typical of the old Inca empire, now acquired added importance because it represented a type of stonecraft shown to be deep-rooted on Easter Island. Some of the stones were fitted with the precision of jigsaw-puzzle pieces, just as in ancient Peru.

It was widely believed that the splendid walls in Peru dated from the late Inca period. This has now been disproven. As was the case with many of their other impressive skills, the Incas had learned the craft of masonry from their predecessors in Tiahuanaco. Bolivian archaeologists have recently started to excavate the earth-covered pyramidal mound at Akapana in Tiahuanaco, revealing it as a terraced pyramid from long before the age of the Incas. It is faced with accurately hewn and artistically joined blocks, just as on Easter Island.

Left: A statue at the foot of Rano Raraku that was only partly uncovered in 1956 was excavated completely in 1987 to let the expedition's photographer obtain a full-length portrait. No one who witnessed this giant in all its majestic size could fail to understand that it was not created by castaway fishermen, who failed to find timber. This was a monument designed by one of the great seafaring civilizations of old. The authorities on the mainland allowed us to keep the giant uncovered just for one day, for fear that somebody might fall into the pit. Later visitors passing this way, like those who went before, will therefore be left with the impression that the monuments are simply eyeless heads. It must have once been an incredible sight: all the giants standing in tall ranks at the foot of the volcano awaiting marching orders to an *ahu,* where they would be given their eye sockets and inlaid eyes.

Top right: The task of digging right down to the base of the stone giant was not without its hazards. We had to keep widening the shaft to avoid being buried under tons of rocky debris once washed down from the quarries uphill.

Bottom right: The author felt very small when he climbed down and found that the giant's fingers were as long as he was tall. The long nails, especially on the thumbs, revealed that the monument represented a person of royal rank not accustomed to physical work. The king lacked any genitalia, which were replaced by a flat relief. This reaffirmed the islanders' explanation that the whole image was a phallic symbol, so the sculptor could not give it a second *ure.*

unique bust of a headless woman which the Long-ears had found thirty years ago merely by digging up the loose sand on the plaza side of this same *ahu.* It was on exhibit in the Kon-Tiki Museum in Oslo. I had bought that headless beauty from the island's mayor. At that time, anybody could buy what the islanders brought, but all we ourselves found through excavations remained Chilean property. The sculptured female torso was of a stone so incredibly hard and heavy that we could not understand how it had been shaped. I could not rid myself of the mad idea that what I now saw in the wall was a section of the same sculpture. All attempts to pull the stone out were in vain, even when we dug out sand and small stones from around it. To the despair of the others, who saw no

Pavel Pavel, a young Czechoslovakian engineer, was invited to join our expedition after having assured the author that he could make a statue "walk" as the islanders had claimed they did. Along with Skjølsvold and the author, he inspected the bases of all the statues that lay toppled and abandoned along the roads. We found that those statues that had not traveled far from the quarry *(bottom left)* had perfectly flat bases; the farther away from the quarry they were, the more convex their bases became, until many of those erected on *ahus* had the edges of their bases completely rounded off from wear *(right)*.

sign of human workmanship in this ugly stone, I clung stubbornly to my suspicion until Sergio allowed me to take the whole wall down. He made the condition that it was to be rebuilt by evening so exactly that nobody could see the difference.

We numbered all the stones in the wall and took a Polaroid photograph of it before we began. Then, with the aid of our excellent foreman, Juan Haoa, and a team of his strongest men we removed all the numbered stones, but still could not move the bewitched block I was after. It went far into the masonry. Wedged deep amid the internal fill that held it in its grip, we discovered a broken Early Period statue of red stone, a torso with arms. No sooner was this extracted from the wall than it became possible to dislodge and pull free the extremely long and slender piece of dark basalt I wanted. We turned it over. It was the strangest face we had ever seen, the more so since it suddenly appeared out of the blue on an island where we were all accustomed to seeing the standard faces made of Rano Raraku stone. The long nose and one ear had been brutally broken off by vandals, who must have worked hard to decapitate the basalt image. The eye sockets were unusually deep and had clearly contained inlays. But the strangest feature was the headgear. It rose upward in a single piece above the forehead, like a vertical diadem or a fan-shaped feather crown, leaving the apex and the back of the head bare. The head with its headgear was just under three feet long, but so heavy that two strong men could barely lift it. With a startled crowd of islanders watching, it was immediately carried into Sergio's museum for safe-keeping, and before sunset the wall was up as before.

As fast as Easter Island's new telephone system allowed, I got the Kon-Tiki Museum in Oslo on the line. The director, Knut Haugland, was to join us on the island in a matter of days. Hoping he could hear my voice, although I could hardly hear his, I shouted to him several times that he should make an imprint or a template of the broken neck of our female bust from Easter Island and bring it with him when he came.

When we met him at the island airstrip a few days later, he came off the plane with a carton that turned out to contain a strangely crooked design. In the village museum, we turned the design back and forth over the broken neck of our newly discovered head. Suddenly the contours fitted exactly. A gasp of surprise was heard all around. The islanders were at first speechless, and I was indeed as

amazed as they. The head we had just found in the royal wall and the body we had brought to Europe a good thirty years earlier made up a complete statue.

"The head belonged to a woman," was all I could think of to say.

"*La Reina,* the queen." This was the immediate response of an old islander. All the others agreed. To them this was *Avareipua,* Hotu Matua's queen. The one and only queen they all still remembered, because she appeared in the songs they had preserved about the first landing in Anakena, when she gave birth to Hotu Matua's son.

Old people wept with emotion. I immediately decided to bring back the body I had bought thirty years ago and return it to the island, so head and body could once again be joined together. Knut and Arne gave me their full support. We could make an immediate decision, as the three of us made up the entire board of the Kon-Tiki Museum. Our sole condition was that we first obtain a cast of this in every sense unique queen to take the place of the headless bust.

A few days later Sonia dug up at great depth another eye fragment, obviously of an image even smaller than any of the usual Early Period statues. It would seem too good to be true if she had found part of the eye of our little queen who would only stand as high as a normal person when the two parts were put together. Casually, I told her to bring her piece to the museum. Shortly after we were interrupted by a messenger in a jeep. It was *not* too good to be true. Sonia had found a piece of the left eye of the queen! Like the giant kings made of Rano Raraku tuff, who had assumed the place of honor on top of the Middle Period *ahu,* the little queen of flint-hard basalt took on a scaringly hypnotic look when we imagined her with complete eye inlays. She was so utterly unlike anything else ever seen on Easter Island, or anything else in the Pacific island world, that everybody's thoughts turned to the advanced cultures of the ancient Americas, if not directly to the Phoenicians or Hittites two oceans away. Nobody thought of Oceania. "This image seems to have dropped from the sky," Sergio said, and everybody agreed. I thought of Camila Laureani's words: The only alternative to an American beginning would be that the image was of extraterrestrial origin. Nothing spoke in favor of such an alternative. This sculpture of the queen had been carved on Easter Island before the Middle Period imagemakers rebuilt the *ahu* in Anakena.

The last day before our group separated, I sat with my good old friends Knut Haugland and Arne Skjølsvold on the terrace of Sergio's bungalow. Chatting over glasses of pisco-sour, we looked out at the now-familiar view of Cook's Bay, where so many of the early explorers had anchored. On the far side of the bay was the reconstructed *ahu* of Tahai, where Bill and Gonzalo had re-erected a row of *moai.* Some were broken, and recalled the days of the civil wars. Despite its modest size, this island had an amazing history.

Knut had never been to Easter Island before, but he had run the Kon-Tiki Museum ever since we sailed that balsa raft together from Peru to Polynesia. Arne had joined me on all my archaeological expeditions ever since the first one to the Galápagos group. Now he was in charge of the research department of the same museum. Here, in a board meeting that would decide our further operations, we literally sat in the midst of the prehistoric battlefield.

Knut wanted to know if the museum would have to back further field research on this particular island. The question was, would there be more to learn through further digging. Arne and I had no doubts about this: there would

On the morning of the day set for the great experiment, Pavel and the author discussed their plans in front of the statue they had chosen to make "walk"; it had been re-erected on the plain of Hotu-iti after the great tsunami.

Leonardo Pakarati repeated what he had said thirty years before, and demonstrated how the stone giants had walked with a waddling gait.

Leonardo's sister Elodia, who used to be Father Sebastian's housekeeper, sang in a low voice a monotonous song in a jerky tempo that matched Leonardo's movements. While she sang an old text and tune she obviously knew by heart, her brother made a string figure like a cat's cradle, which he swung in time to the song. This was repeated during the actual experiment as a kind of magical invocation.

The islanders refused to help Pavel until they had observed the ancient custom of baking a pig and sweet potatoes in an *umu* earth oven. The smell of cooking would placate any unseen *aku-aku*.

always be more to discover under the barren surface of the island. In many places we and other visitors, and the islanders themselves, were walking high above the heads of the people who had once had the answers to all the riddles of Easter Island. The present surface of the sandy plains in Anakena lay thirteen feet above the ground where the first settlers walked. And we had dug twenty feet down—the height of a two-story house—through the debris of Rano Raraku before we reached the ground on which the blind giants had been set up. Nobody could tell what kind of monuments and information a coat of soil as high as a house might still conceal.

The technical problems behind the great stone giants were solved. The mysteries that had confounded visitors and armchair scientists since the days of Roggeveen and Captain Cook existed no more. The genesis of the blind giants dotting the slopes of the volcano was known, and how they walked to the *ahu* before they received their eyes. The way each of these incredible feats had been accomplished with help from neither machinery or outer space—all these former puzzles now had their answers.

One big question emerged: Why had nobody but the islanders themselves taken their ancestral traditions seriously? They would have given us all these answers. I confessed to my two friends that the value of the local oral history was, in a sense, one of the strangest discoveries we had made. A hundred years ago the Easter Islanders had answered all the questions that were put to the elders among them. We from the outside world had recorded what they told us, and saved the answers as primitive fairy-tales:

Once upon a time there were Long-ears and Short-ears. The Long-ears came from the east first, the Short-ears from the west later. The first were industrious and in charge of monuments and the great works. The Short-ears patiently toiled for two hundred years with the monuments in honor of the Long-ears; then they conspired and made revolt. They pushed the Long-ears down into their own burning pyre and ruled the island alone thereafter.

This was the essence of Easter Island tradition. Long-ears from the direction of America first, Short-ears from the direction of Polynesia afterward.

There was more detail to the memories of the nineteenth-century elders on the island. And in the light of what we know today, presumed fables begin to assume the aspect of an epic preserved among the modest heirs to a prehistoric civilization.

Even before the Long-ears had arrived with King Hotu Matua, another king, his "brother," had come from the same direction. Both were losers in battles in a great land to the east and had fled into the ocean in the direction of the sunset looking for an island the location of which was already known to both of them. The first king disappeared, and only traces of his settlement were left on the island. Hotu Matua named the island and his kin survived for a great number of generations, and then they were joined by the Short-ears from the west. The latter abandoned their religion and their culture and began to toil for the Long-ears. For two hundred years. Then they made revolt, burned the Long-ears in their own pyre and took over the island thereafter. But a period of civil war followed, when all the long-eared statues were overthrown and people lived in caves.

The Short-ears had forgotten their own gods, but continued to worship Make-Make, the supreme god of the sky, who was surrounded by the venerated bird-men. They did not venerate the statues, for they represented the chiefs of the

Long-ears. But they had once helped carve them and remembered the procedure. They were all of one type, for those that looked like heads set up at the foot of the quarries had full bodies too, set up temporarily to have their backs finished before they were made to walk to their destinations, blind still, but in an upright position.

Hotu Matua's fatherland was large and divided into several kingdoms, it rose from a scorching hot desert coast into freezing cold altitudes. But when he came to Easter Island it was covered by a green forest with the branches of the trees intertwining above remains of stone-paved roads. He brought the sweet potato, which remained the all-important diet of the island population. But he did not bring the chicken. The chicken was brought with the later arrivals.

All this was plain Easter Island history, which the elders of the island com-

Pavel had indeed worked out the ingenious technique by which the statues were moved—the same technique that we use ourselves to "walk" a heavy refrigerator or a stone too big to carry unaided. The mass of the statue was virtually eliminated, because its whole weight rested on the ground at all times. All that was needed were four ropes. Two were attached to the top of the statue and used to pull it to each side alternately, while the other two were fastened down at the base and alternately pulled foward. As one team pulled on the top rope to make the statue tilt to the right, the other team pulled the left-hand side of the base forward before the giant tipped back again. The teams then changed sides, causing the colossus to waddle along like a drunken man. The technique required great precision and intensive training, but was incredibly effective when the waddling become rhythmic. We reckoned that a well-drilled team of fifteen men could make a twenty-ton statue "walk" at least an average of hundred yards a day.

munity had tried to share with us when asked them, before the original memories petered out at the beginning of the present century. Now what they had told us orally we could give them back written in our own letters and with a stamp of scientific approval.

"Strange," said Arne. "The only thing they had never told us was that the statues had inlaid eyes."

"Not so strange," I said. "Nobody ever asked them. And if they had told us, who would have believed them?"

I smiled, knowing the answer: Nobody had asked that question.

Overleaf: The foreman Juan Haoa signals to the team with the base rope to jerk hard the very moment the team with the top rope tilts the statue over to their side.

The
circle is
closed

Reed boats

Mythological scenes showing reed boats occurred frequently on pottery from the Pacific coast of Peru, especially during the period before the highland Incas conquered the whole coastal region. They put an end to the great seafaring cultures that were typical of the early Mochica period and still persisted to some extent in the Chimu era. Bird-men—human beings with bird heads—play a prominent part in the symbolic motifs of god-kings at sea in reed ships. The bird-men, which were totally unknown to Polynesian religion or art, were just as important in pre-Inca South America as on Easter Island. The idea of making a reed boat look like a sea-monster with gaping jaws was also common to both regions (see also p. 211).

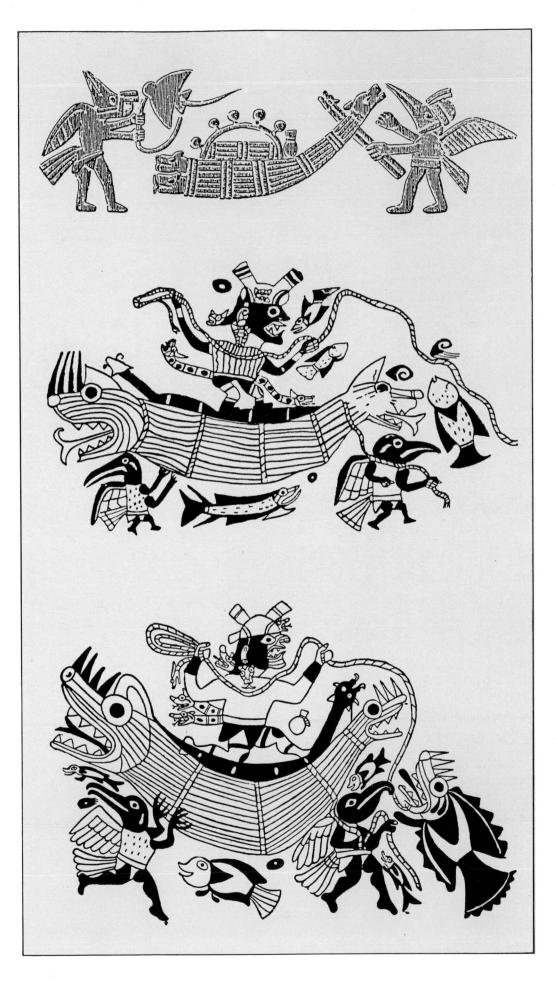

A gilded silver earplug dating from the pre-Inca period, from the coast of northern Peru. It evidently belonged to a prosperous Long-ear of the bird-man religion who had maritime interests, for it is decorated all the way round with typical bird-men sailing in a whole fleet of reed boats. Reed boats, bird-men and ear-lengthening were three phenomena typical of Easter Island and conspicuous by their absence in Polynesia. In this ornament from the coast of Peru we find all three.

The first drillings for pollen samples in the swamps around the crater lakes of Easter Island were conducted by the author in 1955–56 following the instructions of Dr. Olof H. Selling in Stockholm. Selling's analyses provided the first confirmation that trees had once grown on this bare island. Easter Island had had at least as much forest as the nearest islands to the west, while a species of palm absent farther west had been common on the slopes of Rano Raraku. The island was probably deforested because its earliest settlers needed quarries and arable land more than timber.

In 1986, when we dug to examine the roadbed where the heavy statues had walked, we found to everybody's surprise that beneath a thin overlay of gravel and lumps of lava stone was a deep stratum of rich black humus from a former forest. We even found large root holes. Sonia shows Figueroa a sample of the fertile soil, which was compacted as if by a steamroller where the heavy statues had passed.

Great eucalyptus forests now stand on many parts of Easter Island. The sheep-farming that dominated the landscape for a century ended in the 1960s, when a large grove of coconut palms was planted at Anakena Bay. The trees have no problem growing except for the grass fires that the islanders are always lighting. The pollen, the humus and the root holes testify to the former presence of trees, so it cannot have been shortage of timber that inspired the erection of giant monolithic statues and the building of Inca-style walls.

246

Blossoms of a tree which was so rare in 1956 that only one specimen remained on our planet. The toromiro tree, *Sophora toromiro,* was once common on Easter Island, though it did not grow anywhere else in the world. It was always the preferred choice of Easter Island woodcarvers, who used the hard red wood for all their religious emblems and statuettes. The islanders showed the author the last surviving toromiro tree as a curiosity in 1956. All that was left was a dying stump inside the crater of Rano Kao, with a few seedpods on the last living branch. Dr. Selling took charge of these, and planted the seeds in the botanic gardens in Göteborg, Sweden. The last tree on Easter Island died, but three young ones with new blossoms and seeds flourished in Göteborg.

In 1988, the toromiro tree returned to Easter Island and was ceremonially welcomed at the airport. The Swedish botanist Björn Aldén had brought two young plants with him on the plane, a seedling and a rooted cutting, both of which were planted on the island. Two representatives of the island's council of chiefs took part in the ceremony: Alberto Hotu, standing with the author, and Juan Haoa, in a huddle with the island's agronomist Gerardo Velasco and (*right*) Björn Aldén.

A statue comes home

A royal statue comes home. After thirty-two years of exile, the headless trunk of a legendary queen was reunited with her crowned head. The body, of heavy basalt, was found by the mayor of the island in 1956, concealed in the sand on the landward side of Ahu Naunau at Anakena. There was no museum on the island at that time, and the islanders sold all their finds to passing ships. The author bought this unusual fragment of a female bust and exhibited it at the Kon-Tiki Museum in Oslo. He himself in 1988 discovered the broken-off neck of the head, which was visible at the foot of the *ahu* wall after Sergio Rapu's excavations. The head was dug out from under the

wall, and the body was sent back to Easter Island by air. The parts fitted together perfectly, and the female statue was placed in the island's new museum. The islanders immediately gave this unique female monument the name Ava-rei-pua, after the legendary first queen of Easter Island, who landed at Anakena Bay with King Hotu Matua and founded what was to be the island's royal dynasty.

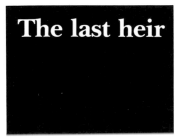

The last heir

The last heir of the red-haired
Long-ears sitting in front of the
red topknot of a giant statue of
one of his ancestors. Young
Venito Hernan Atan can trace his
pedigree on the paternal side in a
direct line back to the legendary
Ororoine, the last of the Long-
ears to survive the massacre in the
fiery trench of Poike. Although
the unmixed line of the Long-ears
ended with Pedro Atan and his
daughter Maria (pp. 68, 201),
Venito has the characteristic red
hair of the Atan family (his mother
comes from the mainland and has
black hair).

Thanks to everyone

Consejo de Korohua, the Council of Elders, is an unofficially elected group of heads of families regarded by the population as the island's chiefs. In 1987, they decided to name the author the island's first honorary chieftain. To celebrate the occasion, the entire council posed for the photographer in front of Ahu Naunau at Anakena, where the island's first royal couple landed.

In that same year, the author was also granted honorary citizenship by the island's official representatives, Governor Sergio Rapu and the new mayor, Lucia Tuki Make, both native Easter Islanders. As a symbol of his new status the governor presented the author with an *ao* paddle of the double-bladed type that has always been a feature of ceremonial occasions on Easter Island. This very type, with a long-eared mask on the upper blade, is unknown elsewhere in the world except on the coast of Peru in pre-Inca times (p. 214).

The full Board of the Kon-Tiki Museum met for the first-time outside Oslo, when the museum's director, *Kon-Tiki* voyager Knut Haugland (*right*), brought the female bust to Easter Island and was met there by the head of the museum's new research department Dr. Skjølsvold (*left*), and the author. The board provisionally decided to stop further excavations on Easter Island, and transfer operations in the near future to archaelogical investigations of the nearest home of other seafaring Long-ears; the coast of Peru.

Easter Island today

The population of Easter Island has grown from 900 in 1955 to about 2,000 in 1988. About half that number have immigrated from Chile in recent years. The construction of an airport capable of receiving even the largest modern jets has opened up this once-remote island to international tourism. In the course of one generation the island community has succeeded in making the difficult transition from a very prinmitive way of life into a modern society with a cash economy. Hospitals, schools, shops, sports-palace, bank, and even two discothéques have grown up with incredible speed, yet without dominating the landscape. A few one-story hotels also stand half-hidden among the now-lush tropical gardens of Hanga-roa, together with nemerous small boarding-houses in the Easter Islander's own modest homes. The little Catholic church, with the graves of Lay Brother Eyraud and Father Sebastican Englert beside its porch, is still the island's most important meeting-place, where everybody who can walk or crawl gathers every Sunday for their own captivating brand of shoral singing.

Tourism is and will remain Easter Islans's sole source of income. But in marked contrast to so many other primitive societies, where sudden contract with the modern world has been a devastating shpock leading to cultural and moral decay, the people of Easter Island have enthusiastically revived much of their ancestral culture.

Bibliography

Alazard, I. *Introduction to Roussel.* 1908.

Beechey, F.W. *Narrative of a Voyage to the Pacific and Beering's Strait . . . in the Years 1825, 26, 27, 28.* 2 vols. London, 1831.

Behrens, C.F. "Der Wohlversuchte Süd-Länder, das ist: ausführliche Reisse-Beschreibungen um die Welt." English translation by *Hakluyt Society* 13 (2nd ser.) 1908. Cambridge.

Bennett, W.C. "Excavations at Tiahuanaco." *Anthropological Papers of the American Museum of Natural History* 34 (3) 1934. New York.

de Betanzos, E. *Suma y narracion de los Incas.* Madrid, 1880.

Brown, J. Macmillan. *The Riddle of the Pacific.* London, 1924.

Buck, P.H. *Vikings of the Sunrise.* New York, 1938.

————— "Ethnology of Mangareva." *B.P. Bishop Museum Bulletin* 157 (1938). Honolulu.

Byam, G. *Wanderings in Some of the Western Republics of America.* London, 1850.

Choris, L. *Voyage Pittoresque Autour du Monde, avec des Portraits des Sauvages.* Paris, 1822.

Christian, F.W. "Vocabulary of the Mangarevan Language." *B.P. Bishop Museum Bulletin* 11 (1924). Honolulu.

————— "Early Maori Migrations as Evidenced by Physical Geography and Language." *Rept. Sixteenth Meet. Australas. Ass. Adv. Sci.* (1924). Wellington, New Zealand.

Clark, B.F. "Reporting calling at Sala-y-Gomez and Easter Islands." Letter to the Commander-in-Chief, written at sea off Easter Island, June 20, 1882. *Proc. Roy. Geogr. Soc. Australasia* 3, pp. 143–46.

Cook, J. *Second Voyage Towards the South Pole and Round the World, Performed in the "Resolution" and "Adventure," 1772–75.* 2 vols. London, 1777.

Cooke, G.H. "Te Pito o Te Henua, known as Rapa Nui, commonly called Easter Island, South Pacific Ocean." *Annual Report Smithsonian Institute* (1899), pp. 691–723. Washington, D.C.

Croft, T. "Letter of April 30, 1874, from Thomas Croft, Papeete, Tahiti, to the President of California Academy of Sciences." *California Academy of Science, Proc.* 5 (1875), pp. 317–23. San Francisco.

Delano, A. *A Narrative of Voyages and Travels in the Northern and Southern Hemispheres.* Boston, 1817.

Ekholm, C.F. "Is American Indian Culture Asiatic?" *Natural History* 59 (8) 1950. New York.

Emory, K.P. "Stone Remains in the Society Islands." *B.P. Bishop Museum Bulletin* 116 (1933). Honolulu.

————— "Oceanian Influence on American Indian Culture: Nordenskiold's View." *Journal of Polynesian Society* 51 (1942).

Englert, P.S. *La tierra de Hotu Matua. Historia, etnologia y lengua de Isla de Pascua.* Imprenta y edit "San Francisca" Padre las Casas. Chile, 1948.

Eyraud, E. "Lettre au T.R.P. Supérieur général de la Congrégation des Sacrés-Coeurs de Jésus et de Marie." Valparasio diciembre 1864. *Ann. Assoc. Propagation de la Foi* 38 (1866), pp. 52–71; 124–38. Lyon.

Ferdon, Jr., E.N. "The Ceremonial Site of Orongo"; "Sites E-4 and E-5"; "Stone Houses in the Terraces of Site E-21"; "Easter Island House Types"; "Site E-6, an Easter Island Hare Moa"; "A Summary of the Excavated Record of Easter Island Prehistory." *Heyerdahl & Ferdon* (1961), pp. 221–55; 305–11; 313–21; 329–38; 381–83; 527–35.

————— "Surface Architecture of the Site Paeke, Taipi Valley, Nukuhiva." *Heyerdahl & Ferdon* (1965).

Forster, G. *A Voyage Around the World, in His Britannic Majesty's Sloop "Resolution," Commanded by Capt. James Cook, During the Years 1772, 73, 74, and 75.* 2 vols. London, 1777.

————— *Observations Made During a Voyage Round the World of Physical Geography, Natural History, and Ethnic Philosophy.* London, 1778.

Frank, V.S. "A Trip to Easter Island." *Journ. Franklin Institute Devoted to Science and Mechanical Arts* 162 (3) 1906. Philadelphia.

Fuentes, J. *Diccionario y grammatica de la lengua de la Isla de Pascua.* Santiago de Chile, 1960.

Geiseler, Kapitänlieutenant. *Die Oster-Insel: Eine Stätte prähistorischer Kultur in der Südsee.* Berlin, 1883.

Gonzalez, F. "The Voyage of Captain Don Felipe Gonzalez on the ship of the San Lorenzo, with the Frigate Santa Rosalia in Company, to Easter Island in 1770–71." *Hakluyt Society* 13 (2nd ser.) 1908. Cambridge.

Graydon, J.J., et al. "Blood Groups and the Polynesians." *Mankind* 4 (3) 1952, pp. 329–39. Sydney.

Gusinde, M. "Bilografia de la Isla de Pascua." *Publ. Mus. Etnologia y Antropología de Chile.* 11 (2) 1920, (3), pp. 261–383. Santiago de Chile.

Handy, E.S.C. "Polynesian Religion." *B.P. Bishop Museum Bulletin* 34 (1927). Honolulu.

de Harlez, D. "Les signes graphiques de l'Ile de Paques." *Le Muséon* 14 (5) pp. 415–25; 15 (1), pp. 68–76; 15 (2), pp. 209–212. Louvain, 1896.

de Hevesy, Guillaume. "The Easter Island and the Indus Valley Scripts." *Anthropos* 23 (1938).

Heyerdahl, T. *American Indians in the Pacific: The Theory Behind the Kon-Tiki Expedition.* Chicago, London, Stockholm; 1952.

————— *Aku-Aku: The Secret of Easter Island.* Oslo, 1957; Chicago, 1958.

————— *Art of Easter Island.* New York, 1975.

————— *Early Man and the Ocean.* London, New York, 1980.

————— *The Maldive Mystery.* London, New York, 1986.

Heyerdahl, T. and Ferdon, E.N., Jr. *Reports of the Norwegian Archaeological Expedition to Easter Island and the East Pacific.* Vol. I: *Archaeology of Easter Island.* Monogr. School Amer. Research and Mus. New Mexico (1961); Vol. II: *Miscellaneous Reports,* Monogr. School Amer. Research and Kon-Tiki Mus. (1965).

Heyerdahl, T. and Skjølsvold, A. "Archaeological Evidence of Pre-Spanish Visits to the Galápagos Islands." *Mem. Soc. Amer. Arch.* 12 (1956). Salt Lake City.

Imbelloni, J. "Einige konkrete Beweise für die Ausserkontinentalen Beziehungen der Indianer Amerikas." *Anthro. Ge. Wien* 58 (1925). Vienna.

Knoche, W. *Die Osterinsel: Eine Zusammenfassung der Chilenischen Osterinsel-expedition des Jahres 1911.* Conception, 1925.

Kotzebue, O.E. *Putesjestvije v jusjynj okean i v beringov proliv dlja otyskanija severo-vostotjnovo morskovo prochoda predpinjatoje v 1815, 1817, i 1818 godach.* Vols. 1–3. St. Petersburg, 1821; (English translation, vols. 1–2. London, 1821).

Langdon, R. "Manioc, a long-concealed key to the enigma of Easter Island." *Geogr. Journ.* 154, No. 3 (Nov. 1988), pp. 324–336. London.

de La Pérouse, J.F.G. *A Voyage Round the World Performed in the Years 1785, 1786, 1787, and 1788.* 2 vols and atlas. Paris, 1797; London, 1798.

Laureani, Ciccarell E. "Los ahu de Isla de

Pascua." *Aisthesis* 14 (1982). Publicaciones Periodicas Pontifica Universidad Catolica de Chile.

———— "Los Moai de Isla de Pascua." *Aisthesis* 18 (1985). Publicaciones Periodicas Pontifica Universidad Catolica de Chile.

Lavachery, H. "La Mission Franco-Belge dans l'Ile de Paques." *Bulletin Soc. Royale de Geogr. d'Anvers* 55 (1935), pp. 313–61. Antwerp.

———— "Easter Island, Polynesia." *Ann. Rept. Bd. of Regents Smithsonian Inst.* (1936), pp. 391–96. Washington, D.C.

———— *Les Petroglyphes de l'Ile de Paques*. 2 vols. Antwerp, 1939.

———— "Thor Heyerdahl et le Pacifique." *Journ. Soc. Oceanistes* 21 (21) 1965, pp. 151–59. Paris.

Lisjanskij, U.F. *Putesjestvije vokrug sveta 1803–1806*. St. Petersburg, 1812. English translation by Lisjanskij. London, 1814.

Lothrop, S.K. "Aboriginal navigation off the West Coast of South America." *Journ. Royal Anthrop. Inst.* 62 (July-Dec.), pp. 229–56. London.

Loti, P. "La Isla de Pascua." *Biblioteca Geogr. e Hist. Chilena* (1903). Santiago de Chile.

———— (alias Viaud, J.) "A l'Ile de Paques." *Cahiers Pierre Loti* 29 (March, 1960). Paris.

———— "Expedition der Fregatte 'La Flore' nach der Osterinsel 1872." *Globus* 23 (5) 1873. Braunschweig.

Markham, C.R. "Notes and Introduction to Garcilasso: Royal Commentaries of the Incas." *Hakluyt Society* 41, 45 (1869). London.

Métraux, A. "Ethnology of Easter Island." *B.P. Bishop Museum Bulletin* 160 (1940). Honolulu.

———— *Easter Island: A Stone Age Civilization of the Pacific*. London, 1957.

Moerenhout, A. *Voyages aux Iles du Grand Ocean*. 2 vols. Paris, 1957.

Morgan, A.E. *Nowhere Was Somewhere*. New York, 1946.

Mulloy, W. "The Ceremonial Center at Vinapu"; "The Tupa of Hiramoko." *Heyerdahl & Ferdon* (1961), pp. 93–180; 323–28.

Palmer, J.L. "Observations on the Inhabitants and the Antiquities of Easter Island." *Ethnol. Soc., London Journal* 1 (1868), pp. 371–77. London.

———— "A Visit to Easter Island, or Rapa Nui." *Roy. Geogr. Soc. Proc.* 14 (1870), pp. 108–19. London.

———— "A Visit to Easter Island, or Rapa Nui, in 1868." *Roy. Geogr. Soc. Journ.* 40 (1870), pp. 167–81. London.

———— "Davis or Easter Island." *Lit. and Phil. Soc. of Liverpool Proc.* 29 (1875), pp. 275–97. London.

du Petit-Thouars, A. *Voyage Autour de Monde sur la frégate la Venus, Pendant les Annees 1836–1839*. Vol. 2 et Atlas Pittoresque. Paris, 1841.

Pinart, A. "Voyage de l'Ile de Paques." *Le Tour de Monde* 36 (1877), 36 (1877), pp. 225–40. Paris, 1878.

———— "Exploration de l'Ile de Paques." *Bull. Soc. Geog.* 6:16 (1878), pp. 193–213. Paris.

Rivet, P. "Relations commerciales précolombiennes entre l'Océanie et l'Amerique." *Festschrift P.W. Schmidt* (1928). Vienna.

———— *Les origines de l'homme américain*. Montreal, 1934.

Roggeveen, M.J. "Extract from the Official Log of the Voyage of Mynheer in the Ships Den Arend, Thienhove, and de Afrikannische Galey in 1721–22, in so far as it relates to the Discovery of Easter Island." *Hakluyt Society* 2:13 (1908). Cambridge.

Roussel, H. "Ile de Paques. Notice par le R.P. Hippolyte Roussel, SS.CC., Apotre de l'Ile de Paques sent to Valparaiso in 1869." *Annales des Sacrés-Coeurs* 305, pp. 355–60; 307; 423–30; 308; 462–66; 309; 495–99. Paris, 1926.

Routledge, K. *The Mystery of Easter Island: The Story of an Expedition*. London, 1919.

Simmons, R.T., Graydon, J.J., Semple, N.M., and Fry, E.O. "A Blood Group Genetical Survey in Cook Islanders, Polynesia, and Comparison with American Indians." *American Journal of Anthropology* New Series 13 (4) (Dec., 1955). Philadelphia.

Skjølsvold, A. "Dwellings of Hoto Matua"; "House of Foundations (Hare Paenga) in Rano Raraku"; "Site E-2, a Circular Stone Dwelling, Anakena"; "The Stone Statues and Quarries of Rano Raraku." *Heyerdahl & Ferdon* (1961), pp. 273–86; 291–93; 295–303; 339–79.

Skottsberg, C. *The Phanerogams of Easter Island: The Natural History of San Juan Fernandez and Easter Island*. Vol. 2. Uppsala, 1921.

———— "Le peuplement des iles pacifiques du Chile: contribution à l'étude de peuplement zoologique et botanique des iles du Pacifique." *Soc. de Biogeogr.* 4 (1934). Paris.

———— *Derivation of the Flora and Fauna of San Juan Fernandez and Easter Island: The Natural History of Juan Fernandez and Easter Island*. Vol. 1, pp. 193–438. Uppsala, 1920–56.

Smith, C.S. "A Temporal Sequence Derived from Certain Ahu"; "Two Habitation Caves"; "The Maunga Ahuhepa House Site"; "Tuu-ko-ihu Village"; "The Poike Ditch"; "Radio Carbon Dates from Easter Island." *Heyerdahl & Ferdon* (1961), pp. 181–219; 257–71; 277–86; 287–89; 385–91; 393–96.

Stephen-Chauvet. *La Isla de Pascua y sus Misterios*. Paris, 1934; Santiago de Chile, 1946.

Thomson, W.J. "Te Pito te Henua, or Easter Island." *Rept. U.S. Nat. Mus.* for the year ending June 30, 1889. Washington, D.C.

Thorsby, E., Colombani, J., Daussett, Ja., Figueroa, J., and Thorsby, A. "HL-A, Blood Group and Serum Type Polymorphism of Natives on Easter Island." *Histocompatability Testing 1972* (1973). Copenhagen.

de Zarate, A. *A History of the Discovery and Conquest of Peru*. Vols. 1–4 translated out of the Spanish by Thomas Nicholas, in 1581. London, 1933.

Zumbohm, G. "Lettres du R.P. Gaspard Zumbohm au directeur des annales, sur la mission de l'Ile de Paques." *Annales de la Congrégation des Sacrés-Coeurs de Jesus et de Marie* 5:46, pp. 660–67 (Oct. 1879); 6:50, pp. 117–31; 52, pp. 231–42; 54, pp. 377–85 (Feb.–June, 1880). Paris.

Picture credits

Illustrations have been collected from the sources listed below. The names of the museums in which objects illustrated may be seen are listed in the captions themselves. All photographs not acknowledged here are from the author's archives.

Attenborough, David 45
Botanical Gardens, Göteborg 247
Bokförlaget Bra Böcker AB 114, 130:1, 193:2
British Museum 44, 47:1–3, 70:2, 71:1–2, 81, 88:2–3
Christchurch 71:3
Galindo, César *Sebrafilm* 12, 13, 18, 20, 26, 30:2, 40:2, 61, 64–65, 82, 83, 97:1, 102:2–3, 116:1, 148, 168, 170:2, 171, 199:3, 218:2, 219, 221, 224:1, 236, 238, 246:2–3, 251:1, 252:4, endpaper photo
García, Henri 2–3, 166, 229:3–4, 253:5
Hamburgisches Museum für Völkerkunde 71:3
Jonsson, Bengt *Sebrafilm* 247:2
Larrain, Sergio 200:1
Leonardi, Walter *Sebrafilm* 16–17, 19, 29, 40:1, 42:1, 43:2, 59, 68, 69, 88:1, 102:1, 108, 130:2, 132–133, 138, 141, 143, 144:1+3, 145:1–3, 154, 157, 181:2, 199:1–2, 226, 227, 228:1, 229:1, 233:2, 234, 235, 240:1, 242–243, 245, 250, 251:2, 252:1+8, 253:4+6
Lidman, Lars, endpaper map
Mario Guillard, Universidad de Chile 116:2, 117:1, 118:1
Museo Nacional de Arqueología, Lima 89
Museum für Völkerkunde, 1 Berlin 33, Dalhem, Arnimallee 23/27 21:4, 47:4–6
Olsen, Kristine 248:2
Olsen, Petter 140, 252:3, 253:2
Peabody Museum Harvard University 33, 34, 98:3, 119
Photo Gecioni 105:2
Reinhard Friedrich Völkerkunde Museum 223:2
Schmidt, Werner 4, 8, 25:1, 38, 41, 130:3, 170:1+3, 203:2, 228:2, 229:2, 232, 233:1, 249, 252:5+7, 253 1+3+7
Scott, Tom, Edinburgh 23
Sebrafilm 240:2–4, 241:1–3
Sepenoski, Margarete 224:3
Skjølsvold, Arne 30:1
Smithsonian Institute Museum of Natural History 105:1
Snare, Knut 248:1, 252:2+6
Übersee Museum, Bremen 101
Ulloa, R 116:3, 117:2, 118:2
Willems, Helge, Urefeld 149:1